FORTY-SEVEN DAYS

FORTY-SEVEN DAYS

HOW PERSHING'S WARRIORS
CAME OF AGE TO DEFEAT THE GERMAN
ARMY IN WORLD WAR I

MITCHELL YOCKELSON

NAL
CALIBER

NAL CALIBER
Published by New American Library,
an imprint of Penguin Random House LLC
375 Hudson Street, New York, New York 10014

This book is an original publication of New American Library.

First Printing, March 2016

LIBRARY OF CONGRESS CATALOGING-IN-PUBLICATION DATA:
Names: Yockelson, Mitchell A., 1962– author.
Title: Forty-seven days: how Pershing's warriors came of age to defeat the German Army in World War I/Mitchell Yockelson.
Description: New York, New York: New American Library, 2016.
Identifiers: LCCN 2015039121 | ISBN 9780451466952
Subjects: LCSH: World War, 1914–1918—United States. | United States. Army. American Expeditionary Forces. | World War, 1914–1918—Campaigns—Western Front.
Classification: LCC D570 .Y63 2016 | DDC 940.4/34—dc23
LC record available at http://lccn.loc.gov/2015039121

Printed in the United States of America
10 9 8 7 6 5 4 3 2 1

Designed by Tiffany Estreicher

Penguin
Random
House

To the memory of John S. D. Eisenhower—
Soldier, Diplomat, Historian, Friend

CONTENTS

Contents

MAPS

PROLOGUE

As darkness fell upon the Argonne Forest, Sergeant Cesar Santini steered his khaki Cadillac along the rain-slicked, shell-pocked Fleury-Varennes Road. German artillery fire lit up the evening sky, and although none of the projectiles hit the automobile directly, shrapnel dented its roof. With the enemy dangerously close, Santini and the orderly seated next to him were prepared for the worst. Both men carried sidearms, and a rifle was strapped on one side of the car. The Cadillac was equipped with several blankets and supplemental fuel tanks, which held forty-two gallons of gasoline. A bag filled with gas masks and helmets was tied to the roof, within easy reach outside the orderly's window.

Santini was born in Digne, France, but was raised in New York

City by Italian immigrant parents. He had joined the Army at Governor's Island in spring 1917 at the age of thirty-five, requesting an assignment as either a driver or engineer. A driver who spoke French was a greater asset to the American Expeditionary Forces (AEF), so Santini was ordered to the Quartermaster Corps and his name was placed on the *Baltic's* passenger manifest. When temporary AEF headquarters were set up in Paris during the middle of June, Santini was assigned as the commander in chief's main driver.

Four white stars decorated the Cadillac's windshield in front of Santini's steering wheel, and to anyone who caught a glimpse of the car, they signified that the passenger in the backseat was none other than General John J. Pershing, commander in chief of the American Expeditionary Forces.

Lieutenant Colonel George S. Patton had seen the AEF commander that evening. Patton and several other men from his tank brigade were hunkered down in ditches by the side of the road, waiting for the heavy concentration of German artillery to finish, when Pershing's car drove by. "Moved by a single impulse we all rose," Patton recorded in his diary, "and, regardless of the shells, stood at salute as he passed us."[1]

The future World War II hero knew Pershing well. Less than two years before, Patton had served as one of Pershing's aides during the Mexican Punitive Expedition, an operation to hunt down Pancho Villa and his followers, who had raided Columbus, New Mexico, on March 9, 1916, and killed eighteen Americans. Patton's cavalry regiment was excluded from the Punitive Expedition, but, desperate to take part in the adventure, Patton badgered two of Pershing's staff for an assignment. Pershing was noncommittal. So the evening before the expedition was set to leave, Patton showed up unannounced at Pershing's quarters to plead his case. I am "good with [newspaper] correspon-

2

dents," Patton begged. "Everyone wants to go," Pershing told him, "so why should I favor you?" Patton fired back: "Because I want to go more than anyone else." Dejected, Patton was sent away without an answer. Around eight thirty the next morning his phone rang. The caller said, "Lieutenant Patton, how long will it take you to get ready?" Patton responded that he was ready right then—his gear was already packed. "I'll be God Dammed," Pershing barked, "you are appointed Aide."[2]

By February 1917, when the expedition was recalled from Mexico, Pershing had emerged a hero. Although Villa eluded capture, Pershing and his Punitive Expedition chased the bandit throughout northern Mexico, badly wounded him, and killed and dispersed most of his band. Through newspaper coverage, Americans followed every detail and embraced John J. Pershing. Patton also achieved notoriety for his exploits, but more important to his career, he impressed Pershing as a talented staff officer and brave soldier. At the end of May 1917, Patton was among the party of 191 officers selected by Pershing to sail with him on the White Star SS *Baltic* for the Army's maiden voyage to Europe. What's more, there was a personal connection: Pershing and Patton's sister, Nita, were engaged.

Pershing's risky nighttime trek through the Argonne Forest carried special importance—he was headed toward the front for last-minute meetings with his corps and division commanders. The next morning they would send over 225,000 untested American soldiers toward the strongest German defenses on the western front, commencing what one journalist would later call "America's Greatest Battle."[3]

By autumn 1918 the western front had been deadlocked for most of the war. On this front the Germans had concentrated most of their forces and held more territory than the Allies. There was little doubt from the beginning that the final outcome of the war would be decided on this front, which comprised Belgium and much of northeastern France. The first major battles of the fifty-one-month-long conflict had been fought here, and many more were to follow. The war had started a month after Austrian archduke Franz Ferdinand was assassinated on June 28, 1914, in Sarajevo. Two opposing alliances—the Allies (France, Great Britain, and Russia) and the Central Powers (Germany and Austria-Hungary)—took up arms and mobilized six million men during an unusually warm European summer. Germany deployed 1.5 million against France, which in turn moved a million men to her own eastern border to try to reclaim the provinces of Alsace and Lorraine that had been lost in the Franco-Prussian War of 1870–71. Britain readied more than 100,000 men for service across the English Channel, while Russia mobilized 1.4 million. Germany countered by sending 500,000 troops to the east.

Of all the belligerents, Germany had the best-trained and -equipped army for fighting a modern war. Since defeating France in 1871, the German general staff had planned for another inevitable encounter with their national rival. Even prior to 1914, German soldiers had practiced with rifles, machine guns, and artillery, and were issued uniforms that were practical for combat. On the battlefield, their bland gray-green attire blended with the terrain, while adversaries like the French, with their long blue coats and red trousers, stood out as easy targets.[4]

In early August 1914 the German armies put their might to the test. Following prewar plans, the bulk of Germany's forces aimed for Paris by sweeping through Belgium and Luxembourg and attacking France from the north. At the same time, France struck along its eastern frontier and southern Belgium to drive German forces across the border. For three weeks, in what was collectively known as the Battle of the

Frontiers, the French, with support from a British contingent that arrived on the Continent just after neutral Belgium was attacked, poked and prodded the Germans before counterattacks sent them into retreat. By this time German troops were occupying Belgium after the neutral country refused to give Germany free passage on its way to France. German soldiers in Belgium treated the civilian population with disdain and for no clear reason inflicted wide-scale murder, rape, and pillage. Germany seemed unstoppable, and it looked as if it would be a short war, probably over by Christmas.[5]

By September 4, German troops were within thirty-five miles of Paris. The city was in a panic and the government prepared to evacuate. Remembering what had happened in 1871, the French expected the Germans to march in and seek surrender terms. Then the unexpected happened. The war saw its first turning point during the Battle of the Marne—so named for the Seine tributary in the region east and southeast of Paris—when British and French forces rolled back the Germans. Over eight days—from September 5 to 12, 1914—500,000 Allied and German soldiers were mowed down near the Marne River. With help from six hundred taxicabs that shuttled French soldiers to the front, Paris was saved and the Allies claimed victory. Exhausted and demoralized, the German armies went mostly on the defensive, and for two weeks withstood British and French counterattacks. In the process they extended the lines from the Aisne River, a tributary of the Oise River that runs roughly parallel to the Marne, to the English Channel. One of the last battles of 1914 took place in the Champagne region, where the well-entrenched Germans demonstrated their effective use of the machine gun against a much larger French army, which refused to give up and continued to attack well into March of the following year.[6] Nineteen fourteen ended with well over a million killed and wounded on the western front. Both sides had dug in and occupied trenches that zigzagged for five hundred miles from the English Channel south to the Swiss border. The Germans enhanced their lines with barbed-wire entanglements, blockhouses, and underground shelters.

Trenches became synonymous with World War I. Constructed of sandbags, wooden frames, and wire mesh, they were supposed to protect inhabitants from artillery, air attacks, and, later on, poison gas. Trenches were almost always muddy and infested with rats and lice. When Allied commanders sent their troops out of the trenches and over the top for an attack, the results were mostly the same. Soldiers charged in orderly rows across the uncontested territory called "no-man's-land." Right away, the Germans responded with machine-gun fire. If the brave men somehow escaped the rapidly spraying bullets, barbed wire was another obstacle; cutting through the wire only attracted more machine-gun blasts. Once inside the enemy's trench, they could expect hand-to-hand combat with bayonets, knives, and grenades.

For a short period in 1914 the war was carried out through maneuvers, but that didn't last and the conflict evolved into trench warfare. Allied commanders predicted that the front would break open the following year, but were sorely mistaken. Throughout 1915 the Allies tried attacking German positions all along the front, only to see any progress driven back by counterattacks. The Germans went on the offensive only once in 1915. It was in April, near the ancient Flemish city of Ypres, Belgium, that the Germans used chlorine gas for the first time. The attack with this new weapon had an immediate effect: British troops temporarily fled from an eight-thousand-yard portion of the line, but eventually they and the other Allies learned how to defend against gas, and added it to their own arsenal.[7]

Meanwhile, the United States, remaining neutral while much of the world found new ways to destroy, maim, and kill, was suddenly drawn into the war. On May 7, 1915, a German U-boat sank the British passenger ship RMS *Lusitania* off the southern coast of Ireland; 128 Americans were among the 1,200 killed. President Woodrow Wilson responded cautiously by protesting the sinking and demanding that in the future Germany protect American lives. Germany rightly argued that the *Lusitania* carried war matériel destined for Great Britain and, therefore, was torpedoed in a war zone; this made the *Lusitania* a legitimate target. Wilson later invoked stronger rhetoric. He warned Berlin that any future sinking of ocean liners would be considered a deliberate and unfriendly act.

Despite growing friction between the United States and Germany, Wilson still wanted no part of the conflict and won reelection in 1916 with the slogan that "he kept us out of war." But America prepared for war anyway. That year the National Defense Act, which would incrementally increase the regular Army to 175,000 and the National Guard to 400,000, was passed. Training camps for officers, such as the Plattsburgh Training Camp in upstate New York, sprang up around the country. By now an untold number of Americans were already fighting in the war. They either went across the border to join the Canadian forces or sailed directly to Europe to serve with the British, French, and Italians as ambulance drivers, doctors, and pilots. The U.S. Army had officers in Europe as observers and attachés, who sent back reports on the latest Allied and German tactics and strategies. Their observations were widely distributed through the Army's professional journals and magazines, and studied at its War College. What became evident was that in previous wars, battles typically lasted between one and three days. Now, on the western front, they continued for weeks or months, and no matter the battle plan or how often it changed, ultimately the outcome was decided by attrition. Nowhere was this more apparent than the bloodbaths of Verdun and the Somme in 1916.

On February 21 the Germans attacked Verdun, a city on the Meuse River that had been heavily fortified since Roman times and was now a threat to German lines of communication. The German general staff anticipated that the French would send as many men as possible to reinforce Verdun, thus allowing Germany the chance to "bleed France white" and force peace negotiations with the Allies. The Germans were correct—French pride kept Verdun from falling. Reinforcements arrived from elsewhere on the western front and the battle lasted for most of 1916. Germany finally gave up in December, and when it was all over, both sides had lost a combined total of over a million casualties.

While Verdun was under siege, the British provided their French allies some relief by attacking on the Somme, and took horrendous losses from the start. On the first day of the battle, July 1, 1916, more than 19,000 British officers and soldiers were killed and another 30,000 were wounded. The offensive continued another four months, with the Allies suffering more than 600,000 casualties, while the Germans lost about 465,000 killed and wounded. On November 18, when the battle ended, there was no clear winner, even though the Allies had penetrated six miles into German-held territory.

In spring 1917, with the western front deadlocked, the French Army made another effort to break the stalemate. Led by General Robert Nivelle, more than a million men, supported by seven thousand pieces of artillery, struck along a forty-mile front between Soissons and Reims, where the Germans had fallen back to their Hindenburg Line. Named after Field Marshal Paul von Hindenburg, the line was constructed in early 1917 from west to east for over two hundred miles and consisted of barbed wire, machine-gun nests, and shelters of all varieties, including farms and other structures. The main thrust was aimed at the Chemin des Dames (the Ladies' Path), a chain of wooded rocky ridges paralleling the front. The offensive was a disaster from the start.

German machine guns in shell holes, in caves, and on the hills never allowed the French soldiers to gain a proper foothold. Yet the attack persisted over the next four days at a cost of 190,000 killed and wounded. French Army morale sank, and soldiers in most of its divisions mutinied. Nivelle was sacked and replaced by General Philippe Pétain, who set about restoring order in the ranks.

While the French reorganized, the British took up the slack. At the end of July 1917, fifty British divisions, helped by six more from the French, assaulted German positions on the high ground south and east of Ypres, where two previous attacks had left the city in ruins and the surrounding landscape a wreck. Somehow, with all of the carnage, red poppies still bloomed in the chalky Flanders soil alongside artillery shells, bullets, and body parts. The current Ypres attack concentrated on Passchendaele, a village east of Ypres and near a vital German railway junction. A ten-day artillery bombardment preceded the attack, with three thousand guns lobbing more than four million shells at the Germans. Unbeknownst to the young British soldiers about to jump off on July 31, 1917, the bombardment was less than accurate. German guns behind Passchendaele Ridge remained intact, and so did the sixty-four strongpoints that protected the left and center of the line.

To make matters worse, heavy rain that lasted for the next seven days straight proved to be the real enemy. The Flanders soil turned into a quagmire. Soldiers were up to their knees in mud. Neither they nor the tanks supporting them could gain any momentum. This didn't stop British commanders from pressing the attacks, and the battle continued through early November. By then the British had taken what was left of Passchendaele and claimed the operation a success, despite losing 310,000 men. German losses were around 200,000.

Passchendaele aside, 1917 was the turning point of the war. Political turmoil in Russia boiled over into a revolution that led to an armistice with Germany. No longer fighting a two-front war, German troops in the eastern theater shifted to the western front.[8] More significantly, the United States finally entered the war. From Germany's perspective, America was already a belligerent because the Wilson administration supported the Allies by sending copious supplies across the Atlantic. In a sense, Germany declared war on the United States when it announced that unrestricted submarine warfare would resume on February 1, 1917. President Wilson answered by breaking diplomatic relations with the German government.

Tension between the two countries rose three weeks later when the White House got wind of the "Zimmermann Telegram," a message sent by German foreign minister Arthur Zimmermann to his ambassador in Mexico that the British intercepted. Zimmermann wished to explore an alliance with the Mexican government in the event that Germany went to war with the United States. Zimmermann also wanted Mexico to declare war on the United States and request that Japan join the alliance. In return, Germany would provide Mexico with financial assistance and help them regain the states of Arizona, New Mexico, and Texas, lost during the Mexican-American War. Wilson released the telegram to the press, and the American people exploded with outrage. This set the wheels in motion for the United States to enter the war. On April 2, 1917, Wilson went before Congress to ask for a declaration of war against Germany. In his war message Wilson made it clear that America "had no quarrel with the German people," only with the German government. American troops would help make the world "safe for democracy." Four days later Wilson received almost unanimous approval and the United States was now at war.

President Wilson committed the United States to war with a skeleton army. The U.S. Army comprised slightly more than 127,000 officers and men in the Regulars and about 67,000 more federalized National Guardsmen. Right after the war declaration, a large number of patriotic Americans rushed to enlist, but there still weren't enough to bolster the meager armed forces. Left with no other choice, Wilson ordered the War Department to organize a draft, with all males between the ages of twenty-one and thirty (later extended to include ages eighteen to forty-five) required to register. Ten million men complied, and the Army eventually drafted 2.7 million.

Training camps were hastily constructed in the South and Southeast, where the new U.S. soldiers would spend six months learning the rudiments of war from officers who in many cases knew only slightly more than they did. Both the British and French helped out by sending officers across the Atlantic to assist with the instruction. It was an eye-opening experience for the foreigners, some of them veterans of Verdun and the Somme. They traveled from one training camp to another, preaching trench warfare to young recruits who carried wooden guns and were without proper uniforms and equipment. It was hard to point out the benefits of grenades, flamethrowers, and artillery when many American troops wouldn't encounter these modern weapons until they reached the western front.

Neither the British nor the French commanders thought the inexperienced American soldiers could contribute much on the battlefield by themselves. They would be a better resource amalgamated with the Allied armies and led by foreign officers. Pershing smartly disagreed and received Wilson's support. American troops had been committed to the war to fight as an independent army and not as cannon fodder for the Allies. Yet Pershing also recognized that he needed the Allies to train American soldiers in quiet sectors on the western front. Along with this arrangement the Allied commanders could utilize these troops in emergencies, such as the Second Battle of the Marne in June and July 1918, when Americans fought alongside the French at Château-Thierry, Belleau Wood, and Soissons.

Not until late summer 1918 were there enough troops and supplies in France for Pershing to organize a large-scale American offensive and fight as an independent army. It had taken a little more than a year to build the AEF, but now Pershing was ready to demonstrate why his men had come to Europe in the first place. They were prepared to engage in a clash that would be known to history as the Meuse-Argonne, since most of the forty-seven-day battle was fought in a sector between the Meuse River and the dense Argonne Forest in northern France. The terrain featured a series of steep hills and ground consisting of porous rock. Heavy rain, which fell frequently in autumn, formed chains of ponds and lakes. Clay soil that easily turned to mud spread throughout the forest like a blanket. Then there were the dense trees; all of this made the ground difficult to traverse.[9] This landscape provided perfect cover for the more than 200,000 German defenders preparing for an onslaught of brave but inexperienced American soldiers. The United States Army would come of age during the horrific battle through trial and error, largely due to the leadership of one single American: John J. Pershing.

1

BLACK JACK

N o officer in the U.S. Army was more qualified to lead the AEF
than fifty-seven-year-old John J. Pershing. Much of his military career had been spent abroad, where he represented his
country as a soldier and a politician. Secretary of War Newton D. Baker
also recognized Pershing's leadership ability, and when he selected him
as AEF commander in May 1917, there was never any indication of re-
gret over this decision, though he did agonize over making the selection. After the war he revealed the ideal partnership between a war
secretary and his commanding general: "Select a commander in whom
you have confidence; give him power and responsibility, and then . . .
work your own head off to get him everything he needs and support
him in every decision he makes."[1]

The only other serious candidate for the position was a former chief
of staff and recipient of the Medal of Honor, Major General Leonard
Wood. Even with his impressive credentials, the Wilson administra-

tion was wary of him. Wood had health concerns and lacked recent field experience, and the scuttlebutt around Washington was that he had presidential aspirations and might be a political threat.[2] He also had close ties to Theodore Roosevelt, whom Wilson despised. Pershing raised none of these concerns.

Standing about six feet tall, Pershing's trim physique was ramrod straight; a full head of sandy hair and a neatly groomed mustache accented a face mostly absent of wrinkles. A widower since 1915, he had aged somewhat from the death of his wife and three of his four children, but Pershing still looked younger than his years and could have served as a model for the army's recruitment posters.[3] Countless Army Signal Corps photographs show only one side of Pershing's demeanor: that of a stern military officer sitting at his desk, on horseback, or reviewing troops in the field. As Lieutenant General Robert Bullard described the AEF commander, "Pershing inspired confidence but not affection. He won followers, but not personal worshipers, plain in word, sane and direct in action."[4] Privately, to those he let into his inner circle, Pershing was sensitive, warm and caring.

Marshal Joseph "Papa" Joffre, who at age sixty-two had saved the French Army at the Marne and now headed the French Military Mission to the United States, took to Pershing right away when they were introduced by Newton Baker:

Mr. Baker now asked leave to present the officer who had just been designated to command the Expeditionary Forces going to France. . . . The Secretary left the room for an instant and returned accompanied by General Pershing. As I held his hand, Mr. Baker sketched for me his brilliant military services. I caught the words New Mexico, Dakota, Cuba, and Mexican Frontier. What struck me immediately in the new Commander-in-Chief was the

*intelligence and energy stamped upon his countenance and ex-
pressed by his whole bearings. Turning to Mr. Baker, I said, "He
is a fine looking soldier."*[5]

Pershing's desire to become a soldier didn't seem logical until he
turned twenty-one and his sister showed him a notice in the weekly
Laclede, Missouri, newspaper. He read that a competitive examination
for selection to the U.S. Military Academy at West Point from his
district was going to be held, and to Pershing, the thought of a free
education seemed appealing. "The idea of entering the country's service," he later wrote, "had never before entered my mind." When he
was eighteen Pershing had turned down a chance to attend the Naval
Academy in Annapolis, but now he had second thoughts about a military education, since it might help further his desire to practice law.
Pershing always had ambition, a trait he learned from his hardworking
father, for whom he had been named.

John Joseph Pershing was born on September 13, 1860, in his parents' home on the outskirts of Laclede, about one hundred miles northeast of Kansas City, Missouri. Reflecting on his childhood, Pershing
vividly recalled witnessing warfare for the first time. On June 18, 1864,
a band of Confederate bushwhackers charged through Laclede, shooting their guns and sacking the town. Missouri was a border state, and
this type of behavior wasn't unusual in the Civil War, but certainly
frightening to a three-year-old. Pershing was at the general store his
father owned in the town square when the raid commenced.

Fearing for his family's safety, John Sr. grabbed a shotgun, cradled
his son, and took him out the back door and down the alley to their
home nearby. From the front-room window the elder Pershing could
see the raiders entering his store. He loaded his gun and pointed it out
the window, but before firing a shot, his wife wrapped her arms around

him. She pleaded with her husband to let them be or he might get killed for defending his property. Pershing's father obliged. Soon afterward a trainload of Union soldiers drove off the bushwhackers, who had carried away three thousand dollars and left two dead townspeople in the Laclede square. Pershing would never forget this scene, even after he had gone to battle numerous times.[6]

The Pershings were not well-off, but by today's standards they would be considered middle-class. That changed after the panic of 1873 hit and they lost the general store and all but one of several farms John Sr. had purchased. He took work as a traveling salesman while his fourteen-year-old son plowed the fields. In the evening the younger Pershing read and kept up with his schoolwork, and at eighteen became a teacher. He also attended classes at a nearby college in hopes of going on to law school. It was then that he took the West Point entrance exam and scored higher than thirteen other applicants.

Pershing entered the U.S. Military Academy in 1882, at age twenty-two, which made him a few years older than most of the other cadets, who often turned to him for advice.[7] Pershing was friendly with everyone, but had few close friends. According to one biographer, he was "more given to listening than talking after a greeting."[8] Pershing was elected class president his first year and remained so until graduation. Academically, he was not especially promising. He struggled in French class and hated reciting lessons in front of his instructors and the other cadets. Outside of the classroom, Pershing excelled. "He was conscientious, took the requirements of the Academy very seriously and gave his best in every element going to make up the sum total of life at that institution," his roommate Charles Walcutt wrote, and at the same time was a "strict disciplinarian who observed very closely his own precepts."[9] West Point taught Pershing loyalty and obedience, which, for a soldier, could be achieved only through discipline, drill, and, most significant, pride in military service and in wearing a uniform.[10] Yet Pershing wasn't all spit and polish. He found pleasure in dancing—his fellow cadets called him a "hop-goer" or "spoony man." With his good looks, Pershing found no shortage of attractive dance partners. He was also known to dish out more than his share of hazing and was referred to as "a champion at deviling plebes."[11] But, most of all, it was personal ambition that drove him as a soldier. Although he struggled with his studies, at West Point Pershing developed a fondness for history as well as sensitivity for other cultures. This was evident throughout his service, no matter where he served.[12]

Pershing also appreciated West Point's history and the alumni who went on to become great Army generals. Boyhood heroes such as Ulysses S. Grant, Robert E. Lee, and William Tecumseh Sherman had set a standard for future cadets, and when the latter came for a visit, Pershing made a point of seeking out Sherman in order to salute him in person.[13] Pershing especially idolized Sam Grant. During the summer of 1885, when Grant's funeral train passed through the nearby Garrison, New York, station on its way to Manhattan, Pershing stood at the head of his class's entire battalion, leading them in salute as Grant's remains rolled by.

Pershing and Grant shared similar class rankings. Grant graduated from West Point twenty-first out of thirty-nine, while Pershing was ranked thirtieth out of seventy-seven. His dismal demerit tally partially accounted for the low position. Pershing received more than two hundred infractions. One time he was called out for studying French after hours and tried to hide this illicit activity by hanging a blanket over the window to block out his lamp. Most of the demerits, however, were for tardiness, a trait that he never remedied.[14]

When Pershing was commissioned second lieutenant by President Grover Cleveland in the spring of 1886, joining him on graduation day were ten future brigadier generals and fifteen future major generals. The bulk of them would later serve in the AEF under their classmate.[15]

After leaving West Point, Pershing was assigned to the 6th Cavalry Regiment on the frontier in New Mexico. On his way out west, Pershing's railcar included others from West Point and a "jollier crowd than ours never traveled," Pershing recalled. "We told stories, sang class songs, cleaned out eating houses, fired at prairie dogs, hazed the peanut boy, and practically ran the train."[16] Pershing found garrison duty was rarely fun and often tedious, but there were moments of excitement, too. He took part in patrols searching for renegade Apaches and Sioux, and although none of the campaigns resulted in capturing the natives, the rides taught the young lieutenant how to conduct field operations far from headquarters. He was also very nurturing to his men, making sure they were properly clothed and fed, and looking out for their overall well-being. For a short period Pershing commanded a company of Indian scouts and saw the Native Americans in a different light than did most other Army officers. By conversing with the Indians and watching their native dance, he quickly learned they weren't savages or inferior to white men, as more senior officers had implied. Pershing firmly believed that educating oneself about other cultures was an essential part of leadership, and he remained dedicated to this approach for the rest of his Army service.

While he was posted with the 6th Cavalry at Fort Niobrara, Nebraska, near the Dakota border, Pershing accepted an assignment with the University of Nebraska as professor of military science and tactics, as well as commandant of cadets. Despite some trepidation about teaching civilians to become soldiers, Pershing found his calling. Both the student body and the faculty adored him. "We tried to walk like Pershing, talk like Pershing, and look like Pershing," one cadet recalled.[17] One of the highlights of his tenure at Nebraska was forming an award-winning drill team that later became the "Pershing Rifles." Always ambitious, he took on more responsibility by teaching math at a university-associated prep school. Two of his students were Dorothy Canfield, who spoke five languages fluently and would be a prolific writer, and Willa Cather, another future writer who became well-known for her novels about frontier life on the Great Plains.

Canfield recalled that Pershing "taught a living subject like geometry as he would have taught a squad of raw recruits he was teaching to drill—that is, by telling them what to do and expecting them to do it. He was the kind who said, 'Lesson for tomorrow will be from page 32 to page 36. All problems must be solved before coming to class.' He never gave us any idea of what geometry was all about, and I now have the impression that he didn't know himself."[18]

While Pershing was at Nebraska, the school's chancellor invited him to study law, and he eagerly accepted. Pershing received his degree in June 1893, which held out a possibility of a career change. He now weighed his options and considered leaving the Army to practice law, but was talked out of it by Charles G. Dawes, a friend who was struggling as an attorney and told Pershing that he was better off in the military. When his university tour of duty ended, Pershing returned to the Army as a troop commander with the 10th Cavalry Regiment, one of four all African American units organized after the Civil War. It was a brief stint and not especially memorable, although Pershing found that African Americans were excellent soldiers and only wanted the same respect afforded white members of the Army. "It was a radical change," Pershing wrote, "to go from the command of a corps of cadets of the caliber from which are drawn the leaders of the nation to a company of regulars composed of citizens who have always had only limited advantages and restricted ambitions."[19]

Much like his view of Native Americans, Pershing's sympathy for black soldiers wasn't entirely shared within the Army. When he returned to West Point as a tactics instructor in 1897 his students loathed him for being so strict in the classroom and behind his back they called him "Nigger Jack," mocking his previous assignment. The nickname was later softened to "Black Jack," and it stuck with him for the rest of his life. Pershing may have deserved some of the ridicule, but not the vicious moniker. Eleven years had passed since he had graduated from the Military Academy and naturally his standards as an officer had risen. Pershing expected the best from his students, even though as a cadet he had been far from perfect. "He seemed a heartless martinet," one biographer wrote, "rigid, unforgiving, always ready to pounce on the slightest departure from perfect performance."[20] But Pershing never saw it this way and blamed the academy's commandant of cadets for being too easy with the students. "Tactical officers under him had little encouragement to extend the scope of their instruction," he wrote, "which continued to remain somewhat monotonous for officers and cadets alike."[21] Teaching at West Point was a miserable experience for Pershing and he couldn't wait to leave. He got his chance in the spring of 1898, when the United States declared war on Spain two months after the USS *Maine* mysteriously exploded in Havana Harbor on February 15, killing 266 American sailors and marines.

Pershing asked to be released from the academy in order to take part in the conflict with Spain, but was turned down. Undeterred, he took leave and headed to Washington, where he met with an acquaintance from Nebraska, Assistant Secretary of War George D. Meiklejohn. Pershing made his case for duty as a field officer and Meiklejohn agreed. He had Pershing reassigned to the 10th Cavalry, which was headed to Cuba with General William R. Shafter's expeditionary force in May. Much to his disappointment, Pershing wasn't given command of a troop, but named regimental quartermaster. Not exactly what he wanted, but still a vital job that required equipping, feeding, and supplying men. The 10th saw combat throughout the Cuban campaign, including the San Juan Hill attack in early July, and Pershing was right there with them. While bullets from the Spanish Mausers zinged around him, Pershing encouraged the troopers to keep fighting as though he were leading them in battle.

During the confusion of battle, African American troopers intermingled with Theodore Roosevelt's Rough Riders and together they crested the Kettle and San Juan Hills and drove off the enemy. It was a proud moment for Pershing and afterward he reveled in the bravery of his men. They "took cover only when ordered to do so," he recorded, and "exposed themselves fearlessly." Regimental commander Colonel Theodore Baldwin was much impressed by Pershing's leadership during the battle. "I have been in many fights through the Civil War," Baldwin told him, "but on my word, you were the coolest and bravest man I ever saw under fire in my life." The United States prevailed in its "Splendid Little War" with Spain and at the turn of the twentieth century transitioned into a colonial empire.

Victory in Cuba and the American acquisition of the Philippines brought with them numerous headaches for the War Department. The Army had responsibility for governing America's new colonial possessions and found the occupation of the Philippines especially difficult. After being under Spanish rule for centuries, the Filipino people and the factions that ruled the country's provinces wanted no part of the U.S. incursion. They retaliated with a bloody insurrection that lasted three years, but further violence against the American occupiers continued for several more years and resulted in mass casualties of soldiers and civilians.

Pershing tasted combat in Cuba and liked the adventure and danger that came with it. He wanted an assignment in the Philippines to get more field experience and perhaps further recognition from his superiors. Once again, Pershing used his Washington contacts and was posted to the Philippines as adjutant general of the District of Zamboanga and later of the District of Mindanao, where problems with the Moros plagued the U.S. Army. Moros were not Catholic like other Filipinos, but Muslim, and they fought as a tribe with primitive weapons. Moro tribesmen were especially adept with long blades that had been handed down through generations of warriors. Pershing's job was largely administrative, but he expanded his role to mediator, engaging the Moro natives as he had done with the Native Americans on the frontier. But the Moros, Pershing recognized, weren't going to obey their Christian invaders so easily. "The Moro is of a peculiar make-up as to character," he wrote, "though the reason is plain when considered, first, that he is a savage, second that he is a Malay; and third that he is a Mohammedan." Furthermore, Pershing reasoned that "in order to control him other than by brute force, one must win his implicit confidence."[22]

Now a captain, Pershing was placed in charge of Camp Vicars, an outpost in Mindanao. There he used his diplomatic skills to learn the native traditions and language, and employed Moros to build schools and roads and instructed his men to purchase goods from the local markets. Slowly, Pershing built a rapport with the Moros. On the Fourth of July he invited tribal leaders to attend a celebration at the camp and ordered his soldiers to mingle with the guests. But Pershing found that goodwill only worked to a point and that brute force spoke volumes against the Moros, who were outmanned and outgunned by Black Jack's army. During a brilliant expedition around Lake Lanao, in west-central Mindanao, Pershing and six hundred men left Camp Vicars on April 3, 1903, in an effort to subjugate the Moros in that district. Pershing described them as "the most warlike people in Mindanao."[23] The march around the lake took two weeks and they encountered minor resistance a few times. Pershing handled it with swift and devastating strength by having his men surround and destroy Moro fortifications. Mostly, Pershing's expedition was greeted warmly and one of the tribal chiefs welcomed the Americans with a feast. Pershing's exploits in the Philippines became legendary in the United States, and Americans thought of him as a hero. So did the Army, and other officers began to speculate that he was about to be promoted. Major General George W. Davis, the commander of U.S. forces in the Philippines, certainly liked the idea and wrote on Pershing's behalf:

When the time comes for the Department to make the selection of general officer for promotion from the grade of captain, I hope that Captain Pershing may be selected for brigadier general. I have frequently brought his merits to the attention of the Department, in routine and in special communications, for gallantry, good judgment, and thorough efficiency in every branch of the soldier's profession. He is the equal of any and superior of most.[24]

Pershing returned home in July 1903, and President Theodore Roosevelt attempted to reward him with a promotion to brigadier general, but couldn't do so without congressional approval; they turned down the request. No one on Capitol Hill disputed whether Black Jack was a stellar officer, but the Army had a seniority list and he was near the bottom. As a compromise, Roosevelt considered making Pershing a colonel, but this was forbidden by law. Disappointed by the turn of events, Pershing nonetheless was optimistic about his future. He accepted a desk officer assignment on the General Staff in Washington and became a celebrity around town. Pershing attended all kinds of social engagements. One of them was a weekly dance at Fort Myer, and it was there, on December 3, 1903, that the forty-three-year-old bachelor met twenty-two-year-old Miss Helen Francis Warren of Cheyenne, Wyoming. She was the oldest child of Senator Francis Emory Warren, who chaired the Senate's Military Affairs Committee. It was love at first sight, although the shy Pershing kept his feelings a secret from Frankie, as he called her, for many months.[25] They became engaged the following year and married in 1905. The Pershing wedding was the social event of that year. A who's who of Washington attended, including the Supreme Court justices, numerous congressmen, and President and Mrs. Roosevelt. After a brief honeymoon in the West, the Pershings headed to Japan for Black Jack's next assignment—service as U.S. attaché and observer of the Mikado's armies, which were embroiled in the Russo-Japanese War. In Manchuria Pershing witnessed the war's carnage: smashed artillery, busted transport wagons, and devastated dwellings.[26] The battlefield was strewn with dead horses, victims to machine guns massed against cavalry.[27] For the first time Pershing witnessed modern war and its associated logistical problems when supply trains, guns, prisoners, and refugees clogged narrow roads. He was destined to confront similar issues with the AEF in 1918.

While Captain John J. Pershing remained on duty in Asia, President Roosevelt once more nominated him to the rank of brigadier general. As before, the appointment needed congressional approval, but this time Pershing had a high-ranking senator on his side. News of Pershing's promotion rocked the War Department. A leap from captain to general was not unheard-of but rare, especially during peacetime. In Pershing's case, he passed over 257 captains who were senior to him, 364 majors, 131 lieutenant colonels, and 110 colonels. Newspapers jumped all over the story, proclaiming the promotion was "political pull" and "selection in marriage."

Eventually Roosevelt was pressured into publishing a letter he wrote to Senator Warren about his son-in-law's rapid advancement:

"The promotion was made purely on the merits, and unless I am mistaken, you never spoke to me on the subject until I had announced that he was to be promoted. . . . To promote a man because he marries a senator's daughter would be an infamy, and to refuse him promotion for the same reason would be an equal infamy."[28]

Meanwhile, Pershing found himself embroiled in a controversy that threatened not only to derail his career but to end his marriage. Newspaper reports claimed that Pershing had acquired a Filipino mistress and had two children with her. He moved quickly to quell the rumors, making public statements, contacting influential friends in the Army and collecting affidavits from those who served him in the Philippines. He even contacted the woman whom he was alleged to have coupled with, and all of them came to Pershing's rescue to proclaim his innocence. But the press was relentless and insisted they had three witnesses who knew otherwise—only one was dead, and the other two backed down when asked to come forward. Eventually the story faded away when the media reported the rumor was set by jealous officers whom Pershing had passed over for promotion.

With his reputation and marriage intact, Pershing left Japan in January 1907 and headed back to the Philippines to command Fort McKinley, outside Manila. For twenty-two months he trained and prepared a full brigade for field operations, the largest concentration of American forces outside the United States. Commanding so many men was awkward at first, but Pershing adapted to the job, and it certainly helped prepare him for later assignments. After leaving the Philippines for Washington in July 1908, Pershing and Frankie took an indirect route through Russia and across Europe. During their visit to Germany Pershing witnessed a small-scale army maneuver and was briefed on German mobilization plans. He noted in his memoirs, "I have never before seen such perfect preparation."

No sooner had Pershing, Frankie, and their new baby girl settled into Washington than he was sent back to the Philippines on November 11, 1909, for a dual military and civilian role as commander of the Department of Mindanao and governor of the Moro Province. Like his earlier stretch in the Philippines, Pershing dealt directly with the Moros, who had become disruptive after he left six years earlier. And as he had done previously, Pershing undertook a combination of sympathetic rule and hard-fisted military action. Pershing also had responsibility for the well-being of about a half million people who lived in the province, thus giving him valuable administrative experience. At the close of 1914, after almost eight years abroad, the Pershings, now a family of six, left the Philippines for the United States. They settled into the Presidio in San Francisco, where he took command of the 8th Infantry Brigade.

It was there, on August 27, 1915, that Pershing's world was swept away by a horror he never fully recovered from. The previous night, a fire had broken out on what was known as the Pershing house on Moraga Street at the Presidio. Occupying the residence were Frankie as well as the Pershings' son, Warren; and daughters, Helen, Anne, and Mary Margaret. The fire was likely ignited from fumes used to repair a floor in the home. Another family was also there that night and vacated at the first sign of flames, but for unknown reasons the Pershings became trapped and died from smoke inhalation. Four months before the fire, Pershing had transferred with the 8th Brigade to Fort Bliss in El Paso, Texas, where tensions on the border between the United States and Mexico had escalated. Frankie and the children were supposed to join Pershing at some point later that year.

Pershing allegedly learned about the fire from Norman Walker, a reporter from the *El Paso Herald*. Scanning the morning Teletypes, Walker and another newsman were struck by a slowly developing story about a fire in the Presidio that destroyed the Pershing house. They eventually learned that the blaze killed Mrs. Pershing and three girls, and that only their son, Warren, had survived. Walker called Fort Bliss for confirmation and believed that the person who answered the phone was Lieutenant James Lawton Collins, Pershing's longtime aide-de-camp. Walker had spoken with him before and thought he had recognized Collins's voice. Walker said, "Lieutenant Collins, I have some more news on the Presidio fire." A trembling voice on the other end responded, "What fire? What has happened?" He repeated, "What fire?" Walker, now realizing it was Pershing on the phone, trembled himself as he read the dispatch from the Teletype. "Oh, God! My God!" Pershing responded. "What's that? Read that again!" Walker obeyed the general's order, and as he read the tragic news again out loud, he could hear Pershing sighing in distress and then exclaiming, "My God! My God! Can it be true?" Walker apologized for mistakenly calling Pershing, who responded, "Thank you, Walker. It was very considerate of you to phone."[29]

Two days after the tragedy, Pershing reached San Francisco and headed to the funeral parlor, where he knelt for about ten minutes in front of each casket. Pershing then insisted upon going to the Presidio so that he could see the house and reconstruct the fire. Afterward, Pershing said, "I am now satisfied that nothing could have been done. They had no chance. I wanted to see that for myself."[30] After tending to the funeral arrangements in Wyoming, where Frankie and his daughters were laid to rest, Pershing returned to Fort Bliss with Warren and one of his sisters who would help take care of her nephew.

Pershing rarely mentioned the heartbreak, ignoring it in the manuscript he wrote about his pre–First World War military service.[31] Occasionally the topic came up with close friends. In 1918, he was in a car with Charles Dawes, and their conversation turned morose. Dawes mentioned his only son, who had drowned, triggering Pershing to think about his own loss. They both turned to each other, tears flowing, and Pershing lamented: "Even this war can't keep it out of my mind."[32]

When he lost his family, a significant part of Pershing died, too. Frankie, with her warm, outgoing personality, had been a wonderful influence on him. Now that she was gone, he reverted back to being introverted and withdrawn. Black Jack socialized from time to time, playing cards and polo, but only with a cadre of folks who made up his limited inner circle of companions. His mailbox at Fort Bliss was flooded with condolence cards from around the world, including one from Pancho Villa, with whom he had a cordial relationship at this point.

Pershing needed to get on with his life, and just as he had done before getting married, his focus was on the Army. He spent the remainder of 1915 and the first part of 1916 attending to the 8th Brigade. But then Pershing found a better distraction. While at Fort Bliss, he first met Lieutenant George S. Patton, a troop commander with the 8th Cavalry Regiment. Patton; his wife, Bea; and their children lived in post quarters, and in early 1916 his sister, Nita, traveled from California for a visit. During a social engagement at the fort, Pershing and Nita were introduced and a romance blossomed. Although still ravaged by the loss of his wife and the girls, Pershing was struck by Nita's resemblance to Frankie, and she provided him the sensitivity and comfort he desperately needed. Their relationship was put on hold, however, when Pancho Villa and around four hundred men raided Columbus, New Mexico, on March 9, 1916, and tangled with the 13th U.S. Cavalry Regiment, who were garrisoned nearby. Villa supporters had been terrorizing Americans in Mexico and conducting border raids for the past year in retaliation for the U.S. backing of President Venustiano Carranza, whom he was embroiled with in a civil war. The day after Villa's invasion, President Wilson "directed that an armed force be sent into

Mexico with the sole purpose of capturing Villa and preventing any further raids by his band, and with scrupulous regard to the sovereignty of Mexico."[33]

Secretary of War Baker, who had just arrived in Washington and knew little about the Army's field officers, asked his general staff to recommend an expedition leader. Army chief of staff Major General Hugh L. Scott and his assistant, Major General Tasker H. Bliss, put Pershing's name forward, and Baker selected him. The other possibility was Major General Frederick Funston, a Medal of Honor recipient and presently commander of the Southern Department out of Fort Sam Houston in San Antonio. Funston outranked Pershing and seemed the obvious choice, but reports that he drank too much ruined his chances. Pershing also had more experience working directly with civilians than any other officer, and that comforted Baker.

Out of all his Army assignments, commanding the Mexican Punitive Expedition was the most difficult. Capturing Villa would be hard enough, considering the bandit knew the terrain better than Pershing and had many allies willing to protect him, but entering Mexico and not inciting its army into a full-scale war would be another challenge. Just after midnight on March 18, 1916, Pershing and the Mexican Punitive Expedition brought the U.S. Army into the modern era of warfare. Accompanying the twelve thousand Regulars were motorized supply trucks, Signal Corps communication equipment, and some airplanes. Pershing split his army into two columns and headed toward the town of Casa Grandes, one hundred miles south of Columbus. A supply base was established at Colonia Dublán and this is where Pershing made his headquarters.

Four weeks into the operation, Pershing's Punitive Expedition had pushed 350 miles into Mexico without snagging Villa, although there had been several skirmishes with his Villistas. On March 29, 1916, 370 troopers from the 7th Cavalry Regiment clashed with Villa's bandits at San Geronimo ranch near the town of Guerrero. Seventy-five Villistas were killed and five Americans wounded. Villa escaped unharmed; it was the closest Pershing's men would get to capturing him. On April 12, a squadron of the 13th Cavalry entered the town of Parral, four hundred miles from the border, where they were swarmed by an angry crowd. Wisely, squadron commander Major Frank Tompkins tried to leave town and was attacked in the process by the local Carranzistas (the name given to Carranza's military forces). Tompkins engaged the Mexicans, and after more American cavalry arrived throughout the day, the outnumbered Carranzistas withdrew. Two Americans died and six were wounded during the standoff. There were many more Mexican casualties, although the exact number is disputed.

Frustrated by failing to locate Villa's whereabouts and fighting Mexican troops in the process, Pershing's men grew tired and aggravated. Cavalry regiments were overly exhausted because much of the landscape they traversed was mountainous and troopers often had to lead the horses on foot. Mexican villagers added to the misery. Pershing ordered his men to treat them with respect and purchase their goods at fair prices, as he had done with the Moros. But locals didn't reciprocate the kindness and snubbed the Americans when asked for help finding Villa. Even more distressing was the Carranza government, which had reluctantly permitted the expedition into Mexican territory under pressure from Wilson, now hoped the Americans would go away.

Pershing thought the 1st Aero Squadron, with its eight Curtiss JN-3 (Jennys) airplanes, led by Captain Benjamin Foulois, could help spot the bandit. He was mistaken. One of the planes crashed on its maiden flight from Columbus to Colonia Dublán, and the other planes either couldn't fly much above the treetops, or suffered from broken propellers, among other failures. Pershing lamented that the "aeroplanes have been of no material benefit . . . either in scouting or as a means of communication. They have not at all met my expectations."[34]

On June 21, the last major battle of the expedition involved Pershing's old regiment, the 10th Cavalry. Once again the enemy was not the Villistas but the Mexican Army. Eleven American soldiers were killed in a skirmish at Carrizal, including the commander of Troop C, Captain Charles Boyd, when the regiment entered the village without approval from the local Carranzista commander. Pershing wanted to retaliate by attacking the Carranzista garrison at Chihuahua, but President Wilson rejected his order for fear it would lead to war between the United States and Mexico and requested that the commander now cease hostile activity. Pershing obeyed and agreed that he would stand down until further notice. Despite the lack of progress and frustrations over equipment failures, Pershing kept his composure and remained professional throughout the expedition. This is apparent in one of the iconic photographs taken of him at the time. Pershing is captured sitting confidently on his horse. A "Montana Peak" campaign hat rests just above his ears, while he wears a crisp shirt and perfectly knotted tie.

With the Punitive Expedition stalled and Pershing waiting for direction from Washington, he still found ways to keep busy. Correspondent Junius Wood observed that the general always seemed energetic. "A light may burn in his tent until early morning," Wood recorded, "while he sits alone reading over reports and planning moves for future days. He may be up at daylight, walking through the sleeping camp and observing with his own eyes." Wood was also amazed at how well Pershing recalled little details. For instance, the correspondent mentioned that he heard fifty horses were killed by lightning. "That's not quite correct," Pershing countered. "Five were killed, one stricken blind, and twelve were stunned."[35]

As 1916 dragged into 1917, there was still no movement by the expedition. Morale within Pershing's army was low and he had a tough time keeping out boredom. Pershing knew that social activities helped combat the doldrums of military life, so he got hold of some projectors and screens to show nightly movies, and encouraged the men to form baseball and polo teams. Soldiers also found their own form of entertainment by way of prostitutes. As long as the Americans had money, women were willing to show Mexican hospitality in bushes and shacks. The longer Pershing's men remained in the camps, the greater the rate of venereal disease. A bishop from a nearby Mormon colony complained to Pershing about the debauchery his ladies witnessed and presented a solution: locate a "restricted district" outside of the Army camp that would be run by a Mexican manager. Pershing liked the idea, made one of his doctors a health inspector, and set up the brothel. A visit with a prostitute was fixed at two dollars and the men flocked to the establishment. Suddenly, Pershing's bold social experiment caused the VD rate to plummet. In response to his critics, who were few in number, Pershing said, "The establishment was necessary and has proved the best way to handle a difficult problem."[36]

Meanwhile, frequent border raids, in some cases led by Carranzista officers, plagued the United States along the Rio Grande. President Wilson responded by ordering 150,000 National Guardsmen to the border, and they were placed under Pershing's control. Because many in the Guard had little or no military training and limited equipment, Pershing refused to make them part of the Punitive Expedition. They remained on patrol in Arizona, New Mexico, and Texas.

At the end of January the Punitive Expedition began to withdraw and returned to Columbus, New Mexico, almost a year after their mission commenced. Even though Villa was still on the loose, the expedition was not all for naught, but a valuable experience for Pershing and the Regular Army. As one historian has noted, "Pershing came out of the Mexican trial a hard, taciturn, competent major general."[37] He gained precious field experience and learned how to operate with the complicated modern tools of war, such as trucks, airplanes, and wireless communication. Mexico was clearly a training ground for future warfare. Two weeks after Pershing returned from Mexico, General Funston died of a heart attack, and Black Jack took over as Southern Department commander at Fort Sam Houston.

Within hours of the United States' declaration of war against Germany, Pershing campaigned for what would be the most coveted assignment in the U.S. Army. He wrote President Wilson and Secretary of War Baker that he was ready and able to take command of an overseas expeditionary force to Europe. He told Wilson, "I am exultant that my life has been spent as a soldier, in camp and field, that I may now the more worthily and more intelligently serve my country and you." To Baker, Pershing said basically the same thing: "My life has been spent as a soldier, much of it on campaign, so I am now fully prepared for the duties of this hour." While Black Jack cooled his heels at Fort Sam Houston, Senator Warren, who remained close to his son-in-law and continued looking out for his best interests, sent him a telegram with this question: "Wire Me Today Whether And How Much You Speak, Read And Write French." Pershing hastily replied that he studied it at West Point and improved on the language when he and Frankie toured Europe and had a stopover in France. Following Senator Warren's telegram were orders to report to chief of staff Major General Hugh Scott in Washington. There, Scott told Pershing that he would command a composite division, but that changed two days later, after meeting with Newton Baker. Pershing would now immediately head to Europe with a small staff who would become the nucleus of what was soon to be called the American Expeditionary Forces.

2

FIRST ARMY IS BORN

On June 8, 1917, following a ten-day journey across the Atlantic, Pershing and his party arrived in England. It was a working trip on board the *Baltic*, and Pershing kept his staff busy outlining plans for the AEF. One of their fundamental concerns was how long would it take to ready American troops for battle and where on the western front were they going to operate. Pershing knew that once he arrived in Europe, the British and French would ask the same question, and for now he didn't have a ready answer.

Greeting Pershing at Liverpool were a small group of dignitaries, a handful of newspapermen, and some soldiers from the Royal Welsh Fusiliers. After exchanging pleasantries, Pershing traveled by train to London, where he met King George V at Buckingham Palace. His stay in London lasted three more days, filled with a church service at Westminster Abbey, a conference with Prime Minister David Lloyd George, and a blunt talk with General Sir William "Wully" Robertson, chief of the Imperial Staff, who insisted that once American soldiers arrived overseas, Pershing would turn them over to the British Army. Pershing respectfully declined, but did ask if Robertson would help secure shipping to get the U.S. Army overseas faster. That was "entirely out of the question," Pershing was told, because there weren't enough ships to fulfill British needs. Their meeting ended with nothing resolved.

Pershing left England early on June 13 and reached Boulogne-sur-Mer at ten a.m. There his party was met by a much larger crowd than in Liverpool, including a band, which, much to Pershing's annoyance, played the "Star-Spangled Banner" over and over again. After that, the "Marseillaise" was played repeatedly while a line of French officers shook hands with Black Jack, who then gave a brief speech. Later in the day Pershing was whisked away to Paris. At the Gare du Nord he was greeted with even more French fanfare and renditions of the two national anthems. Then he left on a two-mile trip from the train station to the Hôtel de Crillon, his residence for the next few days. The short fifteen-minute ride took longer than usual due to the thousands of Parisians who crowded the streets cheering, crying, waving American flags and shouting *"Vive l'Amérique"* as the motorcade passed by. The French viewed the Americans as saviors who would put an end to the suffering of war and bring victory. Pershing was visibly moved by the reception but he knew that right now he could provide little in the way of hope with only a few staff officers and aides. There was no telling when a vast army of Americans would arrive. He lamented later on that the enthusiasm of the French "was most touching and in a sense most pathetic."[1]

Much like his visit to London, Pershing's time in Paris was blocked with visits, meetings, and more lunches and dinners than he would have liked. His talks with French commanders were cordial, especially the one in Compiègne, where he first met General Henri-Philippe Pétain,

N

BELGIUM

Liège

GERMANY

Somme R.

Cantigny

Mézières

Sedan

LUXEMBOURG

Aisne R.

Compiègne

Soissons

Oise R.

Fismes

Reims

Blanc
Mont

Meuse R.

Briey

Aire R.

Belleau
Wood □

Verdun

Souilly

Metz

Paris

Château-
Thierry

Marne R.

Saint-Mihiel

Moselle R.

FRANCE

Toul

Nancy

Seine R.

The American Sector

0   25   50   75
Miles

Chaumont

Map by Chris Robinson

the hero of Verdun and now commander in chief of the French Army. As one of Pershing's biographers observed, there was a great similarity between the two men. Around the same age, both Pétain and Pershing were ambitious, strong-minded, serious, and handsome.[2] When they met on June 16, Pétain stressed his appreciation for the Americans, but said it was imperative that they make an immediate contribution to the war, telling Pershing after lunch: "I hope it is not too late." More than ever, Pétain's sense of urgency made Pershing recognize that the war was close to being lost.

That afternoon Pershing presented the AEF strategy: his troops would fight as an independent army with their own sector. Pershing selected Lorraine, a region stretching between the Argonne Forest and the Vosges Mountains. Lorraine not only borders Germany but also touches on Belgium and Luxembourg. To supply the AEF, the Americans would have access to the ports of Saint-Nazaire, La Pallice, and Bassens on the western coast, as well as French railways that converged in the Lorraine region.

Pétain shook his head in approval and shifted the conversation to where the Americans would launch their first offensive. As both generals pored over a map of the western front, Pershing became fixated on the St. Mihiel Salient. By eliminating this bulge in the line, Black Jack opined, his doughboys could then penetrate deep into German territory and eliminate the rail center at Metz that was used to bring troops and supplies to other parts of the front.* In addition, his troops could

---

* Why American soldiers were called "doughboys" is unclear. Some historians claim it dates to when they marched along the dusty roads of northern Mexico during the Punitive Expedition of 1916–17, and their uniforms turned an adobe color and that was anglicized to "doughboy." Others say they earned the nickname from the globular shape of their buttons. Nonetheless, it became a term of endearment.

capture the coalfields of Saar and the Bassin de Briey, the latter the greatest iron-producing region in the world, providing Germany with 80 percent of its steel to generate armaments.[3] Accomplishing these objectives would break Germany's ability to keep fighting.[4]

For more than four years, experienced French troops had shed significant blood in trying to break the St. Mihiel Salient, and to Pétain, the thought of inexperienced Americans overcoming this obstruction must have seemed foolish. Yet, in Pershing's mind, an American victory in St. Mihiel would prove that the AEF was capable of planning and executing a major operation. Listening patiently, Pétain agreed to Pershing's plan for the moment, but both men knew it might take several months before such an operation could seriously be considered; there weren't enough Americans in France to fight a small skirmish, much less a large-scale battle. Yet Pershing had made an important friend in Pétain. "He has a kindly expression, is most agreeable," Pershing told his diary, "but not especially talkative. His keen sense of humor became apparent from the jokes he told at the expense of some of his staff."[5]

Over the next few months, as more and more Americans arrived in France, Pershing moved AEF headquarters from its crowded location in Paris to Chaumont, a city of fifteen thousand in the countryside of the upper Marne River. A newspaper reporter described Chaumont "as an old and picturesque city, quiet and conservative even beyond French provincialism. It has water and gas and electric lights, but no street railroads and few places of amusement, even in normal times."[6] Pershing's staff took over a four-story, drafty regimental barracks, where Black Jack made do with an eighteen-by-twelve-foot office on the second floor. His modest workspace included a small desk with locks on the drawers to secure classified papers, some chairs, a clock, and maps that almost covered every wall.

Pershing resided four miles from his office at the seventeenth-century Val des Écoliers, a château on the outskirts of Chaumont. His staff prepared a suite for him on the second floor under a baronial tower. Another part of the mansion housed a collection of armor, medieval weaponry, and portraits dating back hundreds of years. Black Jack had the artifacts removed and made use of the space as an office where he could receive reports from the front well into the night.[7]

AEF officers assigned to Chaumont typically roomed with local families. Billeting rates were set by the French Army, and depended on rank: one franc for each officer provided with a bed; twenty centimes for each noncommissioned officer or soldier provided with a bed; and five centimes for each noncommissioned officer, soldier, or animal provided simply with shelter.[8] Chaumont's streets bustled with Americans who spent liberally in the city's shops and dined at its cafés. A favorite eatery was the Restaurant Trampeon on the rue des Tanneries.[9]

At Chaumont, Pershing and his staff directed an expanded AEF that eventually included American military personnel not only in France, but also throughout Europe. To manage this great bureaucracy, Pershing adopted the French system for organizing his general staff. Five branches handled specific AEF functions: G-1 (personnel), G-2 (intelligence), G-3 (operations), G-4 (logistics) and G-5 (training). Each was led by a colonel.

Since early 1918, AEF combat divisions had been spread along the western front for training with the British and French armies, with which many doughboys had served briefly under foreign commanders. Both Britain and France had hoped Pershing would reconsider his plan for an independent army and allow all American troops to fight entirely under Allied leadership. Yet the general fought hard to keep his doughboys. In August, he formally won the battle when newly appointed Allied commander in chief Field Marshal Ferdinand Foch gave Black Jack the go-ahead to organize the American First Army, effective the tenth of that month.

It was a moment of glory for Pershing, and he appointed himself the First Army commander. He now wore two hats, leading the entire AEF as commander in chief while at the same time directing the largest U.S. combat force ever assembled since General Ulysses S. Grant took over the Union Army in 1864. Pershing could now commit his army to an engagement against the German-held St. Mihiel Salient, a triangle formed between two rivers—the Meuse on the west and the Moselle to the east. Before emptying into the Rhine River, the Moselle flows through France, Luxembourg, and finally Germany. The salient overlooked the Woëvre Plain, a low marshland of ponds and streams surrounded by woods of varying size.[10] The salient's three anchor cities were Verdun to the north, St. Mihiel in the south and Pont-à-Mousson twenty-five miles to the east.*

In early September 1914, during the Battle of the Frontiers, German forces unintentionally created the salient, or bulge, in the line when the elements of two armies attacked north of Verdun in an effort to break through the city's fortifications, and cut the important French railroads: the Paris-Châlons-Verdun and Toul-Verdun lines.[11] French defenses held on the right and left of the lines, but the Germans broke through in the center and pushed a wedge, or salient, as far as the town of St. Mihiel. Further attempts to advance were repelled by the French, and this part of the front remained deadlocked. The

---

* Descriptions of distance alternate between miles and kilometers in operations reports, historical narratives, diaries, and other documentation on the Meuse-Argonne campaign. One mile equals 1.609334 kilometers. For the purposes of this book, miles have been used to describe distances unless kilometers have been provided in a direct quote.

Germans recognized its strategic importance in protecting the Briey Iron Works, the Saar coalfields and the city of Metz, just thirty-six miles from St. Mihiel and a key to the entire German defenses along the western front. Therefore, the German High Command reinforced the region's ridges and high ground.[12] Eventually it formed part of the Hindenburg Line.

Repeated attacks by the French in 1915 failed to dislodge the Germans from the salient, including one offensive that resulted in 125,000 wounded and killed. Before the Battle of Verdun in 1916, the salient was considered an inactive front, even with the strong German presence. The French referred to the salient as *l'hernie*, or the hernia. For two years, a strong defensive line the Germans named the Michel Stellung (*stellung* loosely translates as "fortress") prevented the French from breaking through. Dominating the salient was Montsec, a commanding high ground on the south face that gave the Germans an unimpeded view of the Allied lines.

By autumn 1918, Germany's Lieutenant General Georg Fuchs's Army Detachment C held the St. Mihiel Salient. At his disposal were 180 pieces of heavy artillery, 200 airplanes, and 180,000 soldiers. Yet most of the troops assigned to Fuchs were of poor quality, either too old or unhealthy to serve in combat. Hunkered behind deep fortifications along a stretch of woods protected by multiple belts of barbed wire, they were described pejoratively by one historian as "trench troops."[13]

Fuchs reported directly to army group commander General Max von Gallwitz, who, like most high-ranking German officers, was a veteran of the 1870 Franco-Prussian War. A devout Catholic, Gallwitz had spent the first year and a half of World War I on the eastern front commanding the German Twelfth Army. In the eyes of Quartermaster General Erich Ludendorff, who commanded the German army in partnership with Field Marshal Paul von Hindenburg, Gallwitz was a stellar officer. In 1915, Gallwitz was moved to the western front, where he fought in the battles of both the Somme and at Verdun. Sent to the Metz region in 1916, he was eventually assigned to command the Meuse-Moselle (Army Group Gallwitz) sector, where he built a deeply fortified defensive line stretching back several kilometers.[14]

With his army's independence secured, Pershing could now set his sights on an operation against the St. Mihiel Salient. On August 24, he met with Foch at the French commander's Bombon headquarters, a small brick château built on the site where a medieval castle once stood. There, they discussed the general plan and command organization for the forthcoming attack. Pershing left the meeting feeling confident about First Army, but uncertain about his partnership with Marshal Foch.[15] Theirs was a lukewarm union held together out of necessity. France could not continue fighting the war without the Americans, and Pershing couldn't operate without French armaments and French troops, all of which were controlled by Pétain and the French government. Although he was satisfied overall with that day's meeting, Black Jack found their conversations frustrating. After one discussion, Pershing vented in his diary that "Foch never seemed interested when I talked with him of our problems. . . . He was essentially a student and teacher of history and strategy."[16]

Pershing clearly didn't understand the sixty-seven-year-old Foch. Lost Generation writer John Dos Passos described the commander's peculiarities in his work of nonfiction *Mr. Wilson's War*: Foch was a "strutting game cock of a man with gray blue eyes and an abundant grizzled mustache. A punctual man, everything had to be on time. He always attended early Mass. Meals were sacred. Déjeuner à la Fourchette was on the stroke of noon." If a guest was unavoidably late, they waited to be served "after the Marshal had eaten. Dinner was at seven sharp. Early to bed, the members of his staff—known as *La Famille Foch*—reported proudly that during the whole war the old fellow had only spent one night out of bed, during the Battle of the Marne when he had to stretch out on the floor of a small town hall."[17]

Despite his anxiety toward Foch, plans to strike at the St. Mihiel Salient in mid-September were well under way, and Pershing couldn't help but show outward signs of enthusiasm. Pershing's friend from Nebraska, Charles G. Dawes, now a brigadier general in charge of supply procurement and one of Black Jack's few close confidants, noted, "I never saw General Pershing looking or feeling better. He is sleeping well. He is tremendously active."[18]

During the last week in August, Pershing established First Army headquarters at Ligny-en-Barrois, a small town about twenty-five miles west of St. Mihiel. From there the upcoming operation would be directed.[19] Pershing lived aboard what his staff called the "Commander-in-Chief's Field Headquarters Train." Its ten cars included a bedroom, dressing room, and library especially for him, and another four compartments to accommodate overnight guests. The train was presided over by Colonel Earl L. Thornton, who oversaw a staff of eighteen, including six African Americans who had worked as Pullman porters before the war.

Tasked with planning the St. Mihiel attack was Major George C. Marshall, one of the AEF's most promising young officers. A graduate of the Virginia Military Institute (VMI), the thirty-eight-year-old Marshall had arrived in Chaumont in early August after serving as operations officer with the 1st Division. Pershing had witnessed Marshall's staff work when the 1st captured Cantigny in late May. The first American-led operation of the war, the victory showed the apprehensive British and French commanders that the doughboys were in this conflict as combatants, not as spectators on the sidelines.

Marshall rented a room from Ligny's former mayor in a "gloomy château that faced a walled-in garden of damp and unhealthy aspect." His landlord, Marshall recalled, was an unfriendly "curious individual of uncertain age and so stoop-shouldered as to appear deformed." The landlord's wife, on the other hand, was "a sprightly and agreeable old lady." Marshall rarely saw them. Each morning he awoke early and walked to work about two miles away. He arrived around eight and in most instances didn't leave his office until two or three o'clock the following morning.[20]

Marshall's battle plan for St. Mihiel was to direct an attack against the south flank of the salient by Major General Hunter Liggett's I Corps—entailing the 82nd, 90th, 5th, and 2nd Divisions in line right to left, with the 78th in reserve—along with Major General Joseph T. Dickman's IV Corps, consisting of the 89th, 42nd, and 1st Divisions, with the 3rd in reserve.* Hitting the western face of the salient would be Major General George H. Cameron's V Corps, composed of the 26th, the French 15th Colonial, and part of the 4th Division, with the remainder of the 4th in reserve. Cameron's corps was to link up with Liggett's and Dickman's corps, while the French II Colonial Corps with three divisions occupied a sector at the front around the tip of the salient, tasked with supporting the left of the main attack.[21] Marshall's plan emphasized surprise and speed. If the Americans could achieve both, they might be able to break through the German defenses and move eastward across the Woëvre Plain, all the way to Metz, on the

---

* In First Army's battle orders, Marshall refers to H-Hour as the hour the attack would commence, and D-Day as the day the attack would take place. Such designations are closely associated with the Normandy invasion during World War II, but it was during World War I that such code names were first used by an American army.

confluence of the Moselle and Seille Rivers, and capture the vital railroad junction.

AEF divisions fell into three categories: Regular Army (professional troops), National Guard (state troops), and National Army (draftees). Each was designated to have slightly fewer than 28,000 officers and men, about twice the size of Allied and German divisions.[22] An AEF division, commanded by a major general, included three brigades led by brigadier generals. Two of the brigades were designated as infantry, with each composed of two regiments supported by two machine-gun battalions. The other brigade was artillery, with two regiments of French 75mm guns and one regiment of 155mm howitzers. Rounding out a division were various support units, such as engineer, medical, military police, signal, and transportation, which were called trains. Each was typically commanded by a colonel.

Only Hunter Liggett's corps had participated in a major offensive. Back in July on the Château-Thierry front, his divisions, attached to the French, stopped the German advance along the Marne. Some of the same French divisions would now serve adjacent to him at St. Mihiel. This made Liggett the most experienced combat officer in First Army. And even though he didn't look the part, as the war progressed he proved himself the most field-competent commander in the U.S. Army. He had graduated West Point seven years before Black Jack, and, like his boss, had honed his skills during the Spanish-American War and the Philippines. He came to France in April 1917 as commander of the 41st Division, a replacement unit that would not see combat, but was broken up to serve as filler for other divisions. When I Corps was organized in January 1918, Pershing put Liggett in charge.

At first glance, Liggett appeared fat and lazy, yet only the former was true. His weight was in sharp contrast to the ideal set by Pershing as a fit officer, one with the trim physique of a cavalryman. In fact,

Black Jack had considered sending Liggett home in 1917, unconvinced his future corps commander could handle the rigors of war.[23] To impress Pershing, Liggett would leave his Chaumont office every morning for a long walk. Whatever calories he burned were replenished later on, thanks to his personal cook, an immigrant Greek candy maker from Seattle who joined the army as a path toward citizenship.

Journalist Frederick Palmer wasn't kind in his initial description of Liggett: "If ever a soldier looked as though he could 'eat three square meals a day' without indigestion, it was Liggett." Yet at the same time, the I Corps leader's bearing impressed Palmer: "Over six feet in height and generously built, his majestic figure would attract attention in any gathering. There was a depth of experience shining out of his frank eyes, and he radiated mellowness, poise and positive energy."[24]

General Liggett's aide, Colonel Pierpont Stackpole—a Boston attorney in civilian life—recorded in his diary that Liggett suffered from bouts of diarrhea, but this in no way inhibited his ability as a great tactician and commander; if Pershing lost authority over the AEF, Liggett was his obvious replacement. Years before the Great War, when he studied military tactics at the Army War College in Washington and the Command and General Staff College at Fort Leavenworth, Liggett devoured maps of the 1870 Franco-Prussian War and knew the pathway to Sedan better than the French, even though he had never visited the fortress city.[25]

Generals Cameron and Dickman had just been promoted to lead their corps, but both had experience serving under Liggett as division commanders. Four of the nine First Army divisions had not yet seen combat. In the event that the attack went horribly wrong, four divisions were placed in reserve to help out: the 35th, 78th, 80th, and 91st.

August 30 was a busy day for Pershing. During the morning he entertained staff from the French Eighth Army at his headquarters, where they formally presented him control of their sector that bordered the salient. With much delight, the French officers handed Black Jack a two-volume work containing their offensive and defensive plans for the sector. Pershing may have thumbed through a few pages at most; Colonel Marshall had already drawn up First Army's battle plans for St. Mihiel, much more concise at only fourteen pages in length. That afternoon Marshal Foch and his chief of staff, Major General Maxime Weygand, paid a visit to Pershing, and the American general's jubilant mood over the past few days finally turned sour.

Foch started off the dialogue with the usual pleasantries and then eased into the conversation with an explanation of why he called the meeting.* Recently, he said, Allied victories in other fronts had made significant gains, and Foch now believed the Germans were on the verge of collapsing—a far cry from earlier in the year, when Foch proclaimed with much certainty that the war would spill into 1919. Because of these battlefield developments, the commander in chief told Pershing that he either had to reduce the scope of the St. Mihiel attack or abandon it altogether. Pershing was dumbfounded. Before he could respond, Foch declared that a better course of action would be a combined Allied offensive with the British converging on the German lines from north to south, and the French and Americans attacking from the west. An operation against the St. Mihiel Salient was still feasible, Foch assured Pershing, but only a limited attack on the southern face. It would then have to be followed up with a separate attack against

---

* Their conversation had to be translated by interpreters. Even though Pershing took a crash course in French aboard the *Baltic* from a former West Point language instructor, his understanding of Foch's native tongue was limited; the same could be said about the marshal's command of English.

German defenses in the Meuse-Argonne, which Foch believed had more strategic importance than St. Mihiel.[26]

Foch's sudden change of mind was due in part to the influence of British Expeditionary Force commander Field Marshal Sir Douglas Haig. During the spring of 1918 and into the early summer, Pershing had lent the British ten of his American divisions for training and then slowly took them back to form First Army. However, he left Haig with two of his best National Guard outfits. Now five of the divisions in First Army were among the American units Haig's staff had mentored, and the BEF commander was understandably miffed. Haig told Foch that they would be squandered under Pershing's leadership during a meaningless operation at St. Mihiel.

As Foch droned on, Pershing listened intently. When the American general tried to fire back, he was cut off. "I realize that I am presenting a number of new ideas and that you will probably need time to think them over," Foch said, "but I should like your first impressions."

"Well, Marshal, this is a very sudden change," Pershing finally replied. "We are going forward as already recommended to you and approved by you, and I cannot understand why you want these changes." For Black Jack, the crux of the issue was that Foch was trying to break up First Army before it even fired a shot. "The American Government and people expected the army to act as a unit," Pershing said, "and not be dispersed in this way." Foch condescendingly asked Pershing, "Do you wish to take part in this battle?" Pershing responded, "Most assuredly, but as an American Army and in no other way. The American people and the American government expect that the American Army staff shall act as such and shall not be dispersed here and there along the Western Front."[27]

The conversation quickly turned heated. Foch appealed to Pershing's pride, not as an American, but as a soldier just like him. "Your French and English comrades are going into battle," Foch lectured. "Are you coming with them?" Pershing, visibly angry, countered, "Marshal Foch, you have no authority as Allied Commander-in-Chief to call upon me to yield up my command of the American Army and have it scattered among the Allied forces where it will not be an American Army at all." Foch answered just as irately, "I must insist upon the arrangement." Yet Pershing didn't back down: "Marshal Foch, you may insist all you please, but I decline absolutely to agree to your plan. While our army will fight wherever you may decide, it will not fight except as an independent American army."

After arguing for more than two hours, both commanders finally rose from the table. Pershing was exasperated to the point of wanting to punch Foch, but thought better of it. Foch, exhausted and pale after the long exchange, grabbed his maps and papers and headed toward the door. Before leaving, he turned to the American commander, handed him a memorandum of their discussion, and suggested that if he just gave the plan some more thought, Pershing would come to the same conclusion as he had.[28]

After a restless night, Black Jack mulled it over and sent Foch a written response that morning. Pershing reiterated that by no means would he allow the American army to be broken up, and would sacrifice the St. Mihiel operation if necessary. If that were the case, he would comply with Foch and attack only in the Meuse-Argonne—but as a whole American army and nothing less.[29]

Pershing then spoke with Pétain at his headquarters about the messy situation. Always a voice of reason, the French general sympathized with Pershing and agreed that together they would hash out a compromise plan that would be to Foch's liking. Essentially, they proposed that American forces would remain intact while conducting a reduced attack against the St. Mihiel Salient in mid-September, and then strike the Meuse-Argonne two weeks later.

On September 2, Pershing and Pétain met with Foch at Bombon and presented their case. Foch was in a better mood and more reasonable—and for that matter, so was Pershing, perhaps because Pétain was there as a mediator. Foch agreed that the American First Army could execute a restricted attack on the St. Mihiel Salient, but they were not to push forward to Metz; they must stop after the salient had been reduced and prepare for a larger operation west of the Meuse. Foch insisted that the St. Mihiel attack take place no later than September 15, and the Meuse-Argonne operation would launch by September 25.

Pershing had now committed his inexperienced army to undertake two large operations over the course of two weeks. It looked as if Foch were setting Pershing up for failure, but Black Jack couldn't back down from the challenge. Major George C. Marshall was told to resume planning the St. Mihiel operation and commence organizing the more complicated Meuse-Argonne offensive. Immediately after the salient was secured, First Army would need to shift most of the troops engaged in the first battle to a new front sixty miles away and fight jointly with fresh divisions in three corps. Marshall handled this complicated maneuver in a masterly fashion.

With the infantry component set in place, support from artillery, tanks, and planes still needed to be addressed. Foch committed the Allies to assist First Army by providing many of the war tools missing from the AEF arsenal. France promised three thousand pieces of artillery and three million rounds of 75mm shells to be fired by a combination of American and French artillerymen.

Four hundred tanks were also supplied by the French, including 350 Renault light tanks (FT17s), which were placed mostly under

Lieutenant Colonel Patton's command. Renaults were produced by the legendary vehicle manufacturer that was established in 1899. The name Louis Renault, one of the company's founders, was prominently stamped on a plate on the side of the tank. Each machine weighed just less than seven tons and could accommodate two men. Powered by a four-cylinder gasoline, water-cooled, thirty-five-horsepower engine, a Renault reached a top speed of five miles per hour, which was more than four times faster than the speed at which a foot soldier could advance. The tank was armed with 4,800 rounds of ammunition and a Hotchkiss 8mm machine gun that poked out of the turret.[30] "The 'FT17' was the French light tank model. It was also called a 'Baby Tank' and described as 'about as long as a Ford car and as tall as a man.'"[31]

Plans for the air attack were left up to Colonel William "Billy" Mitchell, the face of the Air Service, if not the commander. That job initially went to Major General Benjamin Foulois. Pershing had met Foulois in Mexico when his 1st Aero Squadron supported the Punitive Expedition. Black Jack paid him back with appointment as AEF chief of Air Service in November 1917. Billy Mitchell had assumed that the position was earmarked for him, and had a fit when he was passed over. Prior to the war he had been senior in rank to Foulois, and had been serving in France since October 1917, building the nascent American air program. Mitchell scorned Foulois as a "carpetbagger," and an intense animosity formed between the two. As public figures, the two men were polar opposites. Foulois thought Mitchell brash, annoying, and insubordinate, an opinion shared by many other army officers. Mitchell was "flamboyant, relatively wealthy, and a flashy dresser." Foulois came from "humble origins" and felt more at home in a comfortable "pair of overalls to a neatly tailored uniform." Mitchell craved attention and showed up at dinner parties and other affairs where he might get noticed, while Foulois preferred a stiff drink and a game of poker. [32] As it turned out, Foulois was a poor choice to run the Air Service. He lacked the ability to organize tactical squadrons and keep his branch of the AEF supplied. Simply put, the job was too much for Foulois, and he wanted out. Pershing replaced him with West Point classmate Major General Mason Patrick, and made Foulois second in command.

Aviators were an eccentric bunch, a fraternity of adventure seekers, basking in the glow of danger and glory. Aviation was a young man's game, with many of the pilots in their twenties. Although older than most at age thirty-nine, Mitchell fit right in. He took to the skies in 1916, after several mediocre years as a staff officer that were preceded by service during the Spanish-American War. Mitchell had more passion than just about anyone else in Pershing's army, and he was appointed First Army's chief of Air Service in early August 1918. [33] His dedication to the job was undeniable. He slept less than three hours a night. Reports from squadron commanders didn't usually reach him until ten p.m., and he spent the next few hours drafting orders for the next day. He then rose at five a.m. to watch his planes depart before dawn. [34]

Dedication aside, Mitchell was hard to get along with and had few friends in the AEF. He could never shut up and constantly involved himself in military affairs where he didn't belong. This character trait plagued Mitchell throughout his career. At St. Mihiel, Mitchell was finally presented with a battlefield stage to show the capability of his beloved Air Service. To anyone who would listen, he bragged how his planes would control the skies after the battle started. Visitors to Mitchell's headquarters were shown "an amazing relief map" of the whole salient, designed by French balloon companies who had thoroughly studied the area. At twelve by twelve feet, the map was so large that Mitchell had difficulty finding floor space to accommodate it. "Each hill, woods, road, detached house, large building, railroad yard, ravine—in fact, every incident of the terrain," he later enthused, "was remarkably depicted."[35]

By the time Mitchell completed his preparations, First Army Air Service would utilize 1,481 American, French, British and Italian planes and balloons, spread around fourteen mobile flying fields—the greatest concentration of aircraft during the war.

American planes were the Liberty Engine–powered De Havilland DH-4s. They were notoriously dangerous because the sixty-seven-gallon fuel tank that separated the pilot and observer easily caught fire; aviators deemed them "flying coffins." The four-hundred-pound in-line engines were lubricated by castor oil, which too often leaked out, sprayed, and could find its way into a pilot's stomach, causing severe gas pains and nausea. More preferable were the French Société Provisoire des Aéroplanes Deperdussin (SPAD), and the Blériot or SPAD XIIIs, capable of carrying twenty-pound bombs.[36] Even better were Nieuport 28s, another French aircraft that was maneuverable and had a more reliable 160-horsepower engine that could reach speeds of up to 128 miles per hour.[37]

Regardless of what aircraft they flew, aviators resembled cavalrymen on the western frontier, leaving the fort on scouting expeditions. From the air they provided vital information for combat intelligence officers on terrain and obstacles placed by the enemy.[38] Yet the risks they faced were extreme. Flying in open cockpits without parachutes, pilots were as vulnerable to machine-gun fire as the ground troops they supported.[39] When attacked, they were often left with the choice of a twelve-thousand-foot jump to their deaths or immolation by fire. Aviators stood little chance of survival when their machines, constructed of flimsy wood or metal frames, covered in canvas and marked with highly flammable paint, caught fire after plummeting to the ground. Mitchell knew firsthand the dangers of flying. His brother John, also an aviator, was killed in a training accident in 1917.

Besides a handful of DH-4s, America contributed the fuel used by the attack airplanes. A special grade refined in the United States, the pilots called it "fighting gasoline," "combat gasoline" or "fighting spirits." The Air Service had the fuel shipped across the Atlantic in tankers, and after reaching French ports the fuel was sent to depots by rail and then hauled to the flying fields in small tank wagons or in fifty-five-gallon steel drums.[40]

Many of the pilots Mitchell selected were experienced in aerial combat, having flown in France since 1916 with an all-American French squadron called the Lafayette Escadrille. Mitchell's strategy for the air battle was simple: He would strike at the enemy's rear by massing aircraft on both sides of the salient, "just as a boxer gives a right hook and a left hook successively to his opponent."[41] Yet Mitchell had to be careful where he directed his pilots to attack. The Germans had a custom of placing prisoner of war camps by railroad stations so that Allied bombers would kill their own troops.[42]

Despite Foch's orders to scale back the operation, St. Mihiel was turning into a sizable battle, and an attack of this enormity would be difficult to conceal. A week before D-Day, a meeting was called at Pershing's Ligny headquarters to discuss the length of the artillery assault. First Corps's Hunter Liggett and other staff officers "opposed a bombardment, arguing that the advantages of a complete surprise would outweigh any amount of shell fire."[43] After some debate, it was determined that if Billy Mitchell's aviators could provide First Army with the location of every frontline German division and its nearest reserves, there would be time for a four-hour bombardment without impacting the infantry attack.[44]

Pershing's intelligence staff learned from prisoner interrogations that the Germans expected an attack by the Americans, though they didn't know when or on what scale. Loose-lipped doughboys were the major reason why. Liggett complained that the operation against the salient "was being talked about on the streets of Paris by even the *midinettes*"* despite Pershing's strict orders regarding security. Soldiers were prohibited to display distinctive unit insignia on uniforms, vehicles, and equipment. All letters were censored and could not mention specific geographic areas, only "Somewhere in France." Diaries were absolutely forbidden, although many officers violated this rule, and if caught, the punishment was a trip back to the states.[45]

Yet the looming offensive was "was an open secret in France, England and at home,"[46] and German commanders were preparing for an attack. Nevertheless, Pétain wanted to take no chances, and urged Pershing to come up with a deception to mislead the Germans into thinking the Allied operation would take place somewhere other than the St. Mihiel front. Black Jack's intelligence officers concocted a brilliant plan of deception that unfolded like a plot from a spy novel. Colonel Arthur Conger, a Harvard graduate who was fluent in German, was charged with carrying out the ruse.

On August 28, Pershing commenced the plan by sending Major General Omar Bundy and his VI Corps, along with Colonel Conger, east of the St. Mihiel Salient to the open plateau of the Belfort Gap. On the western end of the gap was the city of Belfort, which remained under French control. On the eastern end was Mulhouse, occupied by the Germans. Historians point out that the Belfort Gap, a narrow passage between the Vosges Mountains and the town of Belfort, was "a

---

* Parisian seamstresses or salesgirls.

logical place to feign an offensive because the area was the nearest Allied point threatening the Rhine and the only point between the east of Metz to Switzerland where an Allied army could advance over open ground."[47] General Bundy was informed that the St. Mihiel attack was actually a deception and that the real plan was to push through Belfort and attack Mulhouse. He wasn't told the truth until the St. Mihiel attack was well under way.[48]

Bundy and his staff took up quarters at Belfort's four-star Grand Hôtel du Tonneau d'Or, where they drew the attention of German spies who had crossed over the nearby Swiss border to congregate at the city's watering holes and cafés. When Colonel Conger arrived at the gap, he put into action a plan to confuse the German troops in Mulhouse: he sent out reconnaissance parties to probe their lines, transmitted fake coded radio messages, and ordered French tanks to roll across the terrain at night, leaving behind tracks that German aerial photographers captured during the day.

To rattle the Germans further, Conger secured a room at the same hotel as General Bundy. Conger sat down at the writing desk in his suite, pulled two sheets of plain paper and one piece of carbon paper from the drawer, and wrote a one-page report to Pershing on the status of the Belfort attack. The report was duplicated with the carbon and both copies were given to a courier. Conger balled up the carbon paper into a tight wad, threw it into a wastebasket next to his desk, then headed downstairs to the bar for a drink. Five minutes later he returned to his room, and as Conger had suspected, the wastebasket had been emptied, most likely by a spy tipped off by the housekeeping staff. Yet the impact of Conger's espionage caper was minimal. German units were evacuated from hospitals and villages near Belfort, and some artillery and a few reserve divisions were brought in, but Gallwitz's main force remained at St. Mihiel.[49]

Later on it was confirmed that while the Germans were certain an attack against the salient was imminent, they didn't expect it until late in September. By then the salient would have been absent of German troops because preparations were already under way to shorten their front. On September 11, the German High Command issued orders for a gradual withdrawal and the destruction of all things of military value that could not be moved. The order had not yet been fully executed when the American attack launched on September 12. The Germans were caught completely by surprise.

3

ST. MIHIEL

On Thursday, September 12, Pershing awoke at three thirty a.m. to a steady rain and headed from Ligny a half hour later with several staff officers to Fort de Gironville, an old French bastion built in 1324. Its heights overlooked the St. Mihiel battlefield from the south, providing a perfect vantage point to watch the operation unfold. First Army artillery had been firing since one a.m. from the southern face of the salient, blanketing key German positions with bombs and shrapnel. At five a.m., the infantry launched the attack from a designated line—an action that soldiers in the First World War referred to as "jumping off." The poor weather hindered the fighting over the next few days, but it was not as bad as some of the First Army commanders had feared.

During a meeting Pershing called the night before that included corps, division, and various other staff officers, First Army Chief of Engineers Brigadier General Jay J. Morrow had pleaded with Black

Jack to postpone the attack. "The rain will slow delivery of ammunition on the railways," Morrow claimed, and would make it difficult to "bring up enough water for the troops." Other commanders in the room, with the exception of Billy Mitchell, nodded in agreement. Mitchell listened to this lame argument and for once said nothing, but noted in his memoirs that "you can always trust an engineer to go on the defensive whenever it is possible."[1] With too much at stake to allow inclement weather to interfere, Pershing gave Morrow's objections no thought and insisted that the operation would take place as scheduled.[2] At Cantigny, Belleau Wood, and Château-Thierry, American doughboys had proved that they were as good as any soldiers on the western front. But those battles had been under French direction. Now, at St. Mihiel, the moment of truth was about to unfold for Pershing. Could the Americans succeed on their own, as he had so desperately wished?

As the infantry climbed from their waterlogged trenches and moved toward the German lines, they encountered little resistance, only sporadic artillery fire. The day before, General Gallwitz had executed Plan Loki, a gradual departure of Army Detachment C to the Michel Stellung at the base of the salient. Along the way, German soldiers were instructed to destroy bridges, roads, and water supplies. While much destruction had been accomplished, the First Army attack had turned Loki from an orderly withdrawal into a chaotic retreat.[3] French soldiers of the II Colonial Corps made matters worse for the enemy by conducting trench raids all around the salient, leaving the confused Germans with no idea which direction the main attack was coming from.[4]

Even though most Germans were running away, several artillery and infantry units remained in the salient and fought back with vigor. On a ridge near the village of Seicheprey, where the 102nd Infantry of the 26th Yankee Division was bloodied on April 20, 1918, the Germans' machine guns and rifle fire poured down on the doughboys of the 42nd Division until artillery and tanks silenced their guns. The American gunners worked "with mechanical rhythm and they loaded and sent the shells to their destination," a London *Daily Mail* reporter observed. This was the case throughout the American lines. Supply trains operating on light-gauge railways ran back and forth, bringing up what appeared to be a never-ending supply of shells.[5]

Pershing had been worried about how the infantry was going to penetrate the wire entanglements draped around the German defenses. Originally, the British offered heavy tanks capable of tearing up the wire, but at the last minute they decided the machines were needed elsewhere. An artillery attack aimed directly at the wire was out of the question—that would have required more than a day of continuous fire and forfeited the element of surprise. Instead, Pershing ordered that the infantry, assisted by small groups of engineers, snip the wire with cutters as they advanced.[6] Black Jack needn't have been so concerned. The first wave of infantry either clipped their way through the wire or, in some cases, walked right over it.[7]

The battle was unfolding just as Colonel Marshall had planned. Hunter Liggett's I Corps ran into little resistance on the southern face of the salient and reached its objectives after only seven hours. The burly commander wanted to continue on toward Metz, but Pershing had already promised Foch that his troops would not go beyond their stated goals for the operation. Liggett might very well have succeeded, because the German lines were in disarray. Accounts from the front reported that German troops were anxiously throwing up earthworks on the incomplete Michel Stellung.[8] Field Marshal von Hindenburg was reportedly so distraught over the American assault, one historian wrote, that he was "unable to carry on a clear and comprehensive discussion." The German commander did manage to tell Gallwitz, "I

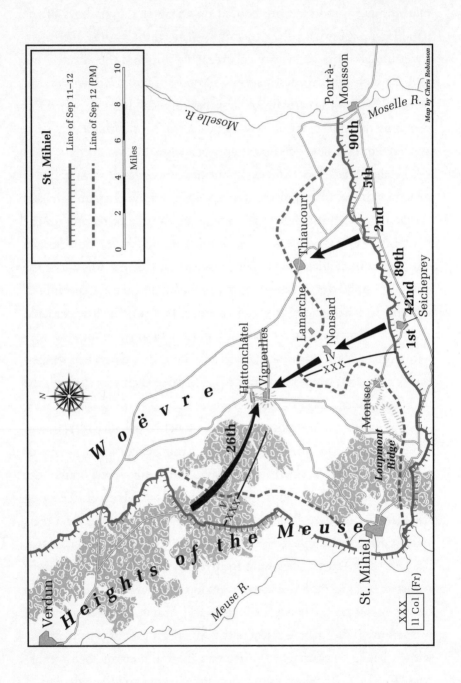

refuse to believe that two German divisions are not a match for an American division."[9]

Major William Donovan's battalion was in the thick of the attack. Serving with the famed 42nd "Rainbow" Division—which also included Father Francis Duffy and the flamboyant Douglas MacArthur— the future director of the Office of Strategic Services, a predecessor to the Central Intelligence Agency, had moved his troops of the 1st Battalion, 165th Infantry Regiment, into position at two thirty a.m. "in one vast circle of flashing skies" from the artillery that commenced earlier that morning. Those close to Donovan knew him as "Wild Bill," a nickname he was given by his men for being such a vigorous trainer. Father Duffy described his friend as "a man in the middle thirties, very attractive in face and manner . . . the athlete who always keeps himself in perfect condition."[10] Wild Bill was confident that St. Mihiel would be an easy operation—"a plum ready for the picking," he wrote.[11]

Within a few hours after jumping off, Donovan's battalion reached the village of St. Benoît, which the Germans had vacated shortly before the Americans arrived. Establishing his headquarters in the village's château, Wild Bill found a cache of valuable paintings, porcelains, and furniture in a courtyard behind the manor house, left by German troops unable to carry them as they fled. Donovan toured the village, where he encountered "poor people who for four years had been with the Germans." That night Donovan and another officer dined with a woman from the village who "had not been out of sight of a German for four years. Every night after she prepared the meals for her officer guests she had to retire to her cellar. This night after she fed us she put on her best skirt and went out to visit her neighbors."[12]

In Essey, a village northeast of St. Mihiel, Brigadier General Douglas MacArthur "saw a sight I shall never forget," he wrote in his memoirs. "Our advance had been so rapid the Germans had evacuated in a panic." He came upon "a German officer's horse saddled and equipped standing in a barn, a battery of guns complete in every detail, and the entire instrumentation and music of a regimental band."[13]

On a little hill overlooking Essey, George S. Patton and Douglas MacArthur met for the first time. After MacArthur's 84th Brigade overran the enemy positions, his men were temporarily held up in the village. He stood on the high ground as the Germans counterattacked with an artillery barrage. Patton's tanks had been supporting the Rainbow Division attack, but, as MacArthur wrote, the machines "soon bogged down . . . [in] mud." Patton sought out MacArthur and joined him on the hill as enemy shells came toward them. MacArthur was sporting his barracks cap and a scarf his mother had knitted for him, while Patton had an ivory-handled Colt .45 strapped to his hip.

MacArthur recalled that Patton flinched when a shell came dangerously close and he told the tank officer: "Don't worry, major [MacArthur misidentified Patton's rank]. You never hear the one that gets you." Patton had much more to say about the event. "I met General MacArthur commanding a brigade," he wrote. "I joined him and the creeping barrage came along towards us, but it was very thin and not dangerous. I think each one wanted to leave but each hated to say so, so we let it come over us. We stood and talked but neither was much interested in what the other said as we could not get our minds off the shells."[14]

Lieutenant Hugh S. Thompson of the 168th Infantry Regiment, also part of the Rainbow Division, led his platoon across no-man's-land "behind a curtain of smoke and flame." They were stopped cold when an "angry gun" opened fire, followed by several more that sprayed bullets in their direction. "The guns were chattering like mad," Thompson remembered. "All thought of controlling the scattered line gave way to fearful self-preservation. We'd be killed if we lay still. There was a gambling chance if we charged ahead." Thompson chose the latter option and escorted his men through the woods and into the enemy trenches, where the frightened German soldiers raised their hands in surrender.[15]

One after another, the doughboys rolled unmolested across the St. Mihiel Salient, their khaki uniforms caked in mud, seizing formerly occupied towns and villages. Hattonchâtel, at the center of the salient, was liberated during the night of September 12–13 by the 102nd Infantry. From the destroyed village the Americans could see flames shooting from the Woëvre Plain in the wake of retreating Germans who had set buildings and supply dumps on fire.

A short distance to the north of Essey, the 89th "Middle West" Division took Bouillonville on the twelfth, and the village was used as a First Army communications command post. Signal Battalion Sergeant Major Arthur I. Wissman, previously a statistical clerk at Southwestern Bell Telephone System in St. Louis, was shocked at what he encountered. "Hardly a house was left standing and the road was pitted with shell holes," Wissman documented. "As our party clattered through the deserted and debris-strewn streets of this town, a faint light was seen in the hallway of what was once a two-story house. Upon coming nearer we found two old French women past fifty years of age, making their way over the piles of brick, at the same time shielding a flickering candle with trembling hands."

When Wissman and the other members of his battalion introduced themselves as Americans and made assurances that they were not going to harm them, the women "burst into tears and exclaimed 'At last, at last; thank God!' They had hid in their cellar that whole day, refusing to go along with the retreating Germans, taking their chances of being killed by shell fire instead." Wissman learned through a translator that the "Boche had been their masters for four years, and when they heard our party coming through the streets, they thought the

Germans were coming back, and they were just coming out to give themselves up."[16]

A group of female Salvation Army workers following First Army motored through the formerly German-occupied villages, and were greeted by the newly freed French citizens with shouts of *"Bonnes Americaines! Bonnes Americaines!* [Good Americans]."[17] The religious-based "Salvationists" came to France shortly after the first American soldiers arrived in the country, following the doughboys to the front and setting up huts where doughnuts, hot chocolate, coffee, cakes and pies were served to remind them of home. They also conducted Bible study classes and helped the wounded at field hospitals.

But it was the French civilians who needed comfort the most. Salvation Army personnel were astonished to see how badly the Germans had treated the French locals, while the Germans themselves lived in relative luxury. Civilians who had nowhere else to go and were forced to remain in the salient had been reduced to begging for food. During the cold winter months, they were allotted only one candle and an hour of electricity per day by the German occupiers. They told of staying in bed for eleven or twelve hours a day because it was too cold to do anything else.[18] In contrast, when the Salvation Army passed by Montsec, they entered the former German lines and came across a collection of log cabin bungalows laid out like a small village. Each bungalow had running water, electric lights, and other modern conveniences to comfort German officers. The "village" also had a dance hall, a billiard room, and several pianos, as well as a well-tended vegetable garden and fully stocked rabbit hutches.[19]

American troops who looked skyward for air support were sadly disappointed. While most First Army divisions reached their objectives on schedule, poor visibility kept Billy Mitchell's pilots grounded for most of the morning. Lieutenant Erwin Bleckley, an aviator with the

50th Aero Squadron, recorded that he took off at 6:15 a.m. but didn't stay up long because the "clouds were so low [I] could not see very much," other than "quite a bit of allied artillery activity." With nothing to report, Bleckley returned to the squadron airdrome two hours later.[20]

Aviator Eddie Rickenbacker fared a little better. A former race car driver from Ohio, Sergeant Rickenbacker had briefly served alongside Cesar Santini in Pershing's chauffeur pool. He found little excitement in motoring staff officers around northern France. With Black Jack's blessing, he transferred to the Air Service and joined the famed 94th "Hat in the Ring" Aero Squadron, a nickname adopted by the unit to signify that, like prizefighters, they were willing to take on any challenge. Rickenbacker and his Nieuport 28 didn't get airborne until noon. Although it was still raining, visibility had improved enough to provide him with a good vantage point over the battlefield. Rickenbacker could see "at 600 feet above ground [flying] straight east to St. Mihiel" that the Germans were soundly defeated. After crossing the Meuse River and turning toward Verdun, Rickenbacker, along with another pilot flying beside him, saw that "many fires were burning under us as we flew, most of them well on the German side of the river. Villages, haystacks, ammunition dumps, and supplies were being set ablaze by the retreating Huns."* Before turning back, Rickenbacker had shot down four German planes, and was well on his way to becoming America's top air ace.[21]

First Lieutenant David E. Putnam might have become better known than Rickenbacker if he hadn't met his demise on September 12. At age nineteen, he was already a veteran flyer with service in the

---

* "Huns" was a derogatory nickname for the Germans adopted by the British and French in reference to Attila the Hun. Allied soldiers also referred to the Germans as Boche, which is French slang for "rascal."

Lafayette Flying Corps before putting on an American uniform and notching twelve victories. Patrolling above the American lines north of St. Mihiel with another pilot from the 139th Aero Squadron, he was ganged up on by seven German planes. Four of them went after Putnam and he was struck in the heart by two machine-gun bullets. The other pilot made it home safely. Putnam's death was a tremendous loss for Mitchell's Air Service.[22]

Over the next few days, as the weather slowly improved, Billy Mitchell's reconnaissance planes reached the German lines, gleaning valuable intelligence about their troop disposition. During the day and night Allied bombers delivered payloads on enemy supply dumps, and in one instance, destroyed the rail lines ahead of Thiaucourt. With nowhere to go, a carload of German soldiers were stuck at the village's train station and became easy prey for an American infantry regiment.[23] Flying at night was especially dangerous because the pilots had to rely on compasses that weren't always accurate, or on the stars, which weren't always visible. Regardless of the time of day the Germans could be counted on to fight back in the skies over the salient. American Air Service losses were reported at forty pilots killed and another sixteen taken prisoner.

Rainfall proved frustrating for the tank corps, whose cumbersome vehicles easily became mired in the sticky mud of the Woëvre Plain.* Lieutenant Colonel Patton watched his machines "coming along and getting stuck in the trenches. It was a most irritating sight," he wrote. "At 7 o'clock I moved forward 2 miles and passed some dead and wounded. I saw one fellow in a shell hole holding his rifle sitting down."

---

* Though Patton's name has become forever linked with America's First World War tanks, the Tank Corps was actually led by Colonel—later Brigadier General—Samuel D. Rockenbach, a former cavalry officer and, like Marshall, a graduate of VMI.

Patton's initial reaction was anger. "I thought he was hiding and went to cuss him out," he recalled with no remorse. Instead, Patton discovered "he had a bullet over his right eye and was dead."[24] Another of Patton's men was shot through the palm of his left hand and sent to the rear for hospitalization, but the officer escaped and walked six miles back to his tank, proclaiming that he could "carry on" with his right hand.[25]

Despite the muddy ground, America's tanks made significant progress on the first day. To keep them fueled, several machines designated as gasoline tanks followed closely behind. When they were put out of action by enemy artillery, Patton's crew improvised. They secured barrels of gasoline to bobsleds and dragged them over the mud toward the stalled tanks.[26]

Besides Patton, Marshall, MacArthur, and Donovan, other future World War II luminaries were well represented on the St. Mihiel battlefield. Major Terry de la Mesa Allen, who eventually led the 1st Division as a general in North Africa and Sicily, commanded a battalion of the 90th Division. Lieutenant Colonel Clarence Huebner, who later took over the 1st Division from Allen in 1943, commanded a battalion of the 28th Infantry Regiment in 1918. Lieutenant Colonel Joseph "Vinegar Joe" Stillwell, the sour-faced commander of the China-Burma-India Theater during World War II, was now IV Corps's intelligence officer. Captain Ernest "Gravel Voice" Harmon, who led Troop F of the 2nd Cavalry Regiment, would later, for about a year, command the 2nd Armored Division in North Africa. At age twenty-nine, Troy Middleton was a colonel in the 4th Division, the youngest officer to hold that rank. During World War II he would command the 45th Infantry Division, gaining notoriety during Operation Cobra and the Battle of the Bulge. Captain Jonathan Wainwright, who in 1942 surrendered his command in the Philippines and served the rest of World War II in a Japanese POW camp, was in 1918 the 82nd Airborne Division's chief of staff.

Out of this group, Terry Allen had the most memorable experience at St. Mihiel. German artillery spotted Allen's 3rd Battalion of the 358th Infantry Regiment as it moved into position for the jump-off, and he was knocked unconscious by shrapnel. Taken to a field hospital in the rear, Allen refused treatment, hopped out of bed, and demanded transportation back to the front. Covered in blood and missing some teeth, Major Allen wandered aimlessly into the Friere Wood, deep in the southeastern part of the German line, looking for his battalion. For some reason he stopped to pick up a German dog tag. When a detachment from the 357th Infantry Regiment saw the confused officer, they thought he was a spy and ordered that Allen empty his pockets. Out dropped the enemy ID and Allen was arrested on the spot. Weak from blood loss, Allen eventually convinced the doughboys he was an American officer, and they had him evacuated back to the hospital.[27]

On the afternoon of September 12, Pershing was back at his Ligny headquarters dealing with problems in the V Corps sector. Specifically, the 26th Division was bogged down and unable to link up at Vigneulles with the 1st Division, which was making great headway from the south. By telephone Black Jack barked out orders to V Corps's Major General George Cameron, demanding that he "push harder" against the western face of the salient. It worked, although not at the pace Black Jack would have liked. One New England regiment didn't reach Vigneulles until three thirty p.m. the next day.[28] Cameron also sent the 2nd Cavalry Regiment, a branch of the army that was all but extinct on the western front, toward Vigneulles. Along the way they found that several smaller villages had been torched. At Viéville, the horse soldiers arrived just in time to prevent the Germans from torching the town and captured a four-gun battery of heavy guns as war booty. In St. Maurice the 2nd Cavalry engaged a German rear guard of mixed troops, killing some of them and taking the rest as prisoners.[29]

Over the next few days it was the same story all over the salient. By the afternoon of the twelfth most of Pershing's warriors were no longer attacking but mopping up. First Army's baptism of fire was a smashing success. Major General John L. Hines, 4th Division commander, wrote in his diary that St. Mihiel "is a thing of the past."[30] Other officers thought First Army should exploit its good fortune and continue on to Metz, regardless of Pershing's promise to Marshal Foch. On the night of September 13, Douglas MacArthur and his adjutant snuck across the lines to the outskirts of the city and found it "practically defenseless for the moment." A golden opportunity, MacArthur thought, "a prize wide open for the taking."[31] George Marshall couldn't have agreed more, but, practically speaking, he advised Pershing's staff against resuming the attack because it "would have rendered impossible the completion of the concentration for the Meuse-Argonne by the date set."[32]

The day after the battle opened, Pershing's desk was stacked high with telegrams congratulating him on his victory at St. Mihiel, as well as birthday greetings—Black Jack turned fifty-eight on September 13. In the pile was a message from President Wilson, who told Pershing that "the boys have done what we expected of them and did it in a way we most admire. We are deeply proud of them and their chief."[33] Wilson wasn't much interested in the military, but he must have felt obliged to write his commander on this important day. At the White House, the president received regular reports about the fighting, but he almost never discussed any aspect of the military's progress with his cabinet.[34]

Also in the stack of messages was a letter that likely had greater importance to Pershing than the one from Wilson; it came from a pretty Romanian named Micheline Resco. Pershing had been introduced to the twenty-three-year-old petite, blond, and blue-eyed Parisian artist at the Crillon Hotel in mid-June 1917. The occasion was a party in his honor, and he was immediately smitten. Three weeks after they met, Pershing and Micheline commenced a regular correspondence, and by September the two were intimate.[35] In his reply to her letter, Black Jack thanked her for the warm sentiments about him and his troops. He closed the note with "I'm sending you a million kisses and I embrace you so tenderly, Yours—JP."[36] Pershing's interest in Nita Patton had clearly faded.

During the next few days Pershing's mailbox was stuffed with hundreds more congratulatory notes that trickled in from the United States—cards, telegrams, and letters from civic organizations, business clubs, schoolchildren, small-town mayors, and the Shriners. Either Pershing or an aide replied to each piece of correspondence.[37] Among them was a letter from Beatrice Patton, George's wife. She told Pershing how much he was now admired in America. "Here in the U.S.A. they call this Hero Day. The papers are full of tales of your present glory and stories of your youthful appetite for pie as told by the old Ladies of Laclede," a reference to Pershing's hometown. She proclaimed the AEF commander "the greatest man in America and one of the greatest in the world today."[38]

Mary Drum, the spouse of his First Army chief of staff Hugh Drum, displayed her admiration for Pershing by writing a letter to the editor of the *Indianapolis Star*. She expressed her frustration over a series of articles in the *Star* that painted an unflattering picture of the AEF commander. In one piece, it was alleged that during a whirlwind inspection of medical facilities, Pershing showed little interest in the patients or staff and left in a hurry. In Mrs. Drum's view, Pershing could do no wrong, and she accused the newspaper editor of ridiculing Black Jack in an effort to "make light of his position of authority or lessen our confidence in him."[39]

Practically every day Pershing and his army were featured on the front page of newspapers all over the United States. From lengthy biographical pieces to articles about his daily interactions and opinions, on some days Pershing received more press than President Wilson. In Paris, his portrait adorned nearly every newspaper with the phrase "Splendid Victory."[40] The general was also on the big screen. Four days before the Battle of St. Mihiel, the Fox Film Corporation released *Why America Will Win*, an epic motion picture about Pershing's life in which he was portrayed by three different actors at various stages: his boyhood, his youth, and as a general.[41]

After St. Mihiel was secure and no longer in danger from German artillery, Pershing spent most of his birthday visiting the front. Georges Clemenceau, prime minister of France, toured the salient with the American commander. Called the "Tiger" for his aggressive stance on diplomatic and political issues, Clemenceau, like Foch, had opposed the formation of an independent American army. But in the wake of the St. Mihiel victory, he put aside his strong opinions and allowed the AEF commander to gloat. Their voyage around the salient went well until the party reached Thiaucourt and got bogged down in a massive traffic jam. Clemenceau, known for his Gallic wit, remarked, "They wanted an American Army. They had it. Anyone who saw, as I saw, the hopeless congestion at Thiaucourt, will bear witness that they may congratulate themselves on not having had it sooner."[42]

Clemenceau wasn't exaggerating. Screenwriter Dale Van Every, who fought at St. Mihiel, put it this way: "At times the roads were blocked for hours. Shadowy lines of vehicles two and three abreast stood motionless or hitched forward a yard at a time. Men and horses and guns, tons of ammunition, tons of food, tons of equipment, were jostled and pressed onward in a movement that had to be as swift as it seemed slow."[43] First Army's inspector general was less kind in his assessment of the problem. He determined that army vehicles were allowed to drive too fast, causing accidents that clogged the roads. More egregious was the issue of "double-banking," where both lanes of a two-way road were occupied by motor transports heading in the same direction. Despite improved efforts by First Army military police to control road congestion, it would only get worse during the Meuse-Argonne.

St. Mihiel was formally declared over on September 16 when it was clear that the Germans were not going to counterattack. The reduction of the salient was not only an important strategic victory but a morale booster for Pershing's newly minted First Army, which had impressed the Allied commander in its first operation. The fact that there were 230,000 American and 110,000 French combatants against only 23,000 Germans certainly made the difference. As a result, First Army in-flicted about 2,000 German casualties (killed and wounded), and captured more than 1,500 prisoners. Among the Germans taken from the battlefield were a mixture of Poles, Prussians, Saxons, and Austrians. One Prussian officer surrendered with his dog, which had been with him at the front for three years. Pershing's men also acquired 443 artil-lery pieces and 752 Maxims and other machine guns. Two hundred square miles of formerly occupied territory were given back to the French, including the Paris and Nancy rail lines. American losses were around 7,000 killed and wounded.[44]

Despite a great showing, the Americans would be in for a more difficult time in the Meuse-Argonne. Major General Liggett recog-nized that at St. Mihiel the German was not at his best, "nor his second best," and Pershing's army was not yet "a well-oiled, fully coordinated machine."[45]

4

PREPARING FOR AMERICA'S GREATEST BATTLE

Secretary of War Newton Baker witnessed First Army's pivotal moment from a seat in Cesar Santini's Cadillac, camouflaged among a grove of trees near Fort Gironville, as Pershing stood nearby. Three days later, Baker and Black Jack met up on the Left Bank of Paris at 73 rue de Varenne, where Pershing had use of a palatial town house owned by wealthy New Yorker Ogden Mills. Pershing's pied-à-terre, set in a garden dating from the time of Louis XV, was so magnificent, T. Bentley Mott recalled, that it was "big enough, indeed, to gallop a horse in." When Colonel Mott, who served on Pershing's staff as liaison officer to Foch, arrived at the Paris house "with a message for the General he would take me out into his garden where we could talk while walking along its paths. This had the advantage of giving Pershing some exercise while at the same time he escaped from the annoyance caused by the feeling that officers were waiting outside the door, each in a hurry to see him."[1]

When Baker arrived at Pershing's residence, he exited his Cadillac looking as though he had just come from combat. An Army-issued steel helmet clenched in one hand, a gas mask in the other, his trench coat, leggings and eyeglasses splattered with mud from the western front, Baker was tailed by a throng of reporters hoping to score the next big headline. They were dissatisfied when Baker simply read a prepared statement: "The people of the United States will be overjoyed that their army, in close cooperation with the Allies, has been able to achieve this striking success."[2]

Baker and Pershing were on friendly terms, primarily because the secretary of war trusted the AEF commander and, for the most part, left him alone. Baker had been on the job for only a year when the United States entered the war. When Wilson offered him the post in 1916, he accepted it with much reluctance. Baker confided to an acquaintance how little he knew about the military. "I had never played even with tin soldiers," he boasted.[3] This was hardly true. In fact, Baker knew quite a bit about armies from the Civil War era. His father was a veteran of the Confederate army who had fought with Jeb Stuart, and his mother had been a blockade runner who smuggled quinine and other valuables to rebel prisoners held at Fort McHenry, Maryland.[4]

Baker was a dedicated public servant who, at various times in his career, served as the lawyer, solicitor, and mayor of Cleveland, Ohio. A Pershing biographer described Baker as "a small, timid-looking man, who sat with one leg under his body and the other barely reaching the floor." Furthermore, he "looked as if he ought to be teaching Latin to some girls' academy." Yet the same biographer also noted that Baker "could be remarkably strong, freewheeling and innovative."[5]

Baker was now on his second visit to France in 1918. In March, he had spent three weeks inspecting AEF training, attempting to gain a clear understanding of what was necessary to build "a great army to vindicate a great cause."[6] The answer was soon obvious: Pershing needed more troops, supplies, and weapons. During his current trip to France, Baker focused mainly on issues hampering Pershing's army. The Services of Supply (SOS) was responsible for the reception, transportation, and distribution of supplies, just about anything the Army needed in a war zone. Supplies came through the French ports of Saint-Nazaire, La Pallice, and Bassens on the west coast, and were then distributed to troops by railroad to base stations in the rear. From there they reached the front by motor transport.

Responsibility over the SOS was in the hands of Major General James Harbord, who had replaced the inefficient Major General Francis J. Kernan in July 1918. A close friend to Pershing, Harbord had until recently commanded the Marine brigade with distinction at Belleau Wood and Soissons. The two men had met right after the Spanish-American War, when Harbord was a quartermaster assigned to the 10th Cavalry. Although Harbord was a more than capable field commander, Pershing correctly recognized his organizational skills and tapped him for the supply job.* On Harbord's first day as SOS head he ordered a special train for inspection trips. Though it is unknown whether he or Pershing first had the idea of a personal train, Harbord's rolling office certainly rivaled his boss's office for its size. Not only did the train have accommodations to eat, sleep, make phone calls and send telegrams; it transported two cars for side excursions. "The car is comfortable; the cook is good," Harbord crowed, "we are quite independent of local people for meals and transportation, and we do business!"[7]

---

* Apparently the position suited Harbord well, because after retiring from the Army in 1922, he had a long career in the private sector, including seven years as president of the Radio Corporation of America (RCA).

Although far from broken, the SOS was not running as smoothly as Black Jack wanted. Soon after taking his new job, Harbord came to the same conclusion and told Pershing that "in general, the S.O.S., the greatest industrial concern that has ever been organized in the history of the world, is not on a firm, business-like basis. . . . Do not get the idea I am weeping over this situation, or that I think that anybody is going to go hungry or naked, but the coincidence of your demands for the First Army, the sudden increase of the A.E.F. program; with the embarrassment which the all infantry and machine gun program of our Allies has given us; certainly gives me cause for the gravest concern."[8] Pershing responded by sending Harbord a reserve division and a large cadre of German prisoners to help at the docks.

Meanwhile, First Army continued to bask in the glory of victory. A French officer who toured the St. Mihiel battlefield told Colonel Marshall "that the evidence on the ground convinced him that our infantry walked over the wire, but he thought perhaps they were assisted in this remarkable performance by the size of their feet."[9] Even Foch chimed in about the American performance with his usual touch of cynicism: "This was where the Americans for the first time showed their worth." But he didn't stop there, and directed a backhanded compliment toward his own army: "In one fell swoop they reduced the famous salient, which during so long we did not know how to approach."[10] Never again did Foch, Haig, or anyone else mention the idea that Pershing's force should fight under British and French command.

On September 21, Pershing moved First Army headquarters from Ligny to Souilly, and set up his office on the town hall's second floor, reached by two sets of wooden stairs worn smooth from three years of French Army boots.[11] In 1916, Pétain had utilized the same office, located at 22 Voie Sacrée, the "Sacred Road," from which he had directed the Battle of Verdun. Pershing's ten-car train was pulled into a railway siding and hidden in a grove of trees not far from the commander's office.[12] Before reaching Souilly, Pershing had stopped off in Verdun, a minor detour of twelve miles. Black Jack felt it necessary to "make a casual inspection of the citadel," which was now part of his command, and toured the destroyed city with a French colonel.[13] They visited what was left of Verdun's best-known landmarks—the cathedral and the bishop's palace.

With St. Mihiel now behind them, Colonel Marshall was fine-tuning the battle plan for the Meuse-Argonne, which was one part of a unified attack all along the Hindenburg Line. Between the American and French armies, the Argonne Forest ran northward for about six miles. The plan was not to make a direct frontal assault upon this forest but to force the enemy out of his defenses by the threat of surrounding it. Pershing's ultimate objective in the battle was the city of Sedan, which the Germans had taken early in the war and turned into a vital railway hub to supply their troops.

If First Army could drive the enemy from Sedan and cut their rail line, German armies would be trapped between the Americans on the Meuse-Argonne front, French forces converging through the Aisne River valley on the left flank of the doughboys, and the British striking northwest in the Somme sector. Pershing would open the attack by advancing through the Aire River valley with the Argonne forest on the left and the east bank of the Meuse on the right. To meet the objective, 225,000 doughboys in three corps made up of three divisions each would attack on a front twenty-five miles wide. Dr. Harvey Cushing, a pioneering brain surgeon before the war and now a colonel in the AEF Medical Corps, expected around 14,000 casualties the first day, including 3,000 dead and 11,000 wounded.[14] Even if Cushing's prediction was way off, there was still a need for adequate hospitals. Forty-four of them were constructed near the front as a precaution.

Sedan was about forty miles from where First Army would jump off, and along the way Pershing's soldiers had to traverse the six-mile-deep Argonne Forest and its assortment of jutting rocks, steep cliffs, and slippery ravines. The Aire valley was just the opposite, with open ground that offered no protection. The river for which it is named flows north for fifteen miles, then curves west to meet the Aisne River at Grandpré, a village with a population of over a thousand, "resting against a bluff of the tongue of ridge which shoots out from the Bourgogne Wood."[15] Grandpré was also called the "Citadel" because the village, with ruins of ancient buildings, jutted out through the forest over the river and was so fortified by the Germans that it was going to be difficult to penetrate.[16]

Over the four years in which they had occupied this sector, the Germans built their defenses around the terrain, but for added protection the Siegfried Stellung, a section of the Hindenburg Line, was raised behind the front. By 1918 the line was the strongest around Cambrai by the Somme River and, because of its proximity to Verdun, the section that ran through the Argonne Forest. Before First Army would even encounter the Hindenburg Line, they had to pass through two frontline positions: the first position with lots of barbed wire and machine guns, and three miles away the intermediate position, consisting of artillery and trenches that stretched to the Aisne River and the surrounding hills called the Meuse Heights.[17]

If First Army's doughboys made it beyond these obstructions, three fortified barriers of the Hindenburg Line awaited them. Each was named for a witch from the operas of Richard Wagner. The first was the Giselher Stellung and contained Montfaucon. The second, called the Kriemhilde Stellung, was five miles away and built along the ridges of the Romagne Heights. Five miles from there was the Freya Stellung, which incorporated the hills adjacent to the village of Buzancy.[18]

Pershing's warriors were to flank the forest on the east, while the French would do the same on the west, and both were to link up to the rear of the forest, from which, by this time, the enemy would have had to withdraw in order to avoid being surrounded. The French and American armies, once joined behind the Argonne, would repeat the process on the wooded hills north of the forest. The two armies would then press northward toward Sedan, while the British, starting from the direction of Cambrai, would press eastward toward the same goal. The combined Allied forces would crowd the German Army, back them up against the Ardennes Forest, and cut the Sedan-Mézières railroad. Trains moved each day between the main part of the rail line, which ran between Carignan, Sedan, and Mézières, carrying German supplies and troops.[19] If it all went as planned, General Ludendorff would have no choice but to surrender the entire German Army by the end of the year.[20] Pershing reportedly said, "Hell, Heaven, or Hoboken by Christmas."[21]

Ludendorff knew the French would attack in the Champagne and his army was prepared for the assault. But from the Argonne to the Meuse, the Germans expected a slight attack, at most. Even though the Germans had taken prisoners and one deserter (their intelligence called him "weak-minded") from several different American divisions, the Germans thought the great effort would be east of the Meuse toward Metz, and had placed 250,000 men in that region. Manning the Argonne front were only six divisions, barely 70,000 men against 225,000 attacking Americans. But the Germans had 85,000 troops in reserve and could move another 70,000 from the Metz front. Similar to the defenders of St. Mihiel, most of the Germans were second- or third-rate troops brought to the Argonne, considered a quiet sector, after having fought elsewhere.[22]

Black Jack and his operations staff visualized the battle in two segments. During the initial attack, First Army would pierce the three German positions, advance another ten miles, then clear the Argonne and link up with the French Fourth Army on the left. The next attack would press forward ten more miles to outflank the enemy defenses along the Aisne River, which would place the Americans in striking distance of Sedan and Mézières on the Meuse. Smaller attacks would clear the enemy from the heights facing the east bank of the Meuse.[23]

Marshall first had to move 500,000 troops, 2,000 guns, and 900,000 tons of ammunition and supplies fifty miles into position for the attack on September 26, but that couldn't be done until the 200,000 French soldiers left the area where the Americans were to jump off. All travel had to be done under cover of night, while airplanes moved either early in the morning or just at dusk to camouflage themselves. In the daytime, nothing was to be seen. The doughboys were concealed in forests, towns, villages, or old dugouts, while Billy Mitchell's aircraft watched for the enemy reconnaissance.[24]

Each cumbersome American division took up twenty miles of road space, as about 25,000 men moved by foot or motor vehicle to the front, followed by a long supply caravan. This complicated maneuver had to be executed without tipping off the Germans. To carry this out, Marshall had the doughboys march toward Bar-le-Duc, twenty-five miles southwest of St. Mihiel, and then turn north until they reached the fringes of the Argonne Forest. From there they were placed on French trucks with no suspension, called *camions*, which were driven by Annamites from French Indochina.

All of this was done in the dark, and it became a nightmare. A constant drizzle from the time First Army left the salient on September 16 until they reached the new front a week later reduced the few available roads to mud. Marian Baldwin, an officer in the Salvation Army, watched as the doughboys headed out on the Bar-le-Duc–Verdun Road, which was "kept as smooth as the top of a billiard table." Following along were "scores of massive guns, rolling along, gracefully draped in their gowns of camouflage and pulled by lumbering snorting trucks."[25] To move supplies to the front, engineers used captured German rolling stock and extended their rail lines, which the Americans called the "St. Mihiel, Argonne and Berlin Railroad." One of the confiscated trains was named the "Argonne Local" by the Germans.

Thousands of horses provided by the French and other Allies collapsed and died. The carcasses, along with a mass of motor vehicles, caused traffic congestion that rivaled the one in St. Mihiel. Marshall witnessed a dreadful jam and personally directed the convoys.[26] "The roadside was fairly well littered with broken trucks, automobiles—particularly Dodge cars and motorcycles." Then, much to his horror, "I saw one aviation truck, from which a longer hangar beam projected, sideswipe two machine gun mules, incapacitating both and injuring the driver."[27] Under the charge of Lieutenant Colonel William Barclay Parsons, who had built New York City's subway system, engineers were busy for hours on end repairing the roads with a hodgepodge of gravel, rocks, mud, and logs.[28] Despite the bedlam of shifting so many men and supplies over rough conditions, Marshall's plan succeeded.

Late on September 25, Santini drove Pershing back to his headquarters at Souilly. Black Jack had spent most of the day visiting corps and division headquarters to sort out any last-minute details about the attack and was exhausted. He told his diary that night that the commanders "were all alert and confident," and it made him feel that "all would go as planned."[29] In his railcar, awaiting the start of the great battle, Pershing likely slept very little that night. Even if he had, a wake-up call by two thousand First Army guns was scheduled at two thirty a.m.; doubtless anyone within range of the bombardment could sleep through the deafening noise.

5

ON WITH THE BATTLE

Precisely on schedule, First Army's artillery erupted with a thunderous roar that was said to have rattled the windows in a house occupied by Max von Gallwitz twenty-five miles from the front.[1] Of the 3,980 guns of all calibers, most of the fire came from the workhorse 75mm. Since 1914, the artillery piece had proved to be an excellent, reliable part of the French arsenal, capable of shooting more than twenty thirteen-pound shells per minute due to its pneumatic recoil system.[2] Also deployed were a smaller number of long-range 105mm and 155mm guns, both French-made; no American-manufactured artillery ever found its way overseas. Three hours before the First Army artillery blazed, a much lesser quantity of 75s were fired by the French Fourth Army from the west of the Argonne Forrest, a deception to make the Germans expect an attack from that direction.

While American and French gunners pounded enemy defenses stretched out over the twenty-four-mile front, First Army's ground troops shivered as much from the morning chill as from fear. Some soldiers crouched behind old trenches, while others bivouacked in wooded areas, sleeping in tents on open ground or lying inside damp shell craters and rifle pits. Every man prayed that German counterfire would miss his position. To one regiment, the noise of shells whirling back and forth across the sky "sounded like a succession of express trains passing overhead."[3] When the Allies' projectiles eventually landed far away in the German lines, the Americans could hear dull thuds as they hit trenches and shelters.

For many doughboys, the Meuse-Argonne battle was their initiation to combat. Yet in short order they became battle-hardened veterans, and they looked the part, with their striking uniforms, arms, and equipment. Uniform shirts were a khaki drab pullover with three buttons down the front and two breast pockets. Pants and jackets were olive drab wool. Brown boots and canvas leggings, later exchanged for wool puttees, completed the ensemble. (This was the same uniform doughboys had worn since the summer. Winter clothes were requisitioned and would not arrive until after the battle had ended.)[4] For cold weather, each soldier was issued a greatcoat that was fastened by two rows of four bronze buttons. Doughboys wore British-pattern steel helmets with a woven lining and adjustable chin straps. The helmets—sometimes called a dishpan hat, tin pan hat, washbasin, or battle bowler—were coated with olive drab paint and a fine layer of sawdust to cut down on glare. Slung across every soldier's chest was a respirator bag, which opened at the front, where a gas mask would be within reach. On his back was a pack that included extra clothes and rubber ponchos, while across one shoulder was a haversack that contained, among other items, a washing-shaving kit.[5]

Around a soldier's waist was an ammunition belt made of khaki-colored webbing that had room for 100 rounds of ammunition, an entrenching tool, a trench knife, a bayonet and scabbard, and a canteen. British- and French-style grenades, which the doughboys called "pineapples," were also found on this accoutrement. Small arms were somewhat complicated. The primary U.S. rifle in World War I was the .30 1903 Model Springfield, while other doughboys were issued a Model 1917 Enfield, manufactured in America for the British. Typically, officers and noncommissioned officers (NCOs) didn't tote rifles; instead, on their belts were single-action, semiautomatic .45 Colt M1911 handguns. Mobile machine gunners hauled the French-made Chauchat (called the "sho-sho" by American soldiers), weighing more than twenty pounds and holding a twenty-round magazine. It was an unreliable contraption that at best jammed, but more than likely fell apart, and its accuracy at long distances was suspect. Better-equipped regiments had the Browning automatic rifle (BAR), a weapon so dependable that a variation was still in use during the Vietnam War.[6]

Doughboys were fed twice a day, the first meal usually at about nine a.m. and the second around seven hours later. Food was either brought up by two men carrying big garbage cans hung on a pole, or by a rolling kitchen.[7] There were two types of rolling food kitchens—horse-drawn and motor-drawn. Each kitchen consisted of a stove and a limber. The stove unit contained a bake oven and three kettles, while the limber contained four bread boxes that were also used as water containers, one cook's chest, four fireless cookers, and four kettles. About seven thousand rolling kitchens of all types were shipped to France.[8]

Just before the war ended, Lieutenant General Robert Lee Bullard recommended that the AEF adopt the French Army's "Marmite Norvégienne." Constructed much like the modern thermos, the "Bullard

Marmite" allowed food to remain at an even temperature for about ten hours. It was shaped and equipped with shoulder straps so a cook could carry it on his back.[9]

Getting freshwater to the front was also clearly thought out. One way was for the mostly African American pioneer regiments to advance before the combat divisions and set up pumping stations at wells or springs, with separate drinking facilities for men and animals. Also, two quartermaster units, the 1st and 2nd Provisional Water Tank Trains, transported water from filling stations in the rear to advanced canvas tanks. On a daily basis during the battle they provided an average of 31,000 gallons of water, which was hauled to the front in carts. Light railways with 2,000-gallon tank cars were also utilized.[10]

First Army ate quite well. As with artillery, planes, and tanks, very little of the food served to American soldiers was produced in the United States. On any given day a doughboy might be served rice, olives, onions, and beans that came from Spain; potatoes from Ireland; or French-made macaroni.[11] Coffee was one of the few staples shipped from America. To roast the beans, the quartermaster established "Coffee Roasting Plant No. 1," in Corbeil-Essonnes, near Paris. It was the largest coffee-roasting and -grinding plant in Europe, with an initial capacity of producing 500,000 rations per day, which, by the time of the armistice, increased threefold.[12]

After eating a quick breakfast on the morning of September 26, 225,000 of Pershing's warriors got in position for the attack. As at St. Mihiel, the Argonne offensive was spearheaded by three corps, each with three divisions. Major General Bullard's III Corps was on the right, with the 4th, 33rd, and 80th Divisions. Cameron's V Corps, composed of the 91st, 37th, and 79th Divisions, was in the middle; and Liggett's I Corps on the left had the 28th, 35th, and 77th Divisions; Frederick Palmer called the corps commanders the "brains of the coming attack."[13] At their disposal were French staff officers who lectured the American corps commanders "about the disposition of the enemy on our front and an innumerable number of details which it is essential to know in planning an attack."[14] This knowledge was vital since five of the nine divisions that kicked off the battle had not yet seen combat, and four of the nine would receive artillery support from regiments they had not yet served with.[15]

Under the cover of darkness, just before the infantry left their start position at five thirty a.m., engineers worked to patch the area's few existing roads, which had seen little traffic since 1914, but plenty of shell fire during the Battle of Verdun.[16] The ground that First Army had to cross, as well as the defenses protecting it, was on everyone's mind. In the days after St. Mihiel, Billy Mitchell's reconnaissance planes brought back clear photographs that showed just how well fortified the sector was. Further proof was provided by POWs from the 14th German Assault Battalion, who advised their American captors "that the Germans expect to make a stand on the Michel I position, which consists of two double rows of wire, with good dugouts."[17]

General Max von Gallwitz, although still in command of Composite Army Group C around Verdun, had placed his immediate subordinate, General Georg von der Marwitz, in charge of the German Fifth Army in the Argonne. A cavalry officer known as a master of mobile defense, Marwitz had gained notoriety by halting Russia's Brusilov offensive in the summer of 1916. At Cambrai in November 1917, when British tanks appeared to have won the day, Marwitz executed a brilliant counteroffensive that turned defeat into German victory. Now under his charge in September 1918 were several under-strength Bavarian and Austrian divisions. This included the 76th Reserve Division, opposing the French Fourth Army, west of the forest, and two divisions in the Argonne, the 2nd and 9th Landwehrs. Close by at Apremont

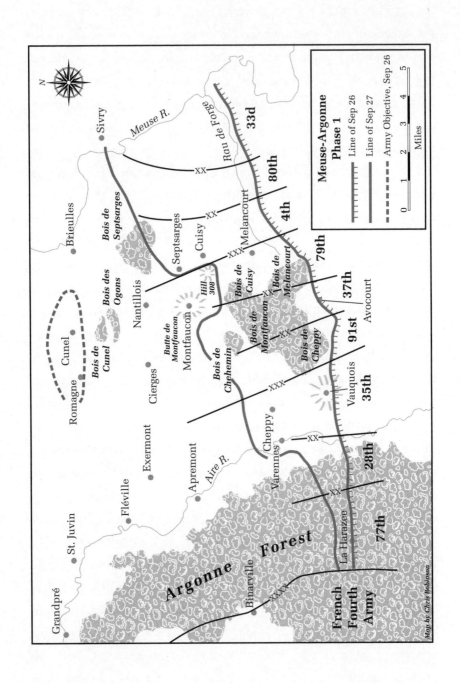

Meuse-Argonne
Phase 1

Line of Sep 26
Line of Sep 27
Army Objective, Sep 26

0 1 2 3 4 5
Miles

Map by Chris Robinson

were the 1st and 5th Guards. An additional five divisions could be brought in at a moment's notice.[18]

Following the early three-hour artillery bombardment, a rolling barrage by division artillery preceded the jump-off from the trenches and open fields. Developed during the Boer War by the British, a rolling barrage laid a curtain of shell fire about one hundred to two hundred yards in front of the infantry and moved forward at a predetermined rate regardless of how fast the soldiers advanced. As in the case of First Army, the divisions, impeded by inexperience, shell craters, broken barbed wire, and a thick fog, could not keep up with the barrage.[19]

Major General Liggett tasked the 35th Division, a National Guard unit made up of men from Kansas and Missouri, with taking Vauquois Hill, which stood prominently in the eastern part of the First Corps sector, between the Cheppy Woods (Bois de Cheppy) and the edge of the Argonne Forest, overlooking the Aire valley. Perhaps he was being biased, but the Missouri-born Pershing had declared the 35th "the best looking lot of men I have in France."[20] On the first day of battle, the division was determined not to let him down.

At the top of Vauquois Hill, the 35th faced Germans who had sealed their trenches, stretching for more than a mile, with concrete to make them bombproof and had constructed tunnels three hundred feet below the point where Vauquois crested. The tunnels connected to galleries filled with high explosives. After attempting to take Vauquois Hill on three occasions in 1914, losing between thirty and forty thousand men in the process, the French had nicknamed the German strongpoint "le mont des morts," or "the hill of the dead."[21] In February 1915, the French tried one last time and again failed to seize the landmark. Now the Americans had their chance to capture the hill.

Commanding the 35th Division was Major General Peter Traub, a

West Point classmate of Pershing's who had seen combat chasing the Sioux in South Dakota and later against the Spanish on San Juan Hill in Cuba. Traub's men were given one of the more difficult tasks on September 26. Once the 35th took Vauquois, his infantry was to proceed on to the village of Cheppy, about two miles ahead of Varennes, and link up with elements of another guard division, the 28th "Keystone" from Pennsylvania, led by its chubby commander, fifty-eight-year-old Major General Charles H. Muir. Supporting the 35th's infantry was an artillery battery commanded by a thirty-four-year-old captain from Independence, Missouri, Harry S. Truman. His rounded steel spectacles made him seem more like a banker than an artillery commander, but such looks were deceiving.

From a young age Truman was passionate about the military, and was captivated by Julius Caesar and Robert E. Lee.[22] Nothing would have thrilled Truman more than to follow in Lee's footsteps by attending West Point, where the Confederate commander had graduated second in his class without incurring a single demerit. But it wasn't meant to be. Truman's military academy application was rejected because of his poor eyesight. Instead, he joined the Missouri National Guard in 1905 and served with a Kansas City artillery battery, but left after six years to work the family's 600-acre farm in Grandview, Missouri.

In April 1917, Truman resumed his military career and was placed in the 129th Field Artillery. After three different commanders either quit or were reassigned, Truman took over Battery D in July 1918, and inherited a roster of rowdy Irish Catholics and German immigrants. Far from intimidating at only five feet eight inches tall and weighing 151 pounds, Truman used a mixture of charm and discipline to tame the unit. He told the battery's noncommissioned officers when they were in France that "I didn't come over here to get along with you.

You've got to get along with me."[23] Yet when asked about the battery commander's personality, one soldier recalled that "his major characteristic was great friendliness, that he had such warmth and a liking for people."[24]

The artillery attack on Vauquois Hill, Truman wrote, "was nothing but a bog. Mud, mud, mud . . ." Positioned on a hilltop near the village of Neuvilly, his battery was ready to open fire when they realized the "guns wouldn't raise high enough to reach [Vauquois]." Forced to improvise, the men placed "the tail of one gun in a shell hole and fired several rounds at the extreme elevation in the general direction of Germany."[25] For four hours Truman's battery fired three thousand rounds of 75mm ammunition toward Vauquois.[26] While trying to keep out of harm's way, one of Truman's men was sitting in a shell hole when "a dud lit right between his legs. If he hasn't a charmed life," Truman joked, "no one has."[27]

After the artillery ceased its main attack, four regiments of infantry followed a rolling barrage and walked slowly across no-man's-land through a "dripping blanket" of heavy fog.[28] At best, visibility was only about thirty to forty feet, and contact between squads was difficult to maintain. Constant shouts from officers to keep the lines straight were in vain. Units intermingled and men stumbled through a maze of broken wire, shell holes, and abandoned trenches. A short distance away, the top of Vauquois Hill peeked through the mist. As the Americans approached their first objective the Germans welcomed them with a hail of machine-gun and small-artillery fire.

The division battle plan called for two infantry regiments—the 139th, followed by the 137th—to attack on the western edge of the hill, while the 140th would assault the eastern slope, followed by the 138th Infantry. The enemy's initial blasts made it seem that the hill was heavily fortified, but in reality Vauquois was manned by an understrength

German division that retreated into the tunnels as soon as elements of the 35th Division began to flank both sides of the hill. What was expected to be a slugfest quickly turned into a rout. Only seventy-five German troops and six light machine guns under command of a young lieutenant, Friedrich von Huellesheim, were defending the hill. With few options before him, Huellesheim considered blowing up Vauquois, but his battalion commander wired orders that he was to hold the hill at all costs. When he tried to regroup his forces, the lieutenant found his men surrounded by one regiment of the 35th with another fast approaching. The French had thought the Americans would need three days to take the hill, but after a forty-minute fight, Huellesheim surrendered the garrison.[29] A battalion of doughboys spent a few moments exploring the "pitted and scarred, scalped and torn" captured ground before moving on to Varennes.[30]

Once a picturesque little village in a bowl-shaped valley on the Aire River—it was here where Louis XVI and Marie Antoinette were stopped in 1791 during the French Revolution and returned to Paris—Varennes was now a wreck.[31] Shells had demolished buildings, and scattered rubble made the streets impassable. At noon the 35th's 137th Infantry entered the town, followed by elements of the 28th Division a short time later. Just after the 35th Division had cleared the eastern part of the town and the 28th took care of the western section, the Americans thought Varennes was abandoned. They were disabused of that notion when Germans who remained in and around the village counterattacked with machine guns. House-to-house combat ensued, and with help from thirty tanks (two companies) belonging to the 345th Tank Battalion, the infantry finally silenced the attack by three p.m.[32] Fifty-year-old Edward Sigerfoos, one of the Keystone's brigade commanders, was mortally wounded during the battle and died eight days later in a base hospital. A graduate of Ohio State University, Brigadier

General Sigerfoos was the highest-ranking officer in the AEF killed during the war.[33]

While infantry from the 28th and 35th Divisions remained in the village to mop up, a tank from the 344th Battalion—crewed by two New Yorkers, Corporal Donald M. Call and Lieutenant John Wesley Castles—ran into trouble. During an attack on machine-gun nests west of Varennes, their tank had half of its turret blown off by a direct hit from a high-explosive shell that also contained poison gas. Choking amid a cloud of fumes, Call left the tank and took cover in a shell hole thirty yards away. After realizing that Castles had not followed him to safety, Call ran back to the tank and pulled him out. The lieutenant was badly wounded and unable to walk, so Call carried him on his shoulder while managing to elude German machine-gun and shell fire until they reached safety a mile away. Call was later promoted to second lieutenant and awarded the Medal of Honor. A Broadway actor prior to the war, Call returned to the New York stage in 1919. Prior to Audie Murphy, the most decorated American veteran of World War II, Call was the only actor to have earned the Medal of Honor. [34]

While three of Major General Traub's regiments remained around Varennes, the 138th Infantry was en route to Cheppy, a few miles away, when it ran into six German machine-gun nests on a bluff above the bank of Buanthe Creek, and two more halfway down on a slope. To the regiment's right, more machine guns protected the creek, which was eight feet deep and ran south through Cheppy. The left flank was blocked by rolls of barbed wire. All of this was supported by yet another machine-gun nest in Cheppy.[35]

Early that morning Lieutenant Colonel Patton's French Renault and Schneider tanks had also reached Cheppy.[36] George Smith Patton

Jr. believed he was destined to be a warrior, and alleged that in past lives he had served with Alexander the Great, in Roman legions, and as an English knight during the Hundred Years' War. Whether or not he had been reincarnated, Patton did come from a long line of Virginia soldiers. Most recently two ancestors died while serving with the Confederacy during the Civil War, and his father graduated from the VMI. By the time Patton was born in 1885, his family had moved to Southern California, and he was raised in lavish surroundings. His mother, Ruth, was the daughter of a wealthy landowner and businessman, and Patton's father, for whom he was named, had been an attorney and politician, among other professions.[37]

Due to dyslexia, Patton was tutored at home until the age of eleven, when he began learning to read and write. With his father's urging, Patton followed him to VMI in 1903. He stayed for only a year, using the school as a stepping-stone to attend West Point, which he entered in 1904 at age nineteen. At the military academy, Patton excelled more in athletics than in academics and had to repeat his plebe year after failing the math exam. Dyslexia was partly to blame for the low grades, but the learning disorder didn't prevent him from devouring books about Napoleon Bonaparte, Stonewall Jackson, and Robert E. Lee. He graduated in 1909, ranked 46 out of 103, and was commissioned as a cavalry officer.

During his first assignment at Fort Sheridan, outside of Chicago, Patton established his character as a no-nonsense commander when leading men on practice marches, bivouacs, and patrols. However, he was better suited for his next post at Fort Myer, Virginia, where most of the Army's top brass were headquartered. His unit, the 15th Cavalry Regiment, was charged with providing escorts at nearby Arlington Cemetery for funerals and looking smart in front of visiting dignitaries at state functions. Patton also got to display his polo skills and socialize with the Washington elite.[38] One of the highlights of his early career was representing the Army in the decathlon at the 1912 Olympics in Stockholm, where he finished a respectable fifth place. By virtue of his fencing skills and an article he authored, Patton became an authority on the U.S. Cavalry saber. But meeting Pershing at Fort Bliss in 1915 was the turning point. Patton idolized Black Jack, who became his mentor and helped set him on a path to become one of the greatest soldiers to serve in the U.S. Army.

Patton saw his first combat during the Punitive Expedition. For the first couple of months he served under Pershing's watchful eye as his aide. Patton tended to scheduling, ordering supplies, and any other administrative task he was told to do. All the while he observed Pershing's command style, and wanted so badly to emulate him. As one of Patton's biographers put it, "Pershing's influence on young Patton cannot be overemphasized. He was the very model of a military commander, whose ideas of duty and discipline meshed perfectly with Patton's own conception."[39] Pershing, too, appreciated the young lieutenant for his energy, ambition, and hunger for action that reminded Black Jack of himself when he had first started out. He brought Patton along during morning horseback rides, and they slowly developed a strong bond. Pershing saw that Patton longed for adventure, and occasionally sent him out in the field as a courier. Besides these small excursions, however, Patton remained at headquarters, helping his boss to keep the expedition organized.[40]

After weeks of little movement, and with Villa and his band still on the loose, Pershing received a credible tip in early May 1916 that General Julio Cárdenas, Villa's trusted bodyguard, was holed up in the vicinity of Rubio. Capturing Cárdenas would be a major coup for Pershing, and Patton wanted to take part in the score. Patton made his pitch; Pershing bought it and temporarily assigned his aide to Troop C of the 13th Cavalry. At daybreak one morning the regiment went looking for Cárdenas. They searched the San Miquelito Ranch, where the Cárdenas family was supposedly living, but only an uncle and some other relative were home. From there the troop scoured the surrounding countryside, but came up empty-handed. Patton was disappointed and vowed to return to the ranch.

His chance came a couple of weeks later when Pershing dispatched three Dodge touring automobiles and loaded them with Patton, ten soldiers from the 6th Infantry, and a couple of civilian guides to purchase corn from a farmer in Rubio. After buying the feed, Patton seized the moment, sending the party to the San Miquelito Ranch, where he hoped Cárdenas had returned from his hideout. Patton ordered the soldiers to surround the dwelling and prepare for a fight. As they crouched with their guns at the ready, three Mexicans ran out the door. The Americans opened fire, killing two of them, including Cárdenas. More shots rang out and a third Mexican was felled. There is no way to tell if the bullets from either Patton's rifle or ivory-handled Colt 1873 single-action .45-caliber revolver killed any of the men. But Patton is credited with initiating the operation and he couldn't wait to tell Pershing, who had no idea what his aide and the other men were up to. Lieutenant Patton and his party rushed back to headquarters with the corpses of the dead Mexicans tied to the hoods of their cars. Patton also carried away Cárdenas's silver-studded saddle and sword as war trophies, which Pershing allowed him to keep. News of Patton's feat blazed in the headlines of newspapers in the United States, which proclaimed him the "Bandit Killer."[41]

Upon his return from Mexico in February 1917, Patton was despondent and anxious about his future. Now thirty-two, he questioned what the peacetime Army had in store for him, and worried if he should continue to rely on Pershing, or someone else, for support. That question was answered in April, when the United States entered the Great War and Pershing brought him to Europe as a staff officer. Patton spent the first few months in France as the adjutant and commandant at Chaumont. Predictably, this job grew tiresome and he patiently waited for a battlefield command. As the AEF inched closer to fielding an army, his perseverance paid off when Pershing opted to establish the U.S. Army Tank Corps. Volunteers were needed, and Patton jumped at the chance to serve with the new combat arm.

With Pershing's blessing, he became a tank officer in November 1917, and spent the next several months observing British and French tanks in action, setting up a light-tank training center, recruiting and organizing tank brigades. He was promoted from captain to major. Five months before leading the tanks into battle at St. Mihiel, Patton wrote his friend Kate Merrill-Smith about his fascination with the machines. "There is I know a general idea that tanks are dangerous but the fact of my being in them disproves that to anyone who knows me," he joked. "They realy [sic] are fine and very interesting and with luck one ought to be able to get quite close to the Bosch. I have always thought I should prefer to see the man who gets me."[42]

Surviving St. Mihiel without a scratch, Patton found his prophecy about death almost realized on the first day of Meuse-Argonne. "I started forward at 6:30 to see what was doing but could see little," he wrote his wife a few days later. "Machine guns were going in every direction in front, behind and on both sides. But no one could tell who they belonged to." Accompanied by two officers and about a dozen runners, Patton walked toward the sound of gunfire to see what was going on. What he saw pleased him. By nine a.m. the tanks had advanced five miles and assisted in capturing Varennes, and were now headed toward Cheppy. As Patton's party approached the village, they were met by shells, machine-gun fire, and panicked American soldiers racing to the rear. Patton stopped the fleeing troops and corralled about a hundred of them into some semblance of order. After enemy fire slowed, he directed the soldiers into a spread formation across the reverse slope of a hill.

Nearby, several tanks were in trouble—unable to cross two large trenches, the massive vehicles were now easy targets for enemy artillery. Patton sent a group of men to break down the trench walls, but shell fire slowed their progress. After watching with disbelief, Patton took charge. Grabbing shovels and picks from the sides of the tanks, he handed them out and urged the men to dig. While bullets flew, the soldiers, more scared of Patton than the Germans, flattened the trenches enough to allow the tanks to go forward. Holding his walking stick above his head, Patton strode right behind the machines, shouting, "Let's go get them. Who is with me?" The group of men still spread along the hill got up and followed their leader to the top, where they were met with blasts of machine-gun fire. Troops fell all around Patton. After the fire died down, Patton got up and again barked, "Let's go." Only six men remained with him, including his orderly, Joe Angelo. After a few steps Patton was felled by a bullet in the thigh. Angelo helped him into a shell hole and tended to his wound, which was bleeding profusely.

Meanwhile, more tanks appeared and Patton ordered Angelo to direct them toward the German machine-gun fire. He also told a sergeant to alert the post command of his wounding and that Captain Sereno Brett, who commanded one of the tank companies attached to Patton's brigade, was now in charge. More tanks arrived and again Angelo sent them to the enemy lines. Eventually a medic passed by, saw Patton, and treated his wound. Because the tanks had yet to silence the Germans, it was still too dangerous to move him out of the shell hole. Not until an hour or so later was he carried by stretcher and placed on a litter. Patton was transported for about two miles until an ambulance company took over. They drove him to 35th Division head-quarters, where he learned that the bullet had entered his left leg and exited "just at the crack of my bottom about two inches to the left of my rectum, leaving a hole about the size of a silver dollar."[43]

Three days after his wounding Patton was sent to Base Hospital 49 in Allerey, far from the front in the Burgundy region of France, where he remained for the next few weeks. Though promoted to the rank of full colonel, Patton's war was over. Angelo, whom Patton claimed was "without a doubt the bravest man in the American Army" and had "never seen his equal," received the Distinguished Service Cross.[44] Patton also received the award, and would lobby unsuccessfully for the Medal of Honor.*

Pershing never publically mentioned the wounding of his friend, but it had to have hit him hard. He wrote of the incident in an October 1918 letter to Beatrice Patton:

I suppose that George has written you of his being wounded. He was exceptionally gallant and was leading a body of men to attack a machine gun nest when he was shot in the leg; I think not very seriously. It was a gallant thing to do, and he has received all sorts of praise from those who know of the incident. You are to be congratulated and should be prouder of him than ever.[45]

---

* Fourteen years after the war, Patton and Angelo were once again on the same battlefield. In the summer of 1932, at the height of the Great Depression, Angelo took part in a demonstration with the Bonus Expeditionary Force in Washington in hopes of obtaining an early payment of a veteran's bonus. Patton was among the Regular Army troops ordered to forcefully disperse their former comrades in arms by then Army chief of staff Major General Douglas MacArthur.

Stories about Patton's escapade spread throughout First Army. Official war artist Harry Everett Townsend heard that the brash lieutenant colonel had died. Townsend was one of eight soldiers designated by the War Department as combat artists, who were permitted to roam through the occupied zones, battlefields, and forward trenches. He jotted down a brief eulogy of Patton in his diary: "He was a most interesting man," Townsend thought, "and most enthusiastic and active and progressive as a Tank Commander."[46] Patton's legacy that day had shown the potential of tanks as vital war machines, but they had a downside, too: their limitations in supporting the infantry. "Tanks can take villages," Major General Bullard complained, "but tanks cannot hold and consolidate the ground they have gained."[47]

At Rarécourt, where Hunter Liggett maintained I Corps headquarters, breaking news from the front, only twelve miles away, was impossible to confirm. According to his aide, Colonel Stackpole, "all morning reports by air, pigeon, wireless, telephone, radio, messengers, liaison officers, and every other means of communication were exceedingly meager." Information finding its way to Liggett's desk turned out to be "inaccurate and conflicting and this was the situation all through the day. 35th Division was most insecure about the position of its front line, and the 28th and 77th slightly less so." Other than the occasional visit to division post commands, Liggett remained in his office playing solitaire with two packs of cards to calm his nerves.[48]

In General Cameron's V Corps sector, Major General Joseph E. Kuhn's 79th "Lorraine" Division had a trying day on September 26. Formerly president of the Army War College, Kuhn had served as an attaché at the German General Headquarters from 1914 to 1916, and personally knew many of the enemy officers.[49] Kuhn was a cheerful fellow and well liked by the men in his division, which was made up of draftees from Maryland, Pennsylvania, and the District of Columbia. The 79th had been at the front for almost a week, taking over trenches vacated by the French in a line roughly four miles long.[50] Each day, the division had stared in the direction of their target for September 26—Montfaucon, or Falcon Mountain.

Rising more than 1,122 feet, Montfaucon loomed over the Meuse-Argonne front like a New York City skyscraper, providing German artillery with direct access to the American lines. Atop the mountain was a village of the same name built around a monastery dating from the sixth century that the Germans had occupied and fortified in 1914. Surrounding this high ground were several deep wooded areas, not only the Argonne Forest to the left, but the Bois de Montfaucon, the Bois de Cheppy, the Bois de Chehemin, and the Bois de Malancourt—all named for nearby villages.

Pershing wanted Montfaucon taken immediately because this natural obstacle blocked First Army's path to Romagne and Cunel, where the Hindenburg Line heavily defended the two villages and was the key to the first row of German defenses. After reading the Meuse-Argonne battle plan, General Pétain told Pershing he thought it would take until Christmas before Montfaucon was in Allied hands, but the American commander in chief thought otherwise and wanted the objective taken on the first day. Practicing Pershing's doctrine of open warfare, by which the enemy was to be driven from his trenches and exposed in no-man's-land, the 313th Infantry Regiment from Baltimore under Colonel Claude B. Sweezey, supported on its left by the 314th from Maryland and Pennsylvania, commanded by Colonel William H. Oury, leaped from the trenches and headed straight toward Montfaucon. On the left of the 79th was the 37th "Buckeye" Division from Ohio, which was also inexperienced. But on the right was the veteran regular 4th Division, under one of Pershing's best combat commanders, Major General John L. Hines.

Less than two miles from the front, war artist Ernest Peixotto stood between the guns of First Army artillery on Hill 304, now silent after their early-morning discharge. The high ground, shadowing the wrecked village of Esnes on its southern slope, gave him an unimpeded view of Montfaucon. Through a pair of binoculars attached to a tripod Peixotto watched the 313th Infantry—a mix of Slavs, Poles, Jews, and Italians known as "Baltimore's Own"—emerge from the woods. "Little khaki-colored toys," he thought, "scattered out in open formation."[51] Ahead of them, Langer's 1st Gas Regiment threw up a heavy screen of black smoke to help camouflage the attack. Yet as the smoke blended with the morning fog, many of the inexperienced troops thought it was a German gas attack and stopped to put on their cumbersome gas masks, or fled to the rear in a panic.[52]

Further troubling the 313th was the ground scarred from the Battle of Verdun in 1916. Major General Kuhn called the landscape a "veritable Gibraltar," with its "overlapping shell holes and tangled forest debris."[53] Adding to the misery were the endless bands of "tangled, twisted barbed wire."[54] Two-man wire-cutting teams had been allotted forty-five minutes to snip the belts, but it actually took them thirty minutes longer, delaying the attack further.[55] Like most First Army units, the 313th couldn't keep up with the rolling barrage. German troops on the high ground somehow spotted the Americans through the thick fog and unleashed a barrage of machine-gun fire from a trench in front of the Bois de Cuisy. They also tormented the doughboys with their 77mm Model 1896 Krupp field cannons, a vicious weapon capable of firing ten rounds a minute of everything from high-explosive, shrapnel, antitank, and illumination shells to poison gas shells.[56]

For several hours, the Maryland regiment was trapped amid a

storm of bullets and shell fire while Sweezey, a West Pointer with thirty years of experience in the Regular Army, roamed the lines, urging his men to move faster. When a young officer told him his men could go no farther, the stone-faced Sweezey stammered back: "Y-e-s y-y-ou will, b-b-y God."[57] By midafternoon, the 313th had advanced two and a half kilometers and made its way into the Bois de Montfaucon, within striking distance of their objective. Fighting in the forest was just as intense as what they had encountered on the open ground. Two of the regiment's battalion commanders were killed. Major Israel Putnam was found shot, lying facedown in a shell hole, while Major Benjamin Franklin Pepper took a bullet through the head from a German sniper near the northern edge of the woods. Meanwhile, Sweezey ran back and forth through the Montfaucon Woods, rallying his men to return fire. Raymond A. Tompkins, a reporter from the *Baltimore Sun*, watched as small groups of Americans attacked German machine-gun nests "in clumps of brush, behind tree-stumps, in little fortresses of rock."[58]

By six p.m. the 313th was barely out of the woods and still had a long way to go. In front of them lay a nine-hundred-foot hill, then a deep valley, and finally Montfaucon. "Not a tree, not a bush, not a boulder between them and the city," Tompkins observed, "just a rolling stretch of open country to be crossed under the eyes of the enemy." With darkness setting in, Sweezey thought it too dangerous to try to advance, so he called off the attack, telling his men to bivouac in the woods for the night.[59]

Twenty-five miles away, Pershing waited anxiously to hear if Montfaucon had been taken. After learning the attack had stalled, he demanded that Major General Cameron get the division moving again. The V Corps commander wrote a scathing note to Kuhn: "The Seventy-ninth Division is holding up the advance of the whole American Army. The Commanding General insists that the attack be pushed more vigorously."[60] Of course, neither Pershing nor Cameron knew what was happening at the front, and Kuhn had done a poor job of keeping them informed. Still, the 79th was by no means holding up the entire First Army. The two divisions close to Kuhn's men, the 4th and 37th, had reached their objectives for the day. The 145th Infantry Regiment of the 37th Division crossed into the 79th Division sector and tried to take Montfaucon, but were driven back. The remainder of the division had penetrated through the woods and was engaged with the enemy at Ivoiry, west of Montfaucon. General Hines's veterans were in an even better position to capture the town, but opted not to try since it wasn't in the III Corps battle plan, and without coordination with the 79th, such an operation could have been dangerous. Instead, the 4th outflanked Montfaucon to the east and attacked the Germans near the village of Nantillois.[61]

Late in the day a member of Kuhn's staff found Sweezey in the Bois de Montfaucon and handed the colonel a note with orders to resume the attack. The news was unsettling. His regiment would have to fight blind against an enemy they couldn't see. Kuhn sent two Renault tanks forward to aid in the attack, but they were of little use. After rolling ahead of the infantry about two hundred yards, the "ghost enemy" deluged them with machine guns, high explosives, and hand grenades. Both French tanks awkwardly turned around and scrambled back to the woods. Sweezey kept the infantry on the open ground to continue fighting, but there was no artillery support because the 75s were too far back. The Germans fired volley after volley at the helpless men. A short time later Sweezey had had enough, and led the regiment back to the woods. He wrote Kuhn a message, tied it to the leg of a pigeon carried by the regiment's intelligence section, and sent the bird toward the division headquarters. But the pigeon flew up into a tree and, refusing to leave the woods, remained perched on a branch all night.

Supporting the infantry advance across the entire Meuse-Argonne front were Billy Mitchell's courageous aviators. Of the eight hundred aircraft that made up Mitchell's fleet, roughly three-fourths would be flown by American pilots. The British, French, and Italians had withdrawn their planes for use in other sectors. Reconnaissance patrols were sent up to scout ahead of the infantry and drop messages to advise attacking infantry units where the enemy was concentrated. In addition, thirteen observation balloons, marked with red, blue, and white circles, looked down upon First Army's doughboys as they jumped off.

Balloons of the First World War, nicknamed "sausages" and "gasbags" by American soldiers, were about ninety-two feet long, constructed of strong rubberized fabric, and fueled by twenty-three thousand cubic feet of flammable hydrogen. They could float as high as four thousand feet above the ground. Balloons were carried at night to a prepared bed and then concealed during daylight from enemy planes with a camouflage covering of tree limbs. Attached to the balloon was a two-man basket tethered to the ground by a steel cable. Once the balloon was airborne, the threat from artillery attack or machine-gun fire from the ground or airplanes was all too real. Parachutes, either worn on the back of the balloonists or stowed in a canister on the side of the basket, offered a chance of escape in the event of an attack, but survival was unlikely.

Mitchell's strategy on the first day of the attack was to rid the skies of German balloons and low-flying planes while harassing German infantry with twenty-pound bombs dropped by the SPADs.[62] Eddie

Rickenbacker, who now commanded the Hat in the Ring Squadron with the rank of captain, departed at 5:20 a.m. with five other planes to seek out German balloons. Because it was still dark at that hour, searchlights were temporarily turned on to help the pilots see the ground as they took off. Once the planes were in the air, the lights were extinguished so as not to draw attention from German planes.

As he reached altitude, Rickenbacker "saw the most marvelous sight my eyes have ever seen." Below him were the Allied guns "belching out their shells with such rapidity that there appeared to be millions of them shooting at the same time." The scene made Rickenbacker "think of a giant switchboard which emitted thousands of electric flashes as invisible hands manipulated the plugs."[63] While flying over Verdun and then the Meuse River, he witnessed two planes from his squadron engaging a German balloon while enemy tracer bullets flashed all around them. Within moments the gasbag burst into flames, and then a second balloon was sent spiraling downward.

Rickenbacker had headed north toward Damvillers, where another balloon had been spotted earlier that week, when off to his right a Fokker was flying beside him "not a hundred yards away." Shocked to see a German plane this early in the day, Rickenbacker tried to regain his composure, but before he knew it the Fokker was heading straight toward him. Bracing for a collision, Rickenbacker clenched the throttle of his SPAD when the German plane suddenly dived under him. Rickenbacker recalled, "I instantly made a reversement [aircraft maneuver] which put me close behind him in a most favorable position for careful aim. Training my sights into the center of his fuselage I pulled both triggers. With one long burst the fight was over." The Fokker plummeted to the ground and Rickenbacker limped back to his airfield with a broken propeller.[64]

Lieutenant Merian Cooper, an aviator with the 20th Aero Squadron, did not have Rickenbacker's good fortune. Cooper and his observer, Lieutenant Edward Leonard, flew their DH4 as part of a seven-plane bombing mission over Dun-sur-Meuse. When the bombers turned back after jettisoning their loads, they were attacked by Fokkers. Five American planes were shot down, including the one piloted by Cooper. Crashing into a field outside the village of Piennes, Cooper and Leonard somehow survived, but were seriously wounded. Cooper's hand and neck were badly burned, while Leonard was bleeding from his neck.

The two Americans were quickly surrounded by enemy infantry and a few curious French civilian onlookers. Then a German plane landed next to them, and its aviator jumped out of the cockpit. He saluted the downed American pilot and his observer and asked if they were French or English, obviously not seeing that the damaged aircraft had American markings. The German officer searched Cooper's plane, looking for flight plans or maps. Finding none, he removed a small framed photograph of a young woman that Cooper had affixed on his instrument panel and placed it in the American aviator's pocket. Cooper and Leonard were taken by automobile to a German field hospital in La Mourie, where they were interrogated separately by an intelligence officer who wrote postcards for them to send to their families stating that they were captured and wounded.

From there Cooper and Leonard were placed in an old cart and driven in the rain to the first of six different POW camps. Most of these prisons were designated for enlisted men, including one that served as a hospital and was full of Russian soldiers who smelled so bad that Cooper insisted on a transfer. By now separated from Leonard, Cooper recalled that the entire time he was a prisoner the treatment wasn't harsh, but the food was of a poor quality, mostly cabbage and barley soups.[65] He didn't return to the American line until after the war had ended.*

At about nine a.m. on September 26, Lieutenant Guy Brown Wiser and his observer, Lieutenant G. C. Richardson, took off in their DH4 with four other 20th Aero Squadron planes to bomb the German rail yards at Dun-sur-Meuse. When they reached an altitude of thirteen thousand feet, Wiser prepared to unleash his payload on the target, but five Fokkers approached and put a stop to the mission. While Wiser tried to maneuver their plane out of harm's way, his observer took the brunt of the dogfight. The German airplanes blasted the DH4 with machine-gun fire, puncturing one of its tanks and spraying Richardson with gas. He tried to return fire, but the drum from his plane's machine gun jammed. The Germans continued shooting and Richardson was hit in the right leg, causing his limb to go numb. Losing altitude, Wiser glided the plane down toward an airdrome that was home of the 13th German Aero Squadron. An enemy pilot rushed over to the downed DH4, administered first aid to Richardson, and then brought the two pilots to the mess hall, where they were fed and given cigarettes. From this point they were now formally declared POWs.

Wiser and Richardson were moved to Germany and incarcerated

---

* After the war Cooper joined the Polish Koscisuzko Squadron and a year later was taken POW again following a forced landing over Bolshevik lines. After nine months in the camp he escaped, and after traveling for twenty-six nights, he crossed the Latvian border into safety and found his way back to Warsaw. Not done with the military, he joined the Army Air Corps during the Second World War and retired with the rank of brigadier general. Cooper's story as an aviator was perhaps just as compelling as *King Kong*, the 1933 film he is best known for directing. During his film career he was instrumental in developing Technicolor and Cinerama. He died in San Diego at the age of seventy-nine.

in a variety of makeshift prisons such as private residences, and for five days in a hotel where Richardson recalled that "the bedding was very unsatisfactory and the rations consisted of soup, black bread, and occasional soggy potato's [*sic*] mixed with codfish." Finally the pair ended up at a twelfth-century castle in Landshut, Bavaria. Even though the conditions were more hospitable, the German guards feared they might escape, so Wiser and Richardson were forced to surrender their shoes each evening at five p.m., and they weren't returned until nine a.m. the next morning.[66] Thanks to a sympathetic guard, Wiser was given a sketchpad and watercolor paints and used the time creating a cartoon archive of his confinement, or as he called it, a "modest records entertainment accorded us while guests of the German Government."[67] After the war, Wiser became a renowned illustrator and painter.

While his doughboys were having a tough go of it on the ground and in the sky, Pershing spent most of the day in his Souilly office. To gain an audience with the commander in chief, one first had to pass through a team of orderlies and adjutants standing guard in front of the town hall. Across the hall from Pershing's office, within shouting distance, was a larger room covered in wall maps that was occupied by chief of staff Hugh Drum.[68] A short man with a large nose, "Drummie," as he was known throughout the AEF, had served for twenty years in the army when the Meuse-Argonne battle started. When Drum was nineteen, his father was killed in combat during the Spanish-American War, and a remorseful President William McKinley offered the grieving son a direct commission. Drum was one of the few officers on Pershing's staff who did not attend West Point. One historian has called him a "man of boundless ambition"; he served another twenty-five years in the military after the First World War ended.

Rumors circulated throughout First Army that "Drummie" acted on Pershing's behalf without his boss's knowledge, sending out orders and memorandums to corps and division headquarters as if he were the commander in chief. Even though Black Jack trusted Drum a great deal and frequently sought his counsel, all important papers, whether or not they were signed by the chief of staff, would have been reviewed by Pershing first. Many of the tens of thousands of documents created by AEF, now in the National Archives, have signs of Pershing's fingerprints all over them, with his notes scribbled in the margins and at the top and bottom of the pages. There are frequent cross-outs of words or complete sentences that he initialed "JJP." It appears that practically every scrap of paper passed through Black Jack's hands. In today's business vernacular he would be called a micromanager. It is unlikely that Drum could have issued anything from Souilly without Pershing's knowledge.

Pershing also controlled how the media would report on the battle. On the night of September 25, fifty or so reporters gathered in Bar-le-Duc were briefed by Major General Fox Conner, another of Pershing's trusted advisers and head of the Operations Branch. First Army had set up press headquarters in a small store on a cobbled side street off the city center. The windows and doors were covered with blackout blankets; only the red glare of burning cigarettes and a few oil lamps and candles provided illumination. With the attack commencing within several hours, strict secrecy was paramount that evening. Conner stood at the front of the room and pointed to a large wall map facing the newspapermen selected by Pershing's intelligence staff. With a pencil he traced the First Army route through the Argonne Forest and across the Meuse River. Connor rested his pencil on Sedan, and told the hushed crowd that this was the key to victory. If the Americans were unable to take the Sedan-Mézières railroad line, the war would be over.

Conner then posed a question to the assembled journalists on behalf of Pershing. Though Black Jack had received hundreds of supportive messages and glowing headlines following his first American victory, he anticipated that the Meuse-Argonne attack would be nothing like St. Mihiel. His doughboys would have to fight hard for every rock, hill, and blade of grass held by the German Army; casualties could be in the tens of thousands. Black Jack wanted to know if the American people had the stomach for heavy losses. Conner received no assurances. Junius B. Wood, who followed Pershing to Mexico in 1916 and now wrote for the *Chicago Daily News*, snidely remarked: "I think the people at home are just beginning to find out there's a war."[69]

One division that stood out on opening day was attached to Bullard's III Corps. The 80th's mountain men from Virginia, Pennsylvania, and West Virginia targeted the town of Brieulles on the Meuse, where the river turns north. By noon they reached the outskirts of their objective after sloshing through a series of marshes. Holding their position for a few hours, the 80th tried advancing toward Brieulles, but German artillery fire from Montfaucon to the west, and Consenvoye Heights and Borne du Cornouiller east of the Meuse, forced them to halt and try again the next day.

In the waning hours of September 26 Pershing reflected on what had happened that day, especially with the 28th, 35th and 37th Divisions, who he surmised were "less satisfactory" when compared with the other divisions. "They were new," he reasoned, "their staffs did not work particularly well, and they generally presented the failings of green troops."[70] All of this was correct. Major General Liggett, on the other hand, felt that First Army could have accomplished more that first day, and it was Pershing who had held them back by ordering his divisions to stop on a line designated as the corps objective. Throughout the Argonne battle and for many years after the contest ended, Liggett wished he had been allowed to fight like Ulysses S. Grant, who relentlessly pursued the Confederates until they were forced to surrender in mid-April 1865. "I thought then, think now, and told General Pershing at my first opportunity," Liggett wrote, "that it was a mistake to stop here until the enemy stopped us."[71] As the next forty-six days showed, Liggett may have been correct. By pushing on, First Army could have had an easier time, but as it stood, there would still be plenty of fighting in what turned out to be the first phase of the battle, and the Germans were far from giving up.

6
ADVANCE!

At dawn on Friday, September 27, Pershing woke to the sound of battle. The earth beneath his sleeper car trembled from his artillery, and when he walked outside he could hear the faint rapid fire of American machine guns and rifles off in the distance. First Army's divisions were once again on the attack. The previous night Pershing had gone to bed satisfied by the significant advances made by I and III Corps, but disappointed by what happened in the V Corps sector. The 79th Division had not yet taken Montfaucon, and by the time it had given up for the night, it had lost many good troops. Medical reports tallied 206 officers and enlisted men killed and another 222 wounded.[1]

Forty miles to the north of Souilly, General von Gallwitz had moved his headquarters from Montmédy to Longuyon, a small factory town and rail junction on the confluence of the Crusnes and Chiers Rivers.[2] The atmosphere there must have been tense. The day before,

Gallwitz had been completely caught off guard by the American attack, and although he quickly bolstered the lines by calling up the 51st and 76th Reserve Divisions and the 52nd Infantry Division, this was a temporary fix. Gallwitz feared that Pershing's attack toward the Argonne might have been a diversion to mask a more concentrated thrust in the direction of the Woëvre or Metz. Not until later in the day would he have a good sense of the American First Army's battle plan after Fifth German Army intelligence interrogated several French deserters and a doughboy captured from the 4th Division. His staff brought him credible information that Pershing was indeed attacking through the Argonne and heading directly to the Meuse River to draw the Germans out in the open. Gallwitz was also told that the Americans had sustained heavy losses, but that mattered little since Pershing's forces still outnumbered his army by a significant margin.[3] Some German divisions could muster only around 3,400 troops, about the size of one First Army infantry regiment.

After two days of clear weather, rain returned to the Argonne front on September 27. Other than caking soldiers' shoes and leggings with sticky mud, the soggy ground had little impact on the infantry, but heavy clouds hampered the Air Service's activity throughout the morning. Lieutenant Erwin Bleckley, a pilot in the 50th Aero Squadron, grumbled in his diary that the "weather was too bad [and] nobody got a chance to fly in [the] a.m.—rained most all morning."[4] By afternoon most planes were able to fly, and even Billy Mitchell went up for a quick view of the battlefield. Soaring over a road leading to Montfaucon, Mitchell's attention was directed toward a cluster of flickering lights in the woods below. Peering closer, he saw they were fires lit by shivering American soldiers trying to keep warm. These men were "new at the game," Mitchell thought, and such carelessness could easily disclose their positions to the enemy. "When I first saw it," he later recalled, "it looked like the best target that I had ever seen for aviation on any field."

Cold, tired, and hungry, the soldiers of the 313th waited throughout the soggy morning for orders to continue the attack against Montfaucon, conserving their food and ammo and protecting the wounded, who lay in the open field. A breakdown in communication between Major General Kuhn and his brigade commanders was causing the delay. The 79th Division commander believed that the best approach when resuming the attack was to deploy two brigades. Brigadier General William Nicholson's 157th would lead off from the left with the 313th, while the 158th, under Brigadier General Robert Noble, with the 314th and 315th, would strike on the right. Noble was instructed to make contact with Hines's 4th Division, which had fought beyond Montfaucon the day before and held the village of Nantillois.

Noble received the written order from Kuhn at one fifteen a.m., and was told to move out immediately. Yet there was one problem: Noble had no idea where his regiments were located. He sent his staff officers to find them, but the party was gone all night. At seven a.m. Kuhn arrived to check on Noble for a progress report and learned that his brigade had not yet moved. Noble explained the delay, arguing that he wanted to avoid an incident of friendly fire between his 314th and 315th. Thinking Noble's excuse was ridiculous, Kuhn fired him on the spot. Brigade command went to Colonel Oury of the 314th, who immediately moved out in the daylight with the other infantry brigade, the 157th.

At around seven thirty the two brigades headed back toward Montfaucon, defended by the 5th and 37th Bavarian Reserves, the 7th German Reserves, and the 117th German Division. Each of them was understrength and composed of "older" troops who had been in the sector for at least a couple of years. Sweezey and the 313th advanced from the left, with support from light artillery and six French light tanks, scraping their way through a heavy blast of machine-gun fire that "Baltimore's Own" eventually silenced with their grenades, bayonets, and a U.S.-made 1916 1.5-pound 37mm cannon mounted on an artillery carriage.[5]

Shortly before noon the ruined village of Montfaucon, as well as the ridge to its left, was in American hands.[6] The 314th, slightly to the rear of the 313th, arrived about fifteen minutes later and cleared the Bois de Tuilerie on the southeast slope of Montfaucon. By the time the other brigade from the 79th (158th) arrived, Gallwitz's troops had completely withdrawn. The only standing structure was an observation post in a tall church tower, used in 1916 by the crown prince of Germany, the eldest of the Kaiser's five sons, to spy on Verdun. His periscope was still intact; after the war the instrument was sent to West Point for the museum collections.[7]

Sweezey once again attempted to send Kuhn a message by carrier pigeon to inform him that Montfaucon had been taken, and this time it worked. Yet it took the bird an hour and forty minutes to reach 79th headquarters some fourteen miles away, and it arrived at its destination bleeding and suffering from a torn left wing. Pigeon 47's message was logged in, but for an unknown reason, it was never delivered to Kuhn. When the general, who had no idea Montfaucon had been taken, saw Nicholson later in the day, he was ready to pounce on his subordinate, as he had with Noble. "Where the hell have you been?" Kuhn demanded. "What do you mean by breaking liaison with me?" Nicholson responded calmly, "I've been taking Montfaucon, that's where I've been."[8] For its efforts, the 79th captured two hundred German soldiers and eleven field guns, but suffered over 3,500 killed and wounded after two days of combat. Sweezey and the 313th spent the night of the twenty-seventh on the northern slopes of Montfaucon, tired, hungry, and thirsty. None of the men had been able to fill their canteens since jumping off the day before. Sweezey had kept his mouth moist by smoking and chewing cigars, one after another, without break.[9]

As difficult as it was for aviators to operate in the rain, the engineers had a far more challenging job. They had the thankless task of trying to repair shell holes on roads before the approaching infantry passed over them. Most of the holes were already overflowing with rainwater from the previous week, and the new storm made matters worse. Engineers used debris from destroyed village walls to patch the craters, but some sections of road were almost impossible to mend because the depressions were too large.[10] Shelling from the Verdun battle had left holes forty to fifty feet deep and one hundred feet wide.[11] Such was the case with Route Nationale 46, a major thoroughfare that crossed through the 35th Division sector.[12] Supply convoys, ambulances, ammunition, and ration trucks headed to the front on this road, but congestion caused the traffic to slow to a crawl.[13] Tractors had to tow motor-driven and some horse-drawn vehicles around the massive craters.[14] Some frustrated drivers abandoned their motor vehicles and resorted to donkeys as a way to get supplies forward. The four-legged creatures were at times stubborn, but with some swift encouragement they managed to cross over muddy holes and other impediments that Ford trucks wouldn't dare attempt.

The Motor Transport Corps, under Major General Harbord's Services of Supply, consisted mostly of Model Ts built by automobile magnate Henry Ford. They had arrived in France painted black due to Ford's antiwar stance, and were repainted olive drab or other colors by the Army. Repairs were handled by skilled mechanics specially recruited for this type of work. The Army had no problem finding mechanics to fix broken trucks, but keeping an ample supply of spare parts on hand was not easy. A typical motor truck had somewhere around

3,500 parts, some of them interchangeable, like tires, springs and bolts.[15] Parts were sent over from America or, if they could be found, purchased locally in France.

On the few roads available to First Army, ambulances were supposed to have the right of way. To accommodate this, Pershing's staff ordered that every tenth truck in a convoy had to display a red disk. There was to be a break between this vehicle and the one in front, large enough for an ambulance to pass through. Yet in the first few days of the battle, with heavy traffic and not enough military police to regulate the flow, this rule was rarely obeyed. In Cameron's V Corps sector, which was crossed by the Esnes-Malancourt Road, bottlenecks were especially bad. By the side of the road, signs with big letters were placed in full view: PLAY THE GAME, BOYS! OBEY THE M.P.![16] One ambulance driver complained that he was at a standstill for twenty-four hours.[17] When darkness set in, regulations forbade using lights or smoking cigarettes so as not to attract German artillery.[18]

To offer some comfort to his soldiers, Pershing sent the Young Men's Christian Association (YMCA) toward the front to provide men with reading material, chocolates, tobacco, and matches. Large tents were loaded on railcars, sent forward and set up as "Y" huts. One of the Y units escorting the 37th Division included an expert tent man "who had traveled for years with Barnum and Bailey."[19]

By the time September 27 came to a close, Pershing was finally able to relax a bit. That evening an Army band formed beside his railcar, serenading the general as a crowd of French poilus gathered and listened to the entertainment.[20] For the most part, his divisions had done all he could ask of them, and in some cases, even more. First Army was now halfway toward the overly ambitious objective he had set for the first day of the battle, which was to reach the Romagne-Cunel Road, which ran through the Kriemhilde Stellung.

On September 28, First Army made even more progress. Major General Hines recorded in his diary that "ammunition artillery and supplies [were] beginning to arrive despite the road congestion, mud and shell holes." By the day's end his division had taken Cuisy, along with 2,045 German prisoners, including 58 officers and many guns.[21] More remarkable over the past two days was the achievement of the 33rd Division. Led by Major General George W. Bell, an 1888 West Point graduate whose round belly, mustache, and goatee made him resemble one of the Three Musketeers, the 33rd from Illinois had spent almost four months with British troops, lending them support in two operations near the Somme River. Now back under American command, Bell's troops advanced down steep slopes and pivoted around the Bois de Forges, which the enemy had considered impregnable, then swung toward the Meuse. In some places duckboards were thrown over enemy barbed wire, while elsewhere the troops waded through swampy ground under intense fire. By noon, however, the division had reached its objectives along the Meuse, having covered a remarkable distance of over four miles. In contrast, the other two divisions of Bullard's III Corps met strong resistance after breaking through the first line of enemy resistance, and suffered particularly from the artillery fire that poured down on them from the east bank of the Meuse.[22]

Word from the 77th "Liberty" Division, draftees out of New York City, was that its advance in the Argonne was progressing slowly. Difficult terrain covered in thick vegetation severely hampered visibility, causing doughboys to inadvertently walk into enemy positions. Led by Major General Robert Alexander, who rose through the Army ranks from private to division commander, the 77th attacked the 2nd German Landwehr Division on a high ridge known as St. Hubert's Pavilion, which the enemy protected with "barbed wire and chicken wire interlaced between the trees."[23] The Germans, well hidden behind the foliage, "could not be seen to be fired at and could only be nosed out and routed by attacking parties that crawled along the ground and scouted from tree-to-tree."[24] At times the line was separated by only a few yards in a sector about one-third of a mile in length. Alexander's men first exchanged rifle fire, then both sides resorted to a hand grenade duel, described by a newspaper reporter "as though they were throwing snowballs in winter." Finally, the 77th engaged the Germans in hand-to-hand combat.[25]

The fighting continued onto a crest called Abri St. Louis, where more German soldiers had taken cover. It "had been a tough nut for them," Colonel Stackpole, Liggett's aid, recorded, "but they had smoked it out and killed occupants." Germans who survived the attack emerged with shouts of "Kamerad" to surrender, but it was a trap: when dough-boys approached, the devious Germans threw grenades at the New Yorkers, causing "losses and disorder." Alexander's men shouted among the ranks, "Retire!" and retreated without taking any prisoners. When Liggett learned about the aborted attack later in the day, he told Stack-pole that "under such circumstances all should be killed as combatants and not taken, and particularly the officers responsible for such a trick; also that anyone, friend or foe, shouting 'Retire' or attempting to cause stampede should be immediately shot."[26]

Temporarily out of trouble, the Liberty Division advanced through the tangled Argonne Forest. On the New Yorkers' left flank, Fourth French Army, under command of General Henri Gouraud, offered protection. Gouraud was a veteran officer with a distinctive appearance: his red beard formed a perfect square, while his lean frame and narrow head made him look like a "big bird with a beak of a nose."[27] It was also hard not to notice that Gouraud's right arm was missing—he had lost it, while suffering two broken legs, as a result of shell fragments during the Gallipoli campaign in June 1915.[28]

Immediately to the French Fourth Army's right was the American 1st Battalion of the 308th Infantry, led by Major Charles Whittlesey, a tall, gangly New Englander who had left a Wall Street law firm to don an Army officer's uniform. At Camp Upton, New York, where the division trained before coming to France, Whittlesey's men made fun of their commander's stiltlike legs, calling him "Galloping Charlie" behind his back.[29] Following close by was the regiment's 2nd Battalion under the command of Captain George McMurtry, a former Wall Street lawyer who had once left Harvard Law School to serve in the Spanish-American War, charging up San Juan Hill with Theodore Roosevelt's Rough Riders.[30]

Whittlesey dragged the two battalions through the dense forest and across a German cemetery, called L'Homme Mort, or "Dead Man's Hill," until darkness and a steady rain kept them from going any farther. The men paused on the far slope of a hill near the cemetery. Not knowing if there was support on his flanks or the whereabouts of the Germans, Whittlesey sent out runners to gather intelligence. At midnight on September 28 one of the runners reported that he had been challenged in the darkness by someone speaking German. Whittlesey then sent out a night patrol to probe even farther, and they returned a short time later with bad news: the battalion was surrounded by enemy machine guns.[31] Whittlesey refused to panic. At daybreak on the twenty-ninth, all was well, when suddenly a German officer and a sergeant appeared from an open space in the forest. They were quickly taken down by American rifles, but before the officer expired, he revealed: "You will meet real opposition up ahead. . . . My company is only seventy men." Whittlesey sent a message by carrier pigeon to the regimental headquarters, stating that he was cut off and needed rations and ammunition.

On September 29, a relief party, led by Lieutenant Colonel Fred E.

Smith of the 308th Infantry, was sent to find Whittlesey's battalion. Along the way, Smith's detachment ran into German machine-gun nests. While his men took cover, Smith unholstered his pistol and fired at the enemy emplacements. Returning to friendly lines, he gathered some grenades and headed back out. Taking a wound in his side, Smith kept shooting at the Germans until he fell dead.[32] For his act of valor, Colonel Smith was awarded a posthumous Medal of Honor.

Additional units from the 77th soon appeared on the scene, and Whittlesey's battalion was rescued. Instead of sending the men back to the rear for rest, Alexander ordered them fed and resupplied so that they could keep pushing deeper into the forest.[33] Three days later Whittlesey and his men would again be cut off in another pocket, although this time the situation was far more serious.

What had happened to Whittlesey's battalion during the previous seventy-two hours, and then the following week, could have been avoided had there been better cooperation between the French 38th Corps on the 77th's left flank and the attached 368th Infantry from the African American 92nd "Buffalo" Division, led by Major General Charles Ballou. Ballou was described by French officers as "a cold, authoritarian man" who at best had "only very superficial ideas about the actual conditions of this war."[34] Commanded by white officers and black NCOs, Ballou's regiment was at a great disadvantage, fighting across difficult terrain with inadequate equipment. The black troops wore U.S. uniforms but French helmets, and were issued French Lebel rifles, which were of poor quality compared with the Enfield 1917 or Springfield 1903 carried by their Caucasian countrymen.

Two hundred thousand black American men served in the AEF, but only about 20 percent were combat troops, including the 93rd Division, with four infantry regiments that served entirely with the French.[35] One of its regiments, the 369th "Harlem Rattlers," spent more time on the front lines than any other AEF unit. Also serving in the 93rd was Corporal Freddie Stowers, who was killed in action on September 28 while rallying the men of Company C, 371st Infantry Regiment, during an assault on Côté 188. Decades later, Stowers became the first African American soldier of the Great War to receive the Medal of Honor when President George H. W. Bush presented it to his two sisters in a White House ceremony.[36]

During this era of military segregation, African Americans were largely relegated to supporting roles and could be found by the thousands in the ports of St. Nazaire and Brest, unloading cargo as stevedores or assigned to labor battalions. While at the front, especially within First Army, General Pershing was more comfortable with white officers leading white enlisted men, despite his experience with African American soldiers early in his career. Pershing tried for racial consistency and allowed black company officers but made sure that there was never a situation in which a white officer would have to take orders from a black superior. He did allow mostly African American pioneer regiments, who were assigned to repair damaged roads and other menial tasks at the front while subjected to artillery fire and constant gas attacks even though most of the troops had not received instructions on how to use their masks.[37]

Little was expected of the 368th Infantry when it jumped off on September 26. The men were to form a link with the French on the western edge of the Argonne in support of the 77th's advance. They were placed directly under the French 1st Dismounted Cavalry with the objective of taking Binarville, a small village at the intersection of two stone-built roads used by the Germans as a supply route. Both roads ran through the forest, and the more important of the two connected the towns of Apremont and Servon in an east-west direction. By the twenty-eighth two of the regimental battalions had cracked from intense shell fire, their men scattered in all directions. After falling back, on September 30 the 1st Battalion of the 368th, under Colonel John N. Merrill, advanced and reached Binarville at around four p.m., twenty minutes after the French had entered the village. But a day later the unit was ordered to withdraw from Binarville. The reasoning for the move was unclear, but the French likely had little confidence in the African American soldiers, who were referred to as "loaned aid" by a staff officer in French 38th Corps.[38] Had Merrill's battalion of eight hundred men been allowed to stay and advance, as well as receive support from the other 92nd Division regiments, the flank of the 77th Division would have been protected.[39]

With Binarville occupied, the Germans were moved off positions on Hill 198.[40] When the French abandoned Binarville, the Germans quietly moved back, and the civilians in the villages of Binarville, Apremont, and Chatel were evacuated and sent to labor camps or to Germany.

Reports on the Americans' combat performance were discussed among the German Imperial General Staff, who made their headquarters at the Hôtel Britannique in the picturesque city of Spa, Belgium; according to one tourist guidebook, it was the oldest bathing place in Europe.[41] Ludendorff and Hindenburg, the two masterminds behind the German Army, were told that Pershing's troops "at the onset of their attacks proved to be strong of nerve, charging in close formation." But "as soon as the Americans encountered lively artillery and machine-gun fire, their charge came to a halt."[42] Ludendorff, now fifty-three, "had risen by sheer ability through the ranks of an army dominated by aristocrats," notes one historian who also wrote that Ludendorff was "a dour professional warrior to every last extremity of his being, he considered war the natural business of mankind."[43]

Hindenburg, seventeen years older than Ludendorff, was in almost every sense the complete opposite of his counterpart. Born into Prussian aristocracy, he sported a name that suited his noble upbringing: Paul Ludwig Hans Anton von Beneckendorff und von Hindenburg. He was a combat veteran who had seen his share of conflict after continuous fighting in the latter third of the 1800s, first against Austria, then France. Hindenburg had retired from military service as a general in 1911, devoting his time to eating, reading, and pipe smoking. But when Germany dressed for war once again in August 1914, he was asked back to the army, and eagerly heeded the call.[44]

How much Hindenburg and Ludendorff told the German emperor, Kaiser Wilhelm II, about the Meuse-Argonne attack is unknown. Described as "lazy and self-indulgent, preferring appearance to reality," Wilhelm had been in power since 1888. At the outbreak of the war his popularity had soared, but by 1917 declined rapidly, with the German people suffering from inflation, food shortages, and labor unrest. A year later his interest in the military had waned, and it was only a matter of days before the kaiser would flee to exile in Holland.[45]

In France, Ferdinand Foch followed the battle's progress at the Château de Trois-Fontaines, about 120 miles east of Paris in the Marne Valley. He often visited with Pétain to complain about the lack of progress made by First Army.[46] Pershing heard of these complaints directly from Colonel Paul Hedrick Clark, his liaison officer with the American Military Mission at French Grand Quartier Général (GQG) in Chantilly, outside of Paris. Clark was one of the smartest soldiers in the AEF. A Chicago native, he took six years to complete West Point due to frequent illness and graduated at the bottom of his class. Yet what made Clark so valuable to Pershing was his knowledge of the French people and his fluency in their language. Colonel Clark was Pershing's eyes and ears among their Gallic allies, and at the end of each day he wrote lengthy memorandums to the general that covered everything from what the French were saying about current operations and the war in general to specific criticism of the AEF and its commander in chief. For instance, two days into the battle Clark reported that "everywhere I go I am pressed for information on the American attack and wherever I go congratulations are offered for the efforts of the American Army."[47] He also relayed bits of information from the French intelligence summaries, such as the Germans' placing of POW camps by railroad stations so that bombing would kill Allied troops, or that Hindenburg visited Metz and ordered additional ordnance and material sent there, believing that First Army was headed in that direction.

As the battle of the Meuse-Argonne unfolded, Pershing would rely heavily on Clark and other staff officers for advice. Yet, at the same time, he managed almost every detail of the battle. If it were feasible, Pershing might have carried a rifle and led his men from the front across no-man's-land himself. Not until the battle eventually ground to a halt did the realization set in that leading both an expeditionary force and a field army was more than one man could handle, especially since some of his division commanders needed more managing than he had thought. This was a steep learning curve for Pershing and his doughboys, and their success depended on having more independence for the corps and division commanders to make decisions on the ground.

7

BEHIND THE LINES

ord of Brigadier General Robert Noble's sacking quickly spread throughout First Army, but no one was completely stunned. Removing incompetent officers had been commonplace since the summer of 1918, when the AEF first engaged in active combat. Any officer in Pershing's army was fair game. Failure to meet an objective pretty much meant a trip to the chopping block. By the end of the war, nearly 1,400 commanders, ranging in rank from second lieutenant to major general, had been either reassigned or sent back to the United States. When the final decision was handed down, the officers were first ordered to the Casual Officers Depot at Blois in the Loire Valley. This depot was initially established by AEF headquarters in January 1918 to handle the large number of officers arriving in France who were not assigned to a particular unit, farming them out to combat outfits as needed. As Pershing carefully watched his combat officers to see how well they and their units performed in battle, actively removing the ones who did not meet his strict standards, Blois took on a new role.

An order to Blois likely meant an officer's career was in danger. In some cases, officers were reassigned to other combat units, but mostly likely they were demoted. Blois, or "Blooey" in AEF vernacular, became synonymous with failure. If an officer was sent to the depot, it was known within the AEF that he had gone "Blooey."[1] Major General Bullard wrote that Pershing was "looking for results. He intends to have them. He will sacrifice any man who does not bring them."[2]

Noble was angered by his dismissal and felt it was unjustified. "I was relieved at dawn after a day and night of the strain of battle," he argued in his own defense, "the first experience of our division in action."[3] Due process was afforded Noble. AEF inspector general Major General Andre W. Brewster, a combat veteran and Medal of Honor recipient, investigated his firing and found "that General Noble failed to take proper steps to carry out his orders; that he was unable to come to a decision and lacked initiative and command." Furthermore, Brewster stated, "I do not believe that General Noble has the leadership and initiative to command a brigade of infantry."[4] Brewster's inquiry carried a lot of weight, and he concluded that Noble had no business being at the front. Pershing let him linger at "Blooey" as a colonel until after the armistice, when Noble served out his time in the SOS.[5]

Pershing was wary of other field commanders and often sent First Army staff officers to the corps, division, and brigade headquarters unannounced to observe their abilities to lead at the front. Nicknamed "periscopes" or "crocodiles," these officers seemed to come out of nowhere at post commands, gathering information for their boss that he later on might use against the field commanders.[6]

Not being able to receive timely and accurate battle reports was a problem that plagued the AEF's efforts in Europe.[7] Pershing had tried to preempt the communication issues when he first established AEF headquarters in Chaumont in 1917. Arriving in France, he found communication switchboards staffed by French telephone operators, creating an obvious language barrier for his Americans. Writing to Army chief of staff Major Peyton C. March in Washington, he requested that the War Department recruit American telephone operators who could speak French. Since nearly all telephone operators in the United States were female, Pershing promised the candidates that "women who go into the service will do as much to help win the war as the men in khaki."[8]

Women were recruited from all over the United States. First, the U.S. Division of Women's War Work, Committee on Public Information, tried to find qualified candidates among women of French descent from Canada and Louisiana. More than three hundred applied, but only six were selected due to the job requirements. The Army Signal Corps then took over the recruiting, and by the spring of 1918 they had received more than 7,600 applications. Out of that pool, 223 were sent overseas, with about half that number staying behind in reserve. To qualify as a telephone operator, applicants had to have competence in French, know how to operate a switchboard, and be in good physical condition. Before each woman was approved, she went through a rigorous psychological test to see if she could handle the pressure of a job that might require answering and transmitting messages at a rapid pace. Since operators would be privy to classified information such as troop movements, each candidate was investigated by the Secret Service to ensure loyalty to her country. Once accepted into service, they trained in New York, Chicago, San Francisco, Philadelphia, and Atlantic City.[9] They were affectionately known as "Hello Girls."

When Pershing established First Army Headquarters at Souilly, he had seven women to handle the lines of communication as telephone operators. Because of the importance of their job in the commander in chief's office, the women were required to follow a certain protocol. Whenever Pershing's light glowed red on the switchboard, the operator must "drop everything, disconnect anyone, and answer within a half second."[10] The women also learned to talk in code. First Army supply area Ligny was known as "Waterfall," while Toul might be "Podunk" one day and "Wabash" the next. The Fourth Corps was known as "Nemo."[11]

There were two types of boards operated by the Hello Girls: one for making local and long-distance calls regarding matters such as supplies and transportation, and the other for messages between frontline units and the commanding officers who directed their movements. "Every order for an infantry advance, a barrage preparatory to the taking of a new objective, and, in fact, for every troop movement came over these 'fighting lines,' as we called them," the chief operator recalled. "These wires connected the front up with the generals and made it possible for the latter to know exactly what was going on at any moment and to direct operations accordingly. It was at the operating board, then, that we seven girls were put when we went into the Argonne."[12]

Mrs. Berthe M. Hunt of Berkeley, California, recalled their arrival:

When we arrived on September 26th, we found ourselves in a French camp that had been used for over four years, including the period of the famous Verdun drive. The barracks were flimsy things that had been lined with old newspapers and maps to keep out the cold. The Y. W. C. A. helped us out by giving us a blanket each, a rug, oilcloth and other comforts. In fact, our sitting room (which we acquired later) was furnished with a piano and other things taken from Boche dugouts in the vicinity. Everyone assisted

in making us as comfortable as possible, considering the fact that
we were in the advance area, where we could see the red and
yellow glare from the shelling and feel the reverberations caused
by the booming of the big guns. The 27th Engineers helped us
get settled and made us shelves for our various belongings, wash
stands, wooden tables and benches, etc.[13]

Pershing referred to the Hello Girls as "real soldiers," a moniker they earned through long hours of important work.[14] Esther Fresnel, from New York, wrote her parents that "we worked day and night, six hours at a stretch, and then ran home to snatch a few hours sleep, then [went] back to work." Berthe Hunt remembered that it was "most thrilling to sit at that board and feel the importance of it." Grace Banker, another New Yorker who served as the chief operator, hated being away from the switchboard. "Soon after 2:00 a.m. I was back in the office with the girls who had left on the earlier shift the night before," Grace recalled. "No one could tell what might happen next; it was like an exciting game—and I couldn't leave."[15]

At times, bombs or thunderstorms would render the lines inoperable, flaring the tempers of the devoted staff. When a fire broke out in the switchboard office, the girls proved their dedication by refusing to leave until forced out by direct military order. After an hour they returned to the smoky room and continued fielding calls.[16]

At Souilly, another message center was set up in a wooden shack with a corrugated iron roof next to Pershing's headquarters and was under direct command of chief of staff Hugh Drum. Within was the AEF code room, where all secret messages were coded or decoded. The code room was staffed by two American and two French officers and a couple of field clerks. From this room, First Army sent not only orders and instructions to the corps and divisions at the front, but also messages in code about the military and political progress of the war from other Allied field commanders.

Several officer couriers assigned to the message center staff were charged with delivering secret field orders or important communications to the American and French commanding generals. Two couriers on motorcycles, either Harley-Davidsons or Indians, were given identical messages, with one rider taking one road while the other was sent by another route to the same destination, so that if one failed to make the delivery, another could be relied on.[17]

Most of the communication staff behind the lines, plus the field signal battalion units attached to divisions, were former Bell System employees, and thus were known as Bell Battalions. Each telegraph battalion assigned to an Army zone was to pick up the lines of communications and carry them forward to corps headquarters, and then eventually bring them forward to divisional headquarters. Recruited were cable splicers, linemen, switchboard operators, and telegraph operators.[18]

Most of the electrical equipment was brought from America. About 39,000 miles of wire were strung on the battlefronts alone, and the entire system comprised of 126,000 miles of wire, which would have encircled the earth more than five times. If he wanted, Pershing could call Americans stationed in England thanks to a cable stretched across the floor of the English Channel.[19]

By the time of the Meuse-Argonne, signal operators carried waterproof radio sets that were so well built and easy to use that the Army called them "ax proof and fool proof." The rear set worked up to one hundred miles, the intermediate worked up to twenty miles, and a small trench set, weighing about thirty pounds and carried on a man's back, had a range of one to three miles. The signalmen did everything from assisting the Air Service with spotting enemy artillery positions to directing troop movements and, on occasion, intercepting and decoding enemy messages. With artillery spotting, the scouting reconnaissance planes had only a transmitter and the artillery commander a receiver. Transmissions often failed, at which point communication from the sky to the ground had to rely on more archaic methods, such as dropping paper messages, then hoping they didn't end up in enemy hands.

Signal operators learned how to tap into the German communication systems and intercept messages. When German officers suspected that the Americans were listening in, they posted warnings in their communication trenches. One poster cautioned "The Enemy Is Listening—Beware of the Telephone," and depicted a spread-eagled German soldier carelessly talking on a handset held between his legs. Of course, the Germans were also snooping on American wires, and First Army had to secure secrecy against German eavesdroppers. The Signal Corps devised the "buzzer-phone," which used a low current to transmit messages in dots and dashes that were read telegraphically.[20] Despite the advanced methods of communicating, all of them were useless to the commanders if they didn't have clear direction from Souilly.

Another issue that occupied Pershing and his staff was dealing with the increasing number of Germans who were captured or who surrendered at the front. During the first two days of combat, First Army took more than eight thousand enemy prisoners. A large percentage of these German POWs carried a "prisoner's bundle,"* indicating that they had anticipated being captured.[21] They were quite a sight for doughboys who had never seen a German up close before. A First Army engineer

---

* This may be a reference to German soldiers carrying extra rations and clothing in case they surrendered or were captured.

wrote in his diary that he had witnessed "three Boche prisoners—just captured—old men around 45 years old—seemed glad to be captured."[22] Major Chester W. Davis, who served in the 1st Pioneer Infantry, a regiment that was a cross between an infantry and an engineer unit, eloquently described a group of German prisoners who had passed near him at the front:

> *Prisoners, some taken by our own regiment, filtered through in bodies of twenty to two hundred, occasionally carrying wounded Americans. Haughty Prussian officers with gold monocles, hard, sulky-looking soldiers, frightened Slavs with rosaries prominently displayed as if to appeal to the feelings of their captors and many boys certainly under sixteen years of age who in happier times would have been romping to school but [were] now clumping along with hanging heads in their green uniforms, round hats and leather boots.*[23]

Bishop Charles Brent, Pershing's chief of chaplains, was informed of an instance of fraternization between Americans and Germans, which was normally forbidden. A colonel told Bishop Brent that he had just come from the front, where he saw "a group of walking wounded from a dressing station," and within the group were many German prisoners. The colonel observed that "every time they stopped to rest, two of the number, one a German and the other an American, sat down and put their heads together, looking at something that lay between them." The colonel, curious by this point, waited a bit until they sat down in a shell hole, went over and found them playing a game of checkers, "each one swearing at the other in his own language."[24]

Upon capture, prisoners of war were immediately disarmed and sent to a brigade headquarters in the rear, where they were searched for concealed weapons and documents not already confiscated at the front. Captured German prisoners, as well as the papers, maps, diaries, and letters taken from them, formed the best source of intelligence for G-2, proving to be more reliable than spies, agents, and intercepted radio messages. It was said that "the best way to find out about the Germans was to ask them."[25]

Prisoners were then placed in division enclosures and interrogated by intelligence officers. Overcoats, blankets, and gas masks were seized, ostensibly for use at salvage depots, but more likely kept as souvenirs by the interrogators. POWs were given serial numbers and made to fill out a postcard to let family members know of their whereabouts. They were housed in tents surrounded by two layers of barbed wire that were patrolled by sentries all day and night.[26]

For long-term imprisonment, POWs were placed in so-called cages, which were actually large wire stockades guarded by doughboys assigned to prisoner of war companies. Most of the camps were in the base sections under Major General Harbord's SOS, although a POW cage was set up just steps from Pershing's office in Souilly. Because German prisoners were deemed such a valuable resource, Pershing insisted they be treated with respect. He issued a standing order that once a prisoner arrived in the rear for confinement, he should be given a meal of bully beef, hardtack, and coffee, along with a sack of tobacco. Eventually German cooks were assigned to feed the incoming prisoners.

While in captivity, German prisoners performed manual labor, such as construction and roadwork, unless a prisoner had clerical or mechanical skills. Noncommissioned officers worked as clerks and interpreters, or supervised enlisted men in their assignments. Officers were not required to work. According to the Hague Convention, prisoners could not be forced to engage in work connected with military operations and could not be employed within thirty kilometers of the front, except when carrying wounded to the rear.

All POWs were paid, though not actually given currency. Instead, each man had a bank account that he could draw on to pay for items from a prison canteen. German prisoners were treated quite well, receiving the same food, clothing, and medical care as the doughboys. For recreation, they were allowed to play sports, with each PW stockade, as they were known, amply supplied with footballs, baseballs, handballs, and boxing gloves. POWs with musical aptitude were given instruments and formed orchestras.[27]

AEF intelligence officers kept a close eye on each batch of incoming prisoners, noting the ones who looked smart, as well as those who looked weak. These men were immediately interrogated. To trick the prisoners into thinking their captors knew more than they did, the interrogators would refer to the man's commanding officer, naming him specifically. Another way to get a POW talking was to promise to send through neutral Switzerland a letter to his family saying that he was in safe hands.[28] Colonel Wiley Howell, First Army chief of intelligence, used ridicule to prod German officers into revealing information. In one instance, when given false information by an enemy officer, Howell staged a "ceremony of degradation" in front of other prisoners and removed the officer's insignia from his uniform. It caused the POW such humiliation that "he broke down and talked."[29]

First Army intelligence generated a counterintelligence scheme to determine if POWs told the truth during interrogation. Recruiting Lance Corporal Alfred Schotze, a German captured during a trench raid just before St. Mihiel, and aviator Alvin Grothe, who crashed his plane behind American lines in the Argonne, intelligence officers dressed the men in German uniforms and told them to mingle with the other prisoners and strike up conversations. "What did they ask you upstairs [in the interrogation room]?" and "Did you tell them the truth?" they asked.

In one instance Schotze figured out that a German major had given false information. The major was hauled out of bed and taken in front of American officers, where his insignia of rank was torn from his uniform. To disgrace the major even further, the act was performed in front of some German privates. He was then sent to an enlisted men's cage for the night, and the next morning forced to work the "dirtiest jobs around headquarters." Schotze and Grothe's spying was kept secret for fear the two might be killed by other prisoners. This happened to another German POW turned spy, who was choked to death when the nature of his work was discovered.

Schotze and Grothe were rewarded by the U.S. government for furnishing "valuable military information to the American Army." As neither wanted to return to Germany, the Military Intelligence Division in Washington, with the cooperation of the Bureau of Immigration, brought them to the United States and gave them new identities and places to live in undisclosed locations.[30] When the men reached America in May 1919, their story was leaked to a *New York Times* reporter and published the next day. A German newspaper took the *Times* article and completely twisted the account. The German people were told that the two prisoners were high-ranking officers said to have held "responsible positions under the Hindenburg command." Before the Meuse-Argonne, the article claimed, American intelligence succeeded in inducing these officers to hand over the German Imperial General Staff's plans for troop movements, probable lines of withdrawal, and other information of great value. The paper further claimed "that these plans made it possible for General Pershing to carry out his operation with the greatest freedom of action, and it is believed that the losses of the Americans were thereby reduced in half."[31]

G-2 also had a cadre of spies, called "train watchers," who were recruited in Germany to hang out at rail stations in cities such as Cologne, Coblenz and Metz. Their mission was to see how many enemy soldiers boarded trains heading to France. Some of the train watchers came directly from the United States and posed as Alsatians, while others were provided by the British and French. Some were crooked German railroad station employees recruited because they could get the intelligence reports out quicker by bribing engineers they were acquainted with. They were specially trained to read diagrams and drawings so that they could "distinguish all the types of German trains, troops and supply." The work could be dangerous because it required spending days on end around railroad stations with the risk of capture from Germans who were on the lookout for spies.[32]

During the Meuse-Argonne one sly train watcher engaged the staff of a German corps that had stopped off in a Rhine rail station. Pretending to be a patriotic German, he pressed the commanding officer to confirm a rumor that the war was about to end and that Germany was capitulating. This only incited the German colonel, who responded in a sharp tone that additional troops were being brought up from Russia and Romania, and that "the Americans could be stood off on a line protecting Luxembourg, Thionville [on the left bank of the Moselle River] and Metz," as shown on a map he proudly produced.[33]

Nolan's staff also made use of intelligence gathered from aerial photography. Almost all of Billy Mitchell's observation planes were equipped to shoot aerial photographs. The cameras were loaded with fifty plates, and weighed about one hundred pounds.[34] Many of the cameras were handheld by an observer in the rear cockpit, who "aimed it laterally," according to one historian, "seeking the best field of view possible through the obstructions formed by wings, struts, and supporting cables." Observers were often exposed "to propeller blast, which could inhibit accurate aim and contribute to camera motion. Oil spray was thrown from the engine and carried by the propeller blast and could fog the lens." The 24th and 91st Aero Squadrons alone shot 1,098 photographs.[35] After landing, the plates were taken for development at the AEF Photographic Section, headed by Edward Steichen, who later became the lead photographer for *Vogue* and *Vanity Fair* magazines.[36]

With cages full of captured Germans giving some observers a sense that the enemy was giving up, Pershing was concerned that his divisions might take the surrenders for granted and not keep up the momentum they had gained during the first days of battle. With this in mind, he had Cesar Santini drive him to the front for briefings with his corps commanders: Liggett, Bullard, and Cameron. Black Jack's first stop was at III Corps headquarters, then on to Varennes for a meeting with the 35th Division's Traub. Brigadier General Lucien G. Berry, the division's artillery commander, whom Pershing observed with "grave doubts as to whether he might not be a millstone about the neck of Traub," was also present. The 35th had made little progress since the September 26, and Black Jack came away with "the impression" that the Missouri-Kansas Division was "somewhat in the air."

At each corps headquarters Pershing "gave orders for the advance to be resumed." He later lamented, "I certainly have done all in my power to instill an aggressive spirit in the different corps headquarters." His last stop was to see Hunter Liggett at I Corps Headquarters, arriving at about seven thirty p.m. "I was not present in the room," Colonel Stackpole told his diary:

but General Liggett said he [Pershing] seemed to be in a rather excited state of mind, with much to say about the enormous importance of our operations and the possibility of ending the war right here if they were successful and the imperative need of drive and push. General Liggett gave him some notion of the terrain, the insidious character of the opposition, and the handicap all the divisions suffered from by reason of inexperience, lack of training, new officers, losses of officers, and poor ones. Pershing said he appreciated this. Liggett said Pershing "seemed to be in good enough humor."[37]

Santini took longer than necessary to drive back to Souilly, giving Pershing a firsthand look at the road problems his troops had suffered since the start of the battle. That evening he noted that because of the "enormous craters it necessitated taking wide detours. There we found jams, which were quite serious." Yet Pershing himself was also to blame for the longer-than-normal trip. He ordered Santini to stop several times as they drove through villages so that he could visit with French children; perhaps they reminded him of his son, Warren, and the three daughters he had lost in 1915.

When he finally returned to his railcar on the evening of the twenty-eighth, Pershing entered in his diary: "Our advance is somewhat checked by rather persistent action of Germans with machine guns. This is due to a certain extent to the lack of experience and lack of push on the part of the division and brigade commanders. On the whole I am not very pleased with the progress made, though it should not be called unsatisfactory."[38]

8

NO PROGRESS

On Sunday, September 29, Pershing's mood was despondent. Over the past seventy-two hours his three corps had made impressive gains after taking key German first-line positions: Vauquois Hill, Varennes, Cheppy, and Montfaucon. But by the third day German resistance stiffened, and First Army was stopped at the Kriemhilde Stellung. Casualties were mounting. Yet despite Pershing's assumptions, his army's delay was not due to lack of trying. Rather, Gallwitz's forces were now "firmly installed on their line," which stretched from the outskirts of Flévillle to the heights up to Cunel and Romagne.[1]

On the morning of the twenty-ninth, Pershing was visited by Marshal Pétain, who had left his Paris headquarters in the War Ministry Building on the Boulevard des Invalides and arrived in Souilly in good spirits.[2] His backhanded reassurance that First Army's slowed advance "was not outstanding and the progress made was good in consideration thereof" was of little comfort to Pershing. Pétain urged the American commander to look on the bright side: the Americans had taken Montfaucon in only two days, an accomplishment the French had never imagined possible.[3]

Even the usually acerbic Clemenceau stopped by Souilly to praise Pershing for capturing Montfaucon. It was Le Tigre's seventy-seventh birthday and he was in an especially good mood. Although he actually cared little for Pershing, Clemenceau had a warm place in his heart for Americans. From 1865 to 1869, he had lived and worked in New York City as a political journalist for a Parisian newspaper, and had taught French and horseback riding at a girls' school in Stamford, Connecticut. There Clemenceau met New Yorker Mary Eliza Plummer, one of his students, whom he married and with whom he raised children.

Clemenceau wanted to visit Montfaucon and see firsthand the village that had caused French forces so much angst during the Battle of Verdun. Even though the high ground was now in American hands, it remained dangerous because German gunners had turned their artillery in that direction. Black Jack tried to talk Clemenceau out of going, but the Frenchman insisted. Pershing sent French Army captain Charles de Marenches to accompany him.[4] The previous year, de Marenches had been assigned to Pershing's personal staff by Pétain.[5]

The Clemenceau party made it to about five miles from Montfaucon before becoming stuck behind a long convoy of American vehicles. Clemenceau grew "very much incensed" and ordered de Marenches to do something to get them going. But the road was too narrow, and the sides too cratered by shells, to move around the traffic. So Clemenceau abandoned the visit to Montfaucon and instead requested a visit with the French Fourth Army, which was also on the day's agenda. Le Tigre leaped out of the car and rapidly walked across the field while shouting at de Marenches to do whatever was possible to move the car forward.

A half hour later, the staff officer gave up and joined Clemenceau, who was a mile ahead on a hill screaming "some strong language." After watching the congestion for a bit, they returned to the car and with great effort de Marenches turned it around and they reached their second destination later that day.[6]

Meanwhile, Pershing frantically tried to get his First Army divisions unraveled and moving. He ordered the division commanders to move their personal headquarters forward so that they would be in closer contact with the units at the front. He instructed each of them to exert "the strongest personal pressure upon all with whom they came in touch, to overcome the difficulties of weather and terrain, to cast aside the depression of fatigue and casualties, and to instill into the troops the determination to force the fight along every foot of the front."[7] Billy Mitchell's planes observed the movement of German convoys in the rear, leading Pershing to believe the enemy was retiring to the north behind the Kriemhilde Line, their last bastion of defense.[8]

Colonel Clark, who had seen his share of misleading intelligence, advised Pershing not to read too much into this. He warned Black Jack to expect firm resistance from the Germans once First Army resumed its attack the next day. "Tomorrow will be the biggest day of the war," Clark promised, "and it is not likely the Boche will be compelled to retire."[9] And Clark was right. Gallwitz rushed more reserve divisions to the front. He now had the veteran 5th Guard Division on the Aire, the 52nd Division near Exermont, the 115th Division near Cierges, the 37th Division west of Nantillois, and the 5th Bavarian just outside the same village.[10]

With fresh German troops in the mix, fighting became heavy in the sector held by the 28th, 35st and 91th Divisions, which extended east from the edge of the Argonne, across the Aire River valley to the high ground beyond. The 35th penetrated as far as the Exermont ravine under the watchful eyes of the Germans, who responded with a heavy enfilade from the flanks above Châtel Chéhéry, a village that a week later would become synonymous with Corporal Alvin York.

Just days before, Pershing had chastised the 79th Division for holding up First Army's advance, but in reality Traub's 35th Division was the problem. Now into their fourth straight day of fighting, the Kansas-Missouri troops were in disarray and needed reorganizing. It was a sad affair and it took months to sort out what actually happened to the division and why they fell apart.

A variety of factors contributed to the breakdown of the 35th Division. Just days before the jump-off on September 26, the division underwent a significant change in command. Traub never really explained why he reorganized the division, but on the eve of Meuse-Argonne, the 35th had a brand-new chief of staff and two new brigade commanders, and three out of four regiments were led by new officers. On September 29, Traub shifted his headquarters to the front, as Pershing had requested. There he became a nervous wreck and exhibited bewildering behavior in front of his men, wrestling with insomnia and subsisting on a diet of cigarettes and coffee. Carrying a swagger stick for no apparent reason, he was seen wandering aimlessly around the battlefield. One time he almost walked into the German lines, and on another occasion he was gassed. Traub was also observed trying to lead troops during an attack, a task normally assigned to an officer of much lower rank.[11]

Yet Traub was only part of the problem. Captain Harry S. Truman blamed the division's artillery, which he was a part of, for the high number of casualties. On the morning of September 29 he reported that "artillery fire was falling short, causing losses among our men." He urged that the barrage be elevated from three hundred to five hundred yards to avoid friendly fire. "During the entire day our troops were

162

continually pelted with our own artillery," Truman wrote, which was "more destructive to our own men than to the enemy."[12]

Traub's men were also sleep deprived. The ground on which they bedded down was soaked from a two-day mist that later turned into a downpour. At night the air turned chilly and the men shivered because there were no blankets to offer them warmth. In addition to these conditions was the fact that the rolling kitchens that were supposed to bring hot food to the front were held back by the poor roads. Men were forced to subsist on hardtack and nasty "bully beef," which gave many of them diarrhea.[13] "In a few days," Frederick Palmer wrote, "sturdy youth with springy steps in the pink of health had become pale and emaciated, looking ten years older as they dragged their feet in painful slowness."[14]

At Cheppy, the 35th hastily organized a field hospital in a cave that the Germans had fixed up and then abandoned. "It was a work of art, that cave," wrote Evangeline Booth of the Salvation Army. "There was a passage-way a hundred feet long with avenues on each side and a place for cots, room enough to accommodate a hundred men." Yet for the Salvation Army workers and the wounded doughboys, it was far from ideal. German planes were relentless in bombing the hospital, and artillery shells hit at twenty-minute intervals. Sleep was almost impossible, as gas alarms blared in the middle of the night, forcing everyone to rush out of the cave and don masks.[15]

Captain Louise Holbrook, also with the Salvation Army, was pressed into service to assist in cleaning up the wounded men and administering anti-tetanus serum, a standard combat medical practice. One of the wounded soldiers Holbrook tended to was a German POW who was naked except for his cap. When asked why he wore just a head cover, he responded that it would prevent him from catching a cold.[16]

There were almost a thousand wounded soldiers to deal with; many were victims of shell shock, exhaustion, and gas attack. "They had come so fast there was scarcely time to get the tents up," Salvationist Alice McAllister recalled. "All the doctors could do was dress the wounds, wrap the men in a blanket and lay them on the ground to await ambulances to take them away. A young officer in one of the tents kept crying out, 'My poor boys, they are all shot to pieces.'"[17]

Traub's medical personnel raced to remove the wounded by ambulances to the rear for treatment, but road congestion forced the drivers to reroute their patients to unfamiliar hospitals. Relying on enlisted men stationed at key points along the routes to give them directions, the drivers in some instances abandoned the motor vehicles and used horse-drawn ambulances, which could cross the trench lines and avoid the crowded roads.[18]

Early on September 29, Brigadier General Malin Craig, Liggett's chief of staff, went to see Traub to tell him that his division should be withdrawn, but the 35th commander initially tossed this suggestion aside—that is, until he realized it was his best option and pretended that he, not Craig, had first proposed pulling his men back. Instead of waiting until dark, Traub began moving his troops that afternoon, right in front of the German 52nd Division, who attacked as the Americans withdrew. After heavy fighting, Traub's men managed to counterattack, and by nightfall they restored their old lines.[19]

Dennis Nolan, Pershing's intelligence commander, appeared at Cheppy. Nolan now held the temporary rank of major general and was detailed to the 28th Division, on the left of the 35th. He wanted to see for himself what was going on with Traub's men, and when he did, it was the same thing everyone else saw: the situation seemed hopeless. Nolan would convey this to Major General Liggett. As he prepared to leave, a handful of German prisoners from the 52nd Division passed by and, "clad in new uniforms with a healthy color upon their faces," stared him "straight in the eye."

"Well," Nolan commented in their direction, "it looks pretty bad for you, doesn't it? We've been pushing you back steadily, six or seven miles!"

The Germans brushed off Nolan's indignant comment, and one of them said, probably in broken English: "Hah, we'll soon stop that. We're the 52nd Division, and we've been in here to stop you Americans, and we're the boys [who] can do it. You may have captured a few of us, but there are a lot more over there like us. More fresh troops are coming. You won't advance anymore." The other POWs "grinned and nodded in agreement."[20]

Although the 35th had advanced more than six miles since September 26, the division paid a terrible toll for the ground it captured, then lost, suffering more than 6,312 casualties. Nearly half its infantry were dead or in the hospital. The other half were overcome from fatigue.[21] No other First Army division had so many casualties this early in the battle. For the most part, the war had ended for Major General Traub and the 35th Division. After some rest, the doughboys from Kansas and Missouri were placed in a quiet sector as a reserve division and remained there until the Armistice.

On the 35th's flank, an advance made by the 91st "Wild West" Division tried to make something out of the disastrous situation, resulting in a brilliant maneuver called a "herculean" effort by George Marshall.[22] With drafted men from all over the western United States, including Alaska, the division was commanded by a former Army paymaster clerk, Major General William Johnson.[23] Early on September 29, after having cleared the woods at Baulny and Les Épinettes the previous day, the 91st went ahead of the divisions on both its flanks, the 35th and 37th, and made it as far as the town of Cierges. German machine guns held them up there for a time before Johnson's troops cleared the nearby woods and pushed north. The division's crusade that day produced an unexpected hero. First Lieutenant Winifred P. McDaniel was a dental surgeon in the medical detachment of the division's 363rd Infantry. He had no business going over the top with his regiment, but he went anyway. After his regiment leaped forward into no-man's-land, McDaniel carried back the unit's first casualty, and by the end of the day he had brought back several more, saving the men's lives. After the war, when asked about his attitude toward military service, McDaniel responded, "Life is what you make of it."[24]

Major General Johnson soon learned that the two divisions on his flanks, the 35th and 37th, were in trouble and withdrawing, leaving the 91st in great danger of being cut off. Johnson sent a messenger to the 37th headquarters with a request that the division move forward far enough to cover his division's right flank. The reply was no, such a movement was impossible. Johnson didn't bother reaching out to the 35th. Left with no other option, the 91st fell back under cover of nightfall. In three days of fighting, the Wild West Division had advanced five miles, but could go no farther without support, and ended up losing some of the ground they had gained.

During the evening of September 29, Pershing announced that the next day there would be a pause in the offensive. For the first time since the battle started, he needed to regroup First Army and go on the defensive. Pershing's decision was a bold but necessary step toward reworking his battle plan. His army was beat-up and needed rest. Though not unusual during intense fighting, halting an attack during a campaign certainly bothered Black Jack. His idol, U. S. Grant, never let up. During the 1864 Virginia Overland Campaign, Grant had struck Lee's Confederates in one bloody battle after another while taking enormous casualties in an effort to wear down his opponent. Pershing was attempting a similar strategy, and found that Gallwitz's troops were just as stubborn as the Rebel army fifty-four years before.

Maybe, as Foch had advised, Pershing was overly ambitious in scheduling the Meuse-Argonne Offensive right after St. Mihiel. Still, pulling back his army must have been a strain on Pershing's ego. It gave the impression that all was not going well for First Army, and suggested that General Pershing, the star of America's military might, was in over his head. Clemenceau's chief of staff, General Jean-Henri Mordacq, visited Pershing and came to the same conclusion. "I could see clearly in his eyes that, at that moment, he realized his mistake. His soldiers were dying bravely, but they were not advancing, or very little, and their losses were heavy."[25]

One of the main reasons First Army was now stalled after three days of fighting was that three of Pershing's most experienced divisions—the 1st, the 26th, and the 42nd—had been idle since St. Mihiel and were being held in reserve near the salient. Pershing rectified this on the afternoon of September 30 when he ordered the 1st Division to relieve the 35th Division at the front, taking its place in Liggett's I Corps. Black Jack wanted the transfer completed that night, and to no one's surprise, Colonel Marshall was assigned the task.

A few weeks before, Marshall had pulled off the gargantuan chore of shifting nine divisions from St. Mihiel to the Argonne front, a feat that even today is marveled at as a logistical masterpiece. It was accomplished despite the fact that there weren't enough French buses and trucks to carry an entire division, much to the anger of many officers. Marshall had to figure out which troops were driven to the front and which ones walked.[26] Yet the problem of how to move an entire division twenty-three miles in one day across crowded roads dumbfounded even Marshall. He later learned that only the infantry would move up, as 1st Division artillery and supply trains were to remain behind for a day or two so that ammunition rations and the wounded would not block the sole road in the I Corps sector.

Although this made the task a little easier, Marshall was still anxious, and headed straight to Hugh Drum's office to see if he could have more time to execute the relief. Marshall stressed "that it was a physical impossibility for the First Division to complete the relief of the Thirty-fifth Division that night," and Drum agreed that only one regiment of the 1st Division, the 26th Infantry, would move to the front that night in motor buses. To accommodate them, all traffic was to be cleared from I Corps's roads. Over the next two days the remainder of the 1st Division would head to the front. But Drum informed Marshall that he also wanted to relieve the 79th and 37th Divisions and replace them with the 3rd and 32nd Divisions, respectively. After a few days, they would then be joined by the 42nd and 29th Divisions. All told, about 140,000 troops were heading to the front, replacing around 45,000.[27]

During the night of September 29, a convoy of French trucks twenty miles long moved doughboys of the 1st Division to Neuvilly, at the front, where they would relieve the downtrodden 35th Division.[28] Colonel Thomas R. Gowenlock, an intelligence officer with the 1st, called his division "a pinch hitter of the AEF." When they reached the sector vacated by the 35th, Gowenlock could see in the darkness that "mangled wheels, harnesses, and swollen horse carcasses lay sprawled where some shell had found its mark."[29]

That final Sunday in September was a somber day for First Army's Air Service. The brotherhood of flyers lost one of its most promising pilots when Lieutenant Frank Luke's military service was cut short near Murvaux, France. Raised in Phoenix, Arizona, by German immigrant parents, Luke had been an adventurous boy, with lots of nervous energy and a natural gift for athletics. He joined the Army's Signal Corps Aviation Service in September 1917, at the age of twenty and, after seven weeks of training at the University of Texas, received his commission and was ordered to France.

Placed in the 27th Aero Squadron under command of Captain Alfred S. Grant, he would spend his first few months in France uneventfully, but that soon changed. On September 18, Luke was credited with five kills: two balloons and three planes. But on the same mission his closest friend and flying partner, Joe Wehner, was killed by a German Fokker. Distraught, Luke became moody and noticeably more arrogant toward other aviators and crew. A rivalry developed between Luke and Eddie Rickenbacker over who shot down the most enemy planes. Rickenbacker would call Luke "the greatest fighting pilot in the war," but he was also jealous of the aggressive aviator when he "shot down in flames thirteen balloons in one day."[30] For a time, Luke's 27th Squadron had more victories than the Hat in the Ring pilots.

Luke was well aware that other aviators saw him as arrogant, but he didn't care because he could back up his words with action. One day in mid-September Luke had flown into the airdrome where the 94th Squadron was headquartered. While walking toward his plane in full view of Rickenbacker and several other pilots, Luke pointed toward two German balloons to the east that were about two miles behind enemy lines and around four miles apart.

"Keep your eyes on these two balloons," Luke announced. "You will see the first one there go up in flames exactly at 7:15 and the other will do likewise at 7:19." Within minutes Luke was airborne. A crowd gathered to watch as the Arizona balloon buster's plane approached the "distant specks in the sky." Suddenly a "flame lighted up the horizon," and the spectators glanced at their watches: it was 7:15 on the dot. As they quickly looked back up at the sky, there was another "burst of flames." This time Luke was a couple of minutes early.[31]

As Rickenbacker put it, "Luke mingled with his disdain for bullets a very similar distaste for the orders of his superior officers." For instance, Luke knew that after each patrol he was to immediately head back to the 27th airdrome. Instead, he would often land at a faraway French field and not return until the following evening.[32]

Two days before his last flight, Luke was grounded for disobedience, but he ignored the order and went airborne the next morning, shooting down an enemy airplane and a balloon. Instead of heading back to his squadron to face likely punishment, Luke landed his SPAD XIII at the flying field of Les Cigognes, France's most celebrated air service unit. Not having alerted his superior officer of his whereabouts, Luke was listed as missing in action. He returned the next day, but promptly took off for the squadron's advance field in Verdun. His commander wanted Luke arrested and planned to court-martial him, though at the same time he recommended the troubled pilot for a Distinguished Service Cross for valor.

As the sun set on September 29, Luke took to the skies for the last time. He flew his SPAD XIII, which was specially equipped with two machine guns—one loaded with standard ammunition, the other one larger and equipped with incendiary bullets—to a nearby American observation balloon and dropped the crew a message, telling them to keep an eye on three enemy sausages hovering over the Meuse near Dun-sur-Meuse. He soon struck a balloon over the town of Dun and continued on toward the next one, which he destroyed as well. While on his way to the third gasbag near the town of Milly, Luke was hit by an Archie and was forced to land in a field near Murvaux.[33]

Circumstances surrounding Luke's death are not entirely clear, and over the decades historians have attempted to unravel truth from fiction. As the most accepted story goes, Luke crash-landed his plane near the village of Murvaux, five miles to the east of the heavily defended Dun-sur-Meuse. Unwilling to surrender, he allegedly fired with his Colt .45 at the German soldiers surrounding him before one man shot the American through the lung. The Germans stripped his body of all identification, threw him in a wooden handcart, and wheeled him to a local graveyard. His corpse lay on the ground until French villagers buried him in an unmarked grave. Other so-called eyewitnesses painted a more heroic picture of what happened to Luke when he reached Murvaux. They claimed that no less than eight Fokkers attacked Luke's plane, and that he successfully downed two of them. Luke then sprayed the village streets with bullets, killing six Germans and wounding several more.[34]

Captain Merian Cooper had a part in the saga of Lieutenant Frank Luke. Fresh from three months' confinement as a POW, Cooper assisted the mother of another aviator who had vanished in the same area as Luke. During a fact-finding trip in 1919, Cooper stopped in Murvaux and interviewed a few of the town's occupants, who told him about "the grave of an unknown aviator killed on Sunday, September twenty-ninth, 1918," in their village. The French civilians who claimed to have seen the deceased aviator described him as "having light hair, young, of medium height, and of heavy stature."[35] Cooper reported what he had learned to the American Graves Registration Service, who sent a team to the spot where he was allegedly buried. His remains were identified from a wristwatch that had been overlooked by the hasty Germans, who did manage to take Luke's shoes, leggings, and money.

Regardless of how he died, Frank Luke's short flying career was impressive. With only thirty hours of combat flying under his belt, Luke downed nineteen enemy aircraft and fifteen observation balloons; only Rickenbacker had more kills.[36] On April 19, 1919, Luke was posthumously awarded the Medal of Honor "for conspicuous gallantry and intrepidity above and beyond the call of duty in action with the enemy near Murvaux, France, September 29, 1918."[37]

Though Frank Luke's contributions to the AEF's war effort were important, First Army's ground troops likely never learned of his death or even knew who he was. As the Meuse-Argonne raged, animosity developed between foot soldiers and aviators. Neither felt the other was contributing their fair share during the battle. Harry Truman wrote his future bride, Bess Wallace, "The easiest and safest place for a man to get is in the Air Service. They fly around a couple of hours a day, sleep in a featherbed at night, eat hotcakes and maple syrup for breakfast, pie and roast beef for supper every day, spend their vacations in Paris or wherever else suits their fancy, and draw 20% extra pay for doing it. Their death rate is about like the quartermaster and ordnance departments and on top of it they are all dubbed the heroes of the war."[38]

Mitchell's aviators had similar opinions about the infantry. "We were experiencing a great deal of trouble with the ground troops in making them answer the signals from the air," he complained, "and properly maintain their radio stations for communicating with our airplanes. Our pilots had to fly right down and almost shake hands with the infantry on the ground to find out where they were." Mitchell grumbled that "it was practically impossible to impress the men in the ranks, through their own officers, as to the value of aviation. They did not even know what the insignia on our plane was in many cases. Wherever possible, we took the infantry battalions back of the line to

our airdromes and took the noncommissioned officers and other soldiers up in the air. This impressed them with the necessity of cooperat-
ing with the airmen as much as possible, and they transmitted it on to
the privates." The cooperation between the air service and the infantry
would never be resolved to anyone's satisfaction at Meuse-Argonne. As
the battle raged, division commanders frequently complained directly
to Mitchell that his pilots had lost control of the skies to the detriment
of the ground troops.

Tuesday, October 1, was a day of healing for First Army, but for Pershing the break in fighting didn't add up to time off from the war.
Since the first shots of battle, Black Jack had spent every night in
Souilly, with no time to sneak away to Paris to see Micheline, who
constantly complained in letters how unhappy she'd been made by his
absence. Black Jack rarely wrote back; he either was too busy or didn't
feel like responding. In a short letter dated September 29 he promised
to see her in Paris at the first opportunity, but couldn't commit to
when that might be.

On occasions when Pershing was able to slip away from his war
duties, it was usually at night, and he instructed Cesar Santini to remove any visible markings from the Cadillac that identified the car
as belonging to the AEF commander. Black Jack enjoyed Micheline's
company. He was a healthy, vibrant man who desired a woman's affection, but physical need was trumped by the war, and their relationship
took a backseat to running an army. Micheline later recounted that
during their evenings together she would hold hands with Pershing,
"neither saying anything, or saying very little, for long periods. When
they talked, it was of everything in general and nothing in particular."
Black Jack rarely spoke of the war, although on one occasion, "he said

with a little sigh, 'I feel like I am carrying the whole world on my shoulders.'"[39]

Pershing no doubt felt this way on October 1, when General Weygand appeared at Souilly carrying a message from Foch. In a plan almost identical to the one the Frenchman and the American had clashed over in August, Foch wanted to take the American divisions in and near the Argonne Forest, such as the 28th and the 77th, and place them under French command. Pershing would still have a token force under his charge.

Black Jack suspected that Clemenceau was behind the scheme, perhaps as retaliation for the traffic fiasco he had encountered during his attempted visit to Montfaucon two days earlier. Pershing thought the French prime minister lacked "expert knowledge of military situations or operations," despite the fact that he had chaired the Supreme War Council, a central command that coordinated Allied strategy. Within this position, Clemenceau had no authority over Marshal Foch, the Allied commander in chief, yet in his capacity as leader of France, he could direct Foch as he wished.

Among the many reasons Pershing opposed Foch's plan was the simple fact that he didn't want the bulk of his army serving under French command. Over lunch Pershing pointed out to Weygand that such a drastic change would impede rather than benefit Allied progress. "General Weygand, I believe," Pershing told his diary, "left thoroughly convinced that my arguments were sound." As protocol dictated, Black Jack would put his response in writing for Foch to mull over. But as far as Pershing was concerned, the idea of relinquishing some of his command was not up for debate.[40]

Elsewhere that day, George Marshall, Hugh Drum, and V Corps's George Cameron traveled by horseback to the front to inspect the traffic problems. Afterward, they rode over to the area of III Corps, where Marshall caught a glimpse of the 79th Division as it left the front. "The drawn, strained expression on the faces of the men and their silence were very noticeable," Marshall remembered, "and gave evidence of the character of the ordeal from which they were just withdrawing."[41] Marshall sympathized with their plight. The command problems of the 79th were no different from those of any other AEF division. Inexperienced junior officers didn't understand how to regroup their units in the heat of combat, an issue that stemmed from a lack of peacetime training. Marshall placed the blame squarely on the shoulders of Congress, which had failed to fund military preparedness before the United States committed its brave young men to war in April 1917. Now the number of experienced officers to be found on American the battlefields was all too few.

To make matters worse, the latest round of officer instruction at the General Staff College in Langres, a few miles south of Chaumont, fell on the eve of the Allied offensives. The purpose of sending officers to school was to have better-trained commanders in the event that the war carried on into 1919, something Pershing expected would happen. To be ready, Black Jack put in an early request for more troops. Three months before Meuse-Argonne, Pershing and Foch sent a joint recommendation to Army chief of staff Major General Peyton C. March that one hundred divisions should be in France by July 1919. March, who often clashed with Pershing throughout the war, concluded that at best he could have eighty divisions ready for deployment by that date, but even this lower number would stress the AEF transportation and supply infrastructure.[42] In the end, none of this mattered, since the war was over well before then. But as an immediate impact of the poor timing of sessions at the officer schools, some of First Army's more experienced line officers were not around during the first few days of Meuse-Argonne, and because of this blunder, the units at the front suffered horribly.[43] A captain in the 77th Division complained that many green infantry officers had trouble reading their maps: "Many a company commander or liaison officer was entirely capable of waving a vague finger over a valley marked on the map, while stating that the troops in question were 'on that hill'; and, if pressed to be more precise, he would give as coordinates figures which represented a point neither in the valley to which he was pointing nor on the hill on which they were."[44]

With a lull in the fighting, enemy soldiers were asked by German war correspondents their opinion of Pershing's troops. "The Americans are cool and daring in attack," they said, "although at times over-rash, and despite losses, will come on again." The Germans were most impressed by the large number of tanks employed by First Army, and said they took pleasure in destroying the machines with tank guns, mines, and hand grenades.[45] Even though Gallwitz recognized that his men were more experienced soldiers, he knew the Americans would keep attacking with more and more troops. In the event that his Army thought otherwise, he issued the following order as a reminder:

According to information in our hands, the enemy intends to attack the 5th Army east of the Meuse. . . .The 5th Army once again may have to bear the brunt of the fighting of the coming weeks on which the security of the Fatherland may depend. The fate of a large portion of the Western Front, perhaps of our nation, depends on the firm holding of the Verdun front. The Fatherland believes that every commander and every soldier realizes the greatness of his task, and that everyone will fulfill his duties to the utmost. If this is done, the enemy's attack will be shattered.[46]

. . .

Impressive gains had been made on the first and second days of battle. First Army troops had broken through two lines of the enemy's defenses and penetrated a third line, the Volker Stellung, before the Germans pushed them back on the third day. General Weygand described Pershing's divisions as "paralyzed."[47]

To help break this paralysis, two air squadrons, each plane crewed with a pilot and observer, dropped more than sixty thousand pieces of "paper bombs" on the battlefield. Rather than explosives, they were large packets of folders and circulars written in German and prepared on a printing press behind the lines. One packet contained a map of the St. Mihiel Salient, showing the ground gained by the Americans and the number of Germans taken prisoner. Other propaganda dropped over German lines included postcards encouraging enemy soldiers to quit fighting and to tell folks back home that the situation at the front was hopeless, as well as pamphlets with photographs exaggerating the number of American, British, and French troops concentrated at the front. G-2 believed the paper bombs had a large impact on German morale, and many POWs were found carrying "well thumbed" copies of the propaganda.[48]

Regardless, First Army still had to contend with well-established German forces along the Hindenburg Line, with Romagne Heights as the dominating position. West of the town of Romagne and southeast of Landres-et-St.-Georges, the Côté Dame Marie offered the Germans a clear line of sight to observe approaching attackers and to make quick retaliation with its flanking artillery. Additionally, the German defensive line included the Cunel Heights and the high ground near the villages of Châtel Chéhéry and Cornay.[49] First Army intelligence learned that Gallwitz added seven more divisions to join the eleven that were already in line. Within the next week they were augmented by nine more divisions, with seventeen in reserve. With the help of narrow-gauge railroads, the Germans added more artillery as well.[50] This meant Pershing's warriors, attacking in the open as he had dictated, somehow would have to outflank the Germans with more skillful leadership than had been exhibited during the first phase of the battle.

9

FIGHTING IN THE ARGONNE

Before the U.S. Army descended upon the Argonne Forest in autumn 1918, the Germans had turned the woodland into a rest area for battle-worn troops plucked from other parts of the front. Beneath rocks that jutted up throughout the hills, they created massive dugouts furnished with electric lighting and bathrooms featuring hot and cold running water. They added pianos, feather beds, and paintings, all stolen from French homes.[1] Separate structures served as smokehouses, in which ham, sausages, and bacon were hung for curing. One German strongpoint contained a soccer field and grandstand, while another had a wine cellar stocked with champagne, schnapps, and other liqueurs.[2]

When the Americans arrived, they discovered burros left behind by the Germans, who had used them to build trenches and transport the dead. When Major General John L. Hines and his staff took over a former German headquarters in Romagne, they found an electric generator powered by two men pedaling away on a bicycle.[3] There was also a German-built railway station used to haul supplies to the front as well as deliver wounded men to a dressing station set up in the town.[4]

But there was a nastier side to the Argonne bunkers. Before vacating them, the Germans set up booby traps. Where they had once lived in comfort, there were now "a multitude of death-dealing devices intended to invite the curiosity of the Yankee souvenir hunters." In one dugout First Army intelligence found a "finely polished" case disguised as a music box, with an alligator handle on top and a monogram on one corner. When the G-2 men carefully lifted the lid they saw "two squash-shaped grenades" along with Cheddite, a yellow powder described as "eight times as powerful as dynamite." Attached to the grenades were four friction handles connected to the alligator handle, designed to detonate the box when lifted. In case the intended victim decided not to open the box by its handle, a two-second fuse was attached to the end of each grenade and extended into the Cheddite compartment. This would set off the charge when the lid was removed.[5] Fortunately, the sabotage failed.

Behind the lines, General Pershing was still dealing with another lethal situation, in the form of Marshal Foch and his continuing attempts to break up First Army. Weygand returned to Souilly on the morning of October 2, wanting a reply to Foch's proposition from the day before. Pershing consented to withdraw divisions from the Woëvre Plain, but emphasized that "to introduce a new army between me and the 4th Army, and to turn over some of the divisions would, instead of hastening, very much retard the resumption of the advance, because I will be ready to advance in a day or two, whereas the 2nd Army could not possibly be installed in anything like that time."

Weygand listened intently and asked Pershing to put his response in writing. Then, as there was no tension between them, Weygand and Pershing sat down for lunch aboard the AEF commander's train. Later that day Weygand returned to Foch's headquarters and provided his boss with Pershing's response. Foch replied to Pershing the next day. The marshal would allow Pershing a pass, "provided that an attack should be resumed at once, and that there be permitted no halt such as had taken place in the previous attack." Pershing was outraged over Foch's critique, telling his diary that Foch's "functions are strategical and he has not the authority whatsoever to interfere in tactical questions. Any observations from him as to my way of carrying out my attacks are all out of place."[6]

Whatever acrimony existed between Pershing and Foch was kept from the war correspondents at Bar-le-Duc. Since the commencement of the battle, motorcycle couriers had delivered army and corps headquarters reports written by press officers to the reporters, who struggled with what to do with this information. During the first day of the attack, as the Americans made steady progress, it was easy to write an upbeat story, but in the days that followed it became difficult to put a positive spin on the faltering battle. Headlines such as "YANKS BIG DRIVE FAILS!" or "OUR BOYS SUFFER BLOODY REPULSE!" would send Pershing into a rage, not to mention cause "endless misery and anxiety to those at home with someone over there," in the words of journalist Thomas Johnson. To avoid worry or anger, dispatches were toned down and edited. "Rain, mud and other causes have temporarily slowed up the American offensive from the Argonne to the Meuse," read one, while another story proclaimed, "There is no doubt now that the Germans are preparing to oppose us here with a defense as desperate as anywhere. It is the universal opinion that in the future the American forces will have to win every yard of advance with clenched teeth." Reporters were encouraged to stress that "whatever ought to be done, whatever will, courage, determination could do, the American Army would do for the American people."[7]

The Press Division was under AEF Intelligence and designated as G-2-D. Press officers would send information to GHQ, who would in turn disseminate the information to all of the press corps. G-2-D officers also briefed the journalists the night before about upcoming operations.[8] Each story generated by the correspondents was vetted by a field censor, who carefully read the article and redacted anything that might seem detrimental to the war effort. At least one journalist was wounded during the Meuse-Argonne. Joseph Timmons, a Los Angeles reporter, was on a hillside outside Épinonville when a shell fragment hit him in the face. He was taken to a field dressing station, where medical officers diagnosed the wound as minor and patched him up.[9]

Major General Alexander's soldiers had spent more time in the thick Argonne Forest than any other American division. Wednesday, October 2, was supposed to be a day of rest for First Army, yet Alexander's 77th Division continued to grind its way through the dense woods, consolidating the unit's lines for a future attack. The New Yorkers weaved across deadly terrain protected by German barbed wire, machine-gun nests, short-range mortars, and a host of other killing devices. For long-distance shelling, the enemy used an Austrian high-velocity gun that Allied soldiers called a "whiz-bang," named for its shell, which whizzed by at a high rate of speed, bursting with a tremendous crash.[10]

The previous evening, Major Charles Whittlesey of the 308th Infantry was called to the headquarters of regimental commander Colonel Cromwell Stacey to discuss an attack that would take place the next morning. Whittlesey was in no mood to discuss a new operation.

Only a week before, his battalion had huddled for three days, cut off from escape, as the Germans prowled nearby. Earlier this day, he had tried to advance from the high ground near L'Homme Mort across a deep wooded ravine toward the German defenses at La Palette, a hill that was much taller and defended by machine guns. On Whittlesey's right, the 307th Infantry had been charged with taking another piece of high ground, Hill 198. Neither attack went well, especially against La Palette, where Whittlesey's battalion took heavy casualties.[11]

Despite his fatigue, Whittlesey listened as Colonel Stacey relayed precise orders that had been drawn up by the 154th Brigade commander, Brigadier General Evan Johnson. Whittlesey's battalion, Stacey instructed, was to jump off the next morning at six thirty and "proceed straight ahead, then bear westward up the ravine from the valley of Charlevaux Brook. On the crest above lies the Giselher-Stellung. Take it; push on to the road on the opposite slope above Charlevaux Valley. There dig in, establish liaison left and right, and await further orders." Furthermore, Whittlesey was to go forward with George McMurtry's 2nd Battalion "without regard to his flanks." Implied in these orders was that the major should not expect help from the French Army on his left, nor the 307th to his right.[12]

Whittlesey was apprehensive about the plan, protesting to Stacey that his battalion was at half strength, down to about four hundred men, and lacked rations, blankets, and raincoats. He suggested that the operation be delayed. Stacey agreed and passed on the recommendation to General Johnson, who also thought it was reasonable and called the division commander by field telephone. Yet Major General Alexander, who had made his headquarters in what one historian described as "an elaborate German complex equipped with kitchens and mess hall," as well as bathhouses, a bowling alley, and a movie theater, couldn't relate to the situation at the front.[13] "Damn it, General," Alexander exploded at Johnson. "There will be no dallying or delaying! Headquarters wants action and they shall have it. Either attack on schedule or I'll relieve you on the spot and put in somebody with guts! Do I make myself clear?"[14]

Early on October 2, Major Whittlesey's battle-weary doughboys were made even more miserable as a steady rain was joined from the east by a cold wind. Field kitchens that were supposed to bring hot food never appeared, and the men had to rely on hardtack and canned beef that the Americans soldiers called "corned willy." In preparation for the day's mission, at six a.m. two artillery regiments of 75s opened fire, pummeling enemy lines. What damage they inflicted on the Germans in a half hour of shelling is unknown, but the fusillade certainly alerted them that an attack was imminent.[15]

When the shelling ceased, Whittlesey, wielding his Model 1911 .45 caliber Colt pistol, led three companies along the east side of a deep ravine, followed by Captain McMurtry's 2nd Battalion, also with three companies. One company from each battalion followed on the west side of the ravine. Eventually, the troops came together and halted in a spot that was to become known as "the pocket."[16] First Lieutenant Maurice V. Griffith, a signal officer in the 308th Infantry, called the new campsite that was under constant German bombardment, positioned on the south slope of a hill nearly a mile northeast of Binarville, "just this side of hell."[17] Whittlesey's and McMurtry's battalions totaled only 679 men, including a number of replacements who had only two months of training, and no experience in throwing hand grenades or firing their Enfield 1917 rifles.[18]

Unbeknownst to Whittlesey, German troops had quickly filtered in behind his men and returned to Hill 198, stringing barbed wire across the ravine to further cut off and trap Whittlesey's men. The bat-

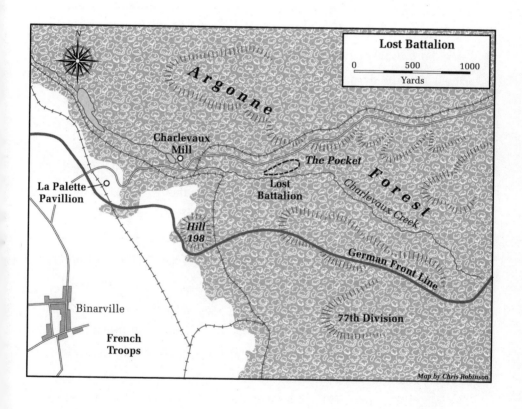

Lost Battalion

0   500   1000
Yards

Argonne

Charlevaux
Mill

La Palette
Pavillion

The Pocket

Lost
Battalion

Forest

Charlevaux Creek

Hill
198

German Front Line

Binarville

77th Division

French
Troops

Map by Chris Robinson

talion commander didn't realize until the following day how bad a predicament they were in.[19]

Bright and early on October 3, Whittlesey ordered Company K, under the command of Captain Nelson Holderman, to cross the Charlevaux Brook and proceed up Hill 198. Holderman's orders were to see if it was possible to get back to the 77th headquarters from that direction. Holderman's men encountered German snipers and enfilade fire on a small road at the foot of the hill. The captain wisely delayed for an hour, waiting for the enemy to move on, then brought his company across the narrow trail a few men at a time. Taking only a few casualties, Company K made it up the hill, but encountered resistance when Holderman sent out patrols and scouts to see if there was a way out of the pocket. After passing through barbed wire, the party was hit by a barrage of German rifle and machine-gun fire. They responded with their own guns, but when they ran into another stretch of barbed wire, it was obvious the company was surrounded.

Again, Holderman's entire company engaged the enemy. When it was safe, the men withdrew two hundred yards, where Whittlesey was waiting for them.[20] Afterward, Whittlesey and McMurtry discussed the dire situation, and a difficult decision was made. Whittlesey wrote out a message and passed it around to the company commanders: "Our mission is to hold this position at all costs. Have this understood by every man in the command."[21]

Behind the lines, Whittlesey's plight was soon leaked by Lieutenant Kidder Mead, a former *New York World* reporter serving as a I Corps press officer. While reading the intelligence bulletins and following the progress of 77th Division, Mead could see that a mixed battalion was cut off in the Argonne. Surely this was big news and would play well in the headlines, so he sent a dispatch to the Press Corps at Bar-le-Duc. The first to pick it up was United Press correspondent Fred S. Ferguson, who cabled the story to his editor in the United States, Harold D. Jacobs, who coined the phrase "Lost Battalion," though Whittlesey's men were not lost, nor were they even a true battalion, since the unit was a conglomeration of mixed companies. Regardless, it was a great story and other newspapers picked up on it.[22]

Fifteen miles west of the Lost Battalion, two American divisions were engaged against German positions in the Champagne region. At the request of Marshal Foch, they had been sent to General Gouraud's French Fourth Army as reinforcements a few days before Meuse-Argonne commenced. Pershing selected the 2nd and 36th Divisions, and they were assigned to the French 38th Corps, but held in reserve when Gouraud's forces attacked concurrently with First Army to drive the Germans from a heavily fortified line of ridges—the highest of which was Blanc Mont, or "White Mountain," at 250 feet.[23] Like the Argonne, the Germans had occupied Blanc Mont since 1914, and over time continually strengthened their position in the Champagne district. Northeast of Reims, Blanc Mont rose high above the landscape, affording Germans troops a clear view of the Argonne Forest to the east and the spires of Reims Cathedral toward the west.

By the autumn of 1918, after four years of German bombardment, not much was left of the cathedral. Colonel Avery Andrews from Pershing's staff and another officer stopped by the picturesque city on their way to Chaumont and found its "ruined cathedral enclosed by a rough board fence." Guarding the city's landmark were two crippled French soldiers, who prevented passage through the fence "on account of danger from crumbling roof and walls." Not to be deterred, when Andrews and his companion "exhibited a package of cheap smoking tobacco, all objections to their entrance upon the part of the French veterans seemed to vanish in smoke." Within, in a pile of rubble in the nave, the two Americans found a ten- or twelve-inch German shell that had failed to explode. Andrews guessed that, had it detonated, "little if anything would have been left standing of the magnificent Reims cathedral where so many kings of France have been crowned."[24]

While the Americans struck toward the Argonne on September 26, Gouraud's French Fourth Army attack started off well. The first day French soldiers advanced north from Navarin Farm, marching five kilometers before running out of steam. Over the next few days Gouraud pushed his men harder, and they got as far as three kilometers south of Blanc Mont Ridge before enemy resistance stiffened. At this point Gouraud called off the attack and requested that the American 2nd "Indianhead" Division, now commanded by Major General John Lejeune, take over.

Lejeune was unlike any of Pershing's other division commanders. A U.S. Marine who had graduated second in his class from Annapolis, the short, dark-skinned French Creole had grown up in Bayou Teche, Louisiana, where his ancestors had migrated from Nova Scotia.[25] Lejeune had attended the Army War College, where he had met many of the officers now serving on Pershing's staff. Harbord called him a "splendid man," while others labeled him a "Marine's Marine" and the "greatest of Leathernecks."[26]

Gouraud also thought Lejeune impressive. After they were first introduced at Gouraud's Marie-sur-Marne headquarters, the Frenchman, supposedly eager to mimic the American officer, said "that he too, was a Marine, as indicated by the khaki-colored uniform which he wore." Lejeune was equally taken by Gouraud. "He was a man of power," the American recorded, and "I acquired confidence in his judgment." During their discussions, Gouraud stressed that driving the Germans from Blanc Mont would not only get the French moving

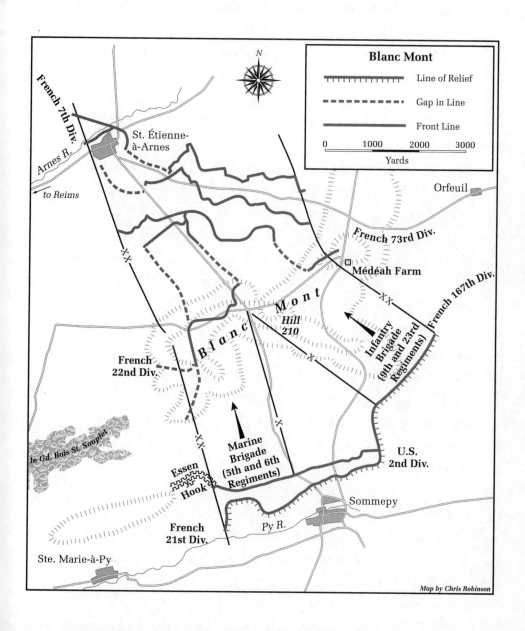

Blanc Mont

|||||| Line of Relief

- - - - Gap in Line

───── Front Line

0   1000   2000   3000
Yards

N

French 7th Div.

Arnes R.

to Reims

St. Étienne-
à-Arnes

Orfeuil

French 73rd Div.

Médéah Farm

French 167th Div.

B l a n c   M o n t

Hill
210

Infantry Brigade
(9th and 23rd Regiments)

French
22nd Div.

le Gd. Bois St. Souplet

Marine
Brigade
(5th and 6th
Regiments)

Essen
Hook

U.S.
2nd Div.

Sommepy

French
21st Div.

Py R.

Ste. Marie-à-Py

Map by Chris Robinson

again but would force the enemy to the Aisne River, twenty miles to the rear.[27] Lejeune, worried that his division might be split up and farmed out as brigades to various French divisions, promised Gouraud that if the 2nd remained intact and was "allowed to attack on a narrow front, I am confident it could take Blanc Mont Ridge in a single assault."[28]

At Lejeune's disposal were a brigade of Marines, the 5th and 6th Regiments, and two regiments of infantry, the 9th and 23rd. The almost eight thousand Marines attached to 2nd Division were unique among the AEF. Secretary of the Navy Josephus Daniels had sent them to Pershing under pressure from the commandant of the Marine Corps, General George Barnett. Pershing, unsure what to do with this unique band of troops, at first refused to place them with a combat division. Instead he ordered them to the rear for guard duty, where they remained until October 1917, until an incensed Barnett intervened and Pershing was forced by members of Congress and Daniels to organize the Marines into a brigade. Assigned to the 2nd Division, the leathernecks were bloodied, but victorious, at Belleau Wood in June and July 1918. Daniels, impressed by the Marines' grit and hard fighting, proudly proclaimed, "They saved Paris."[29] German troops thought the Marines' tenacity in battle was ferocious, and called them *Teufel Hunden,* or "devil dogs."

At Belleau Wood the Marines had fought in wheat fields and meadows, but in Champagne the terrain was far different. The chalk-limestone soil of the region offered a difficult battleground. The flaky white earth easily broke into chunks, which German soldiers carved with pocketknives, crafting crude picture frames, ink blotters, and ashtrays as souvenirs for the folks back home. As the soft soil was easy to shovel, the Germans carved bombproof dugouts into the hills south of Py Brook, with numerous exits and cavernous passages manned by veteran troops, some of whom had been there since autumn 1914.[30] After four years of steady shelling, the Champagne region was reduced to "a wilderness of craters, large and small," an American Marine wrote, "wherein no yard of earth lay untouched."[31]

Blanc Mont was an L-shaped ridge protected by three lines of German defenses, including a series of trenches five hundred feet wide running north and scores of concrete machine-gun emplacements that stretched as far as the eye could see. Preceding Blanc Mont Ridge was a strong trench system that shattered any French units that dared to take them.

Opposing the 2nd Division were the XII Saxon Army Corps (Group Py), commanded by General of Cavalry Hans Krug von Nidda. Attached to the German Third Army, Krug von Nidda had three divisions: the 51st Reserve, the 200th, and the 213th. American intelligence reports said they were understrength, with low morale, even "apathetic and indifferent," according to a captured battalion commander.[32] Yet even a despondent German division fought hard, to which the French could attest, and Lejeune knew his men would be in for a difficult time. To make matters worse, any element of surprise had been lost after German planes were spotted flying over American troops motoring to the front with French tanks in tow.[33]

Originally the 2nd Division was set to attack Blanc Mont on October 2, but Lejeune was able to postpone the operation by one day to ensure that the artillery was in place and that the infantry could clear out enemy outposts and machine guns immediately facing the jump-off.[34] Lejeune had paid close attention to the First Army attacks in the Argonne, and was determined not to repeat their mistakes. Infantrymen, following Pershing's philosophy of open warfare, were mowed down because either the artillery didn't get far enough to the front to reach the German machine guns or advancing troops couldn't keep up with the rolling barrage. Too often it was a combination of both. Lejeune, more than any other AEF division commander, knew that open warfare would work only if infantry and artillery coordinated their attacks.[35]

The extra day helped significantly. At six thirty in the evening on October 2, the Marine brigade (5th and 6th Regiments) now led by Brigadier General Wendell Cushing Neville, a Medal of Honor recipient and future commandant of the corps, joined the infantry brigade (9th and 23rd) under Brigadier General Hanson Ely, a "gruff, forceful, former West Point football player," and together they advanced to gain a jump-off position for the next morning's attack.[36] The 2nd inherited trenches previously held by the 61st French Division, whose companies were reduced to the size of platoons after days of hard fighting.[37] On the way to the front, the Americans took heavy fire on the left flank from the jagged, rocky Essen Trench, which curved northward over higher ground and was called Essen Hook on the French maps.[38] Dead center between the American jump-off line and Blanc Mont was the Bois de la Vipère, or Viper Wood, an appropriately named dense forest filled with deadly machine-gun emplacements.[39] By nightfall, the 9th and 23rd Infantry, along with the 5th and 6th Marines, were spread out along the line, so far apart, one observer wrote, that they looked like "four little islands in a turbulent Boche sea."[40]

On the morning of October 3, French and American artillery "opened with one world-shaking crash." Off in the distance, doughboys could see the effects of the shells from the 75s as they landed in the German trenches. Red flames turned into large black clouds. Closer to Blanc Mont, a terrific explosion shook the ground when an ammunition dump was hit. Then "a broad column of smoke shot up hundreds of feet, and hung in the air, spreading out at the top like some unearthly tree."[41] Confident that the artillery had dented the German defenses, at 5:50 a.m. Lejeune sent the 2nd, with the infantry on the right and Marines on the left, over the top. They rushed toward Blanc Mont with support from both a rolling barrage and the French 2nd and 3rd Light Tank Battalions. German machine guns on the right blazed from the edges of Viper Wood, but Ely's men skirted around the forest. Shortly after leaving the trenches, the 9th Infantry made it to the slopes of Blanc Mont, then scaled it while the Germans countered with heavy fire. Undeterred, the 9th kept coming, overwhelming the enemy positions at the top of the hill and digging in along the northern slope of Blanc Mont.

Meanwhile, the Marines following on the left were slowed by considerable fire from the western slope of Blanc Mont. Two French divisions, the 21st and 167th, remained at the front to assist in the Marine attack, but couldn't keep pace with the assault. The Germans fired uninterrupted from Essen Hook until the 17th Company of the 5th Marines took it upon themselves to clear the strongpoint, then moved on toward Blanc Mont. The trench system was now occupied by the French, who managed to lose it to a German counterattack that afternoon. Around nine p.m. a 2nd Division signal unit flashed its position, and Lejeune knew that Blanc Mont was in American hands.[42]

By capturing Blanc Mont Ridge, the 2nd Division had sliced through one of the most difficult German strongholds on the western front.[43] The French were ecstatic. Gouraud called the attack "brilliant." Pétain remarked that the victory "was the greatest single achievement of the 1918 campaign" and appointed Lejuene a commander of the French Legion of Honor.[44]

Although driven from the ridge, the Germans had not gone far, and the fight was far from over. At dawn the next morning, October 4, another 2nd Division attack was planned. Just after midnight a German soldier who had deserted from his unit crawled into the American lines. He told his captors that the Germans were planning their own attack—against the American flanks—and that a fresh Prussian division had been brought up for that purpose. Major George Hamilton, in command of the 1st Battalion, 5th Marines, brushed off the news. Our "orders are to attack," he announced, "and by God, we'll attack."[45]

And attack they did. Later that morning, the Marines pushed north and by midday were on par with Ely's line, but across Blanc Mont Ridge. Together both 2nd Division brigades advanced farther and gained some ground, but soon lost most of it to German counterattacks from the vicinity of Médéah Farm and the village of St. Étienne. But at the end of the day the Germans abandoned the ridge, having received orders from Hindenburg to fall back to the Aisne River, where they would make a stand.[46] Left behind were four German officers and 284 men as POWs of the 2nd Division, as well as eighty-five machine guns and fifty trench mortars—not to mention a listening post on the pinnacle of the ridge that over the past four years had signaled Allied advances.[47]

An exact count of how many Indianhead Division soldiers had thus far been killed or wounded is unknown, but to care for casualties, the 2nd Division set up a field hospital under the command of surgeon Richard Derby in a "shell-proof dugout" at Souain-Perthes-les-Hurlus, a twenty-minute ride from the front by ambulance.[48] One of Derby's patients, a young Marine, complained that his wounding resulted because "those d——d 'Frogs' never came up on our left and we ran into cross fire."[49]

Off in the distance, Charles Whittlesey probably heard the fighting around Blanc Mont, but he had his own worries to contend with. A German plane had flown over the battalion, and within a half hour the pocket was taking hits from the big German guns. Whittlesey sent out his first message by pigeon: "We are being shelled by German artillery. Can we have artillery support? Fire is coming from the Northwest." The message apparently reached division headquarters, because a short time later the 77th counter-battery took out the German guns.[50]

Pigeons were the unsung heroes of World War I. France and Great Britain had been successfully using carrier pigeons throughout the war. The U.S. Army—which had experimented with pigeons in 1878, when a number of birds were sent to support the 5th Infantry Regiment in the Dakota Territory, only to have them preyed upon by hungry hawks—were encouraged to duplicate their allies' success.[51] The Signal Corps managed the effort, and in 1916 sent birds to Pershing for use in the Punitive Expedition. A year later, a formal Pigeon Service was established, and about six hundred specimens were sold to the Army by British bird breeders.

When the AEF marched into battle, pigeons and their handlers were assigned to each corps and division. Once released, a pigeon would carry a message in a lightweight canister fastened to its leg. When the bird landed in its coop behind the lines, a bell or buzzer would signal that a message had arrived.[52] By the end of the war, more than fifteen thousand birds had served on the western front in support of the doughboys.[53]

In the coming days, pigeons would prove vital to Whittlesey's survival and the hopes of rescue for his trapped battalion.

10

THERE IS MUCH FIGHTING AHEAD

riday, October 4, was an active day all over the front with the commencement of phase two of the Meuse-Argonne campaign.

The previous day, Pershing had made his usual visits to see his corps commanders—Liggett, Bullard, and Cameron—and their respective staffs. His message was simple: "drive forward with all possible force."[1] Division commanders, he instructed, needed to move their personal headquarters forward, wrote George C. Marshall, who was traveling with Pershing. "They should be in close contact with the fighting line, and exert the strongest personal pressure upon all whom he [the division commander] came in touch." Pershing preached that they must "overcome the difficulties of weather and terrain, to cast aside the depression of fatigue and casualties, and to instill into the troops the determination to force the fight along every foot of the front."[2]

Pershing returned to Souilly that night feeling confident. After dining with Charles Dawes and Major General James W. McAndrew, the AEF chief of staff, Pershing explained his plan for the upcoming attack. Dawes was impressed with Pershing's "grasp of the situation. . . . Every foot of the ground over which the attack was to occur he knew. He is intensely concentrated mentally."[3]

Major General Charles Summerall's 1st Division would lead the October 4 assault in the I Corps sector. So far in the war, the fifty-one-year-old West Point graduate had compiled an impressive résumé. Formerly an artillery brigade commander in the 42nd Division, he had taken command of the 1st Division in mid-July 1918. A couple of days prior to the charge on the Romagne Heights, the division had settled into its jump-off area, a two-and-a-half-mile front that extended to the Aire River. In replacing the decimated 35th Division, their objective was to take back ground lost by the Kansas-Missouri men.

Summerall's division was ordered to advance through Montrebeau Woods and across wide-open ground until it reached the Exermont Ravine, where a wall of hills three miles wide and just as deep awaited them, protected by the usual German killing machines. From there the 1st was to proceed to Montrefagne Hill. For this attack there would be no preceding artillery fire, only a rolling barrage that extended for about a mile.[4]

At five thirty a.m. on October 4, under the cover of darkness, two brigades from the 1st Division jumped off for the first time since St. Mihiel. As the infantrymen passed through ground that had been temporarily occupied by the 35th Division, they found American corpses, left untouched since the survivors had vacated the front.[5] Summerall's doughboys were supported for a time by forty-seven Renault tanks from the 1st Tank Brigade, until most became disabled and were of no use. The brigade on the left reached the Exermont Ravine and Fléville, a village on a bluff by the Aire River, but they didn't stay long, because intense German machine-gun fire from the flanks held back the supporting brigade on the right. The following day, Summerall ordered another attack to bring his right brigade in line with the left. Aided by an artillery smoke screen, the two brigades were on equal ground late in the morning after an intense fight that resulted in heavy losses among the ranks. "Stretcher-bearers are marching to the rear in long files," an officer in the 1st observed, "bearing figures white with pain. More than once a pair of bearers with their moaning burden is blown to bits by a direct hit."[6]

Montrefagne Hill, which guarded the Exermont Ravine, proved to be one of the toughest objectives to take during the entire Argonne fight. "German forces fought with might and main," said a journalist who witnessed the struggle. When the Americans took possession of the east, west, and south slopes of the hill, the unwavering Germans sent up reinforcements from the north, where they had placed artillery. Enemy wagons carrying ammunition attempted to reach their bottled-up army, but American rifle fire killed many of the horses and drivers. Why the Germans were so adamant about retaining the heights was obvious to the doughboys who slogged bit by bit, little by little, toward the summit, often pulling themselves up by clinging to brush and small trees.[7] Much like Montfaucon, Montrefagne Hill offered a commanding observation of the landscape. Through high-powered telescopes, the Germans could see for miles in the direction west of the Meuse.

Waiting on top of the hill were shell-pocked stone farmhouses divided into machine-gun nests. The hill, "shaped like an inverted cup . . . honeycombed with dugouts," resembled "an Indian village of Arizona."[8] Each dugout was strengthened by earthworks propped up by wood and steel. The only way the Americans were going to take the hill was to divide their forces and flank the heights on both sides. The operation took all day, and the last German machine gunners didn't surrender until evening, after American artillery had pummeled the enemy from all sides with shells that reached all the way to the top of the hill. Early in the fight on October 4, the soldiers of 1st Division thought the Germans were giving up when they raised a white flag from atop the hill, but as the doughboys approached, "the enemy's guns re-opened fire." An American counterattack brought the battle to a close.[9]

One 1st Division warrior who performed just as fearlessly as the dough-boys in khaki was a four-legged creature named Rags, under the care of Private John Donovan, a signal specialist in the 26th Infantry. Donovan had found Rags while sightseeing in Paris in July, and trained the dog as a runner, to carry messages in his collar between the infantry and supporting artillery. During the fighting in Argonne, Rags earned the entire division's respect. On October 2, he carried a message from the 1st Battalion of the 26th requesting that the division's 7th Field Artillery lay a barrage that resulted in the capture of the Very-Épinon-ville Road, a vital objective that day. A week later, on October 9, the combat service of both Donovan and Rags came to an abrupt end. As the 1st pushed through Le Petit Bois, a communication wire was severed by enemy artillery, and Donovan was tasked with relaying a message. As Rags ran beside the private, the two were hit by German gas shells. Donovan quickly donned his gas mask and carried the dog forward, but they were soon struck down by shrapnel, the force of the explosion rolling the animal into a shell hole.

Rags was badly wounded, with cuts on his right paw, right ear, and right eye. Donovan was in even worse shape. His gas mask had been shot from his face, both his arms and legs were sliced open by shell splinters, and blood poured from his forehead into his eyes. Donovan and Rags were carried from the battlefield, placed in an ambulance, and transported to a dressing station. Although Rags recovered, Donovan eventually succumbed to his wounds in 1919.[10]

Other First Army units also adopted dogs as mascots. The 313th Infantry had Murphy, who gave birth to two puppies, "Verdun" and "Montfaucon." The 102nd Infantry brought to France a short, brindle bull terrier named Stubby, who served admirably with his regiment at the front. He was especially valuable in detecting gas attacks, but more heroically, on one occasion the dog sniffed out a German soldier hiding near the lines. With a ferocious growl Stubby held the scared German captive until doughboys took him prisoner. As a reward, the POW's Iron Cross was stripped from his uniform and pinned on a blanket that Stubby wore for most of his life. He was also promoted to the rank of sergeant by the regimental commander. In 1921, Pershing added a Dog Hero's Medal on Sergeant Stubby's blanket, to go with other decorations the mascot received after the war.[11]

General Pershing sounded matter-of-fact about First Army's progress when he wrote in his diary on October 4: "Attack resumed at 5:25 this morning. Met durable resistance, advance very slow. Our men have had to fight for every 100 yards they have gained, and it looks as though we will have a hard, slow advance. There is no course except to fight it out, taking the best possible advantage of the ground which now lays to the advantage of the Germans."[12]

That same day Jean-Henri Mordacq, a member of Clemenceau's entourage, met with Pershing at Souilly. "I could read clearly in his [Pershing's] eyes," Mordacq recorded, "that, at that moment, he realized his mistake. His soldiers were dying bravely, but they were not advancing, or very little, and their losses were heavy."[13]

Also on October 4, Bullard's III Corps slogged toward Cunel, making it as far as the Bois de Fays. Meanwhile, Cameron's Fifth Corps struggled in the center of the line as his divisions tried to flank the Romagne Heights. Pershing ordered his two corps commanders to attack again the next day, but German artillery fire coming from the heights of the Meuse to the east kept Cunel and Romagne out of American hands, at least for the time being.[14]

Behind German lines, Gallwitz had formed a different opinion about the latest American setback: Pershing's troops had collapsed "under the brave and obstinate resistance of our infantry and the performance of our artillery."[15]

11
PROGRESS WAS MADE

By October 5, Germans under General Krug von Nidda finally retreated from Blanc Mont Ridge and formed a new line along the Aisne, but left behind were a few enemy troops who needed to be removed. To clear the ridge, a battalion of Marines jumped off behind a rolling barrage at five a.m. As the morning progressed, Major George K. Shuler's men "hit the hill and went up the side. Not a man had dropped."

> *[They] began to get into the pine trees that fringed the ridge and still there were no causalities. Slowly, carefully we followed on. Then the signal came for the lifting of the barrage, and before the last gun had ceased booming, those marines were at the entrances of the deep dugouts, their bayonets on the alert—their voices shouting for surrender.*

"Hey, you Boche," one of them shouted in German, "come on out and I'll get you a job with the government at a dollar a day!"[1]

Shuler's Marine battalion became entangled in another vicious battle that took place the next day in and around St. Étienne. At six a.m. the Americans surprised the 213th German Division, which thought it had the village secured. Fighting continued throughout the day with hand-to-hand combat on the streets. The Americans were driven beyond the south edge of town while the Germans lobbed artillery at them. By the afternoon, the Germans had enough and abandoned the village.

Blanc Mont was now completely secure, but the fighting to take the ridge had done nothing to help First Army, which remained mired on the Argonne front. Pershing's October 5 diary entry read: "Attack resumed with little headway." Pétain came to Souilly that day and told Black Jack over lunch, "This is something which might have happened to anyone, and there is only one course left and that is to keep on driving."[2]

During the next few days the 2nd Division was slowly relieved by the 36th Division, National Guardsmen from Oklahoma and Texas under the command of Major General William R. Smith. Major General Lejeune kept his forces in place to help Smith's green troops become acclimated. As they marched toward the front, one of Smith's doughboys, who had yet to see combat, remarked that the Marines were "a battered, filthy, ragged crew: they did not look like soldiers. . . . Bristly growth ringed around their lips, silent mouths helped frame weary eyes that had a glare of madness in their depths." This was "in contrast to the "fast-stepping column" of "tall, clean-cut fellows, walking rapidly toward the guns."[3]

A week after Blanc Mont was taken, Billy Mitchell flew over the

Champagne battlefield to make his "usual inspection and reconnaissance" in the air. Taking off from the Souilly Airdrome on October 14, Mitchell and his observer had reached an altitude of thirteen thousand feet when they passed over the chalky landscape. "I had been looking carefully for the well remembered roads to the East of Somme-Py; they no longer existed," he wrote after the war. "I looked for the villages; they were not to be seen. Never on any field has the ground been so completely obliterated as it was here. It is seldom that a place is so destroyed, particularly a road, that it cannot be quickly seen from the air. Glancing to the left, we saw the place where our gallant 2nd Division [and 36th] had broken the German line while acting with General Gouraud's army. No Man's Land, here, was the worst desert I have ever seen, and it will be remembered that this section in times past saw innumerable Roman battles, saw Attila and his Huns defeated, and, during the present war has been a perfect charnel house for human beings." Mitchell imagined "that more men have been killed in this section of Champagne than in any other area of corresponding size in the world."[4]

Blanc Mont's capture gave Pershing and First Army reason to beam, but it had no impact on Charles Whittlesey and his Lost Battalion. After days with little food, supplies, or medical care, they found themselves in desperate circumstances. Not until October 5 did Major General Alexander come up with a plan to rescue them. First, Johnson's brigade on the left would attack, with help from the French. Airplanes were to try to drop provisions and munitions to Whittlesey while divisional artillery would fire on the surrounding Germans. Later Alexander updated the plan to include a message dropped by plane to the Lost Battalion, directing them to attack from the rear at the same time Johnson's men advanced, thus trapping the Germans on Hill 198, east of the ravine. Of course, this assumed that Whittlesey's men had the strength to carry out an attack. Alexander had no idea of their condition, nor did it matter. All he knew was that six hundred of his men were trapped, and the situation caused much angst within the division, First Army, and, most specifically, for General Pershing.[5]

Johnson was ordered to prepare for an attack, and he relayed this message to Stacey, his overstressed regimental commander. Stacey was less than thrilled to learn his 308th Infantry would go on the offensive once again. "It is impossible to push through with these tired, disorganized men," he responded to Johnson. "Fresh troops will have to do the job. Request I be relieved." Denied, Stacey came up with one excuse after another, complaining about the inadequacies of his regiment. It had poorly trained officers, he claimed, who had no idea how to scout and patrol because they "have no instruction and equipment, and they are now tired and thoroughly disorganized. I don't believe the General understands the shape my regiment is in. I must refuse to assume responsibility for any further attacks until we have some equipment and reinforcements."[6]

Johnson timidly relayed Stacey's response to Alexander and received a quick rebuke from the general. "Relieve him! You should have done that without reporting to me," Alexander shouted. "The responsibility for this attack is not on Stacey but on me. I'm ordering it."

"But relieving the Colonel will leave the regiment under the command of an emergency captain," Johnson pleaded. "The major is up there in the pocket, and after all, Stacey is a regular officer with twenty years' service."[7]

Alexander cut him off before he could speak further. "I don't care if it leaves the regiment in command of an emergency corporal, as long as he'll fight. Relieve that man at once and send him back to headquarters and relieve any other officer who talks that way. You will take personal command of the attack." Johnson heeded Alexander's demands and appointed Captain Lucien Breckinridge as Stacey's replacement.[8] Stacey was sent to a field hospital, where he was diagnosed with nervous exhaustion. His military career was in ruins; it took four years and a special court of inquiry to restore his name.[9]

Yet the chaos in the rear in no way matched the horror Whittlesey's men were experiencing in the forest. Lieutenant Griffith recalled that "we were in shell holes all of the time, in groups according to the size of the hole—some held two, some four and some larger ones held a dozen men. It rained almost constantly and we wallowed in mud, but the mud made our bed softer. While we were cut off we had no rations and were forced to eat brush, leaves and roots. When our supply of tobacco was exhausted we smoked dry leaves. Our water supply was mostly from shell holes, although at night some of the men would crawl out to a little slough at the foot of the hill and fill their canteens. Dead soldiers were lying all around. The Germans crept up on us. They were so close we could hear them talking and they would occasionally throw over a hand grenade. Sometimes we could toss them back before they exploded."[10] German grenades and artillery were so effective because the Americans had bunched together, instead of spreading out.

On October 5, the 50th Aero Squadron made two attempts, once in the morning and then in the afternoon, to parachute baskets of chocolates, cigarettes, ammunition, and medical supplies to the trapped soldiers before they were chased away by German antiaircraft guns. Whittlesey had previously used white cloths to signal airplanes but chose not to use them at this time; instead, his men waved, shouted, and fired tracers in the air, but to no avail.[11] Unfortunately, the supplies fell within the enemy lines and were eagerly grabbed by German soldiers. When another American plane appeared overhead, a German machine gunner who had the DH4 within his sights was wrestled to the ground by another soldier and told not to "shoot the delicatessen-flyers."[12]

Private Robert Dodd, a Native American from the Paiute tribe, volunteered, along with eight other men, to retrieve the misdirected parcels of food and supplies. They were soon cut off by German soldiers, who killed five of the doughboys and captured the other four. Dodd was interrogated by his captors, but he divulged little information on the Lost Battalion despite suffering wounds in his ankle and shoulder.*

Alexander ordered the 50th Aero Squadron to try again the next day. Lieutenant Erwin R. Bleckley, a bank teller from Wichita, Kansas, and his observer, Lieutenant Harold E. Goettler from Chicago, took off in the early afternoon of October 6. Upon reaching the site of the Lost Battalion, Bleckley and Goettler's DH4 came under German machine-gun fire. Undeterred, Bleckley flew even lower, and when they were just over the treetops, Germans bullets blasted the plane. Goettler was killed instantly with a shot to the head, while Bleckley may have been wounded. The Kansan managed to get the plane back toward Allied lines, but crashed not far from Gouraud's French Fourth Army. He was thrown from the plane and died on his way to the hospital. Both aviators were posthumously awarded the Medal of Honor.

On the afternoon of October 7, a doughboy who had been taken prisoner when he and several others had left the pocket without permission to go find food dropped by the American planes was blindfolded, led out of the German lines, and given a stick with a scrap of

---

* In addition to Dodd, the 77th included a Native American physician, Lieutenant Josiah A. Powless, who was killed that October while treating the wounds of another medical officer while exposing himself to intense German machine-gun fire. Powless was posthumously awarded the Distinguished Service Cross. There were a total of 891 Native Americans who fought with First Army in the Meuse-Argonne.

LEFT: Fresh from the Mexican Punitive Expedition, in June 1917, General John J. Pershing was selected by Secretary of War Newton Baker to lead the American Expeditionary Forces (AEF). Pershing withstood pressure from Allied military and political leaders to relinquish control of the American army in France and led the Americans to victory in Meuse-Argonne.

BELOW: Throughout the war Colonel Pierpont Stackpole, a Boston lawyer turned aid to Lieutenant General Hunter Liggett, maintained a diary that provides insight into his boss and is critical of many AEF officers.

A French family, liberated by the Americans in the St. Mihiel Salient, holds gas masks in case the retreating Germans counterattacked.

German prisoners are escorted to the rear by doughboys in the St. Mihiel Salient while an American motion picture cameraman records the scene.

Liberated by the Americans in the St. Mihiel Salient, French citizens return home after being held prisoner by the Germans.

Army Group Commander General Max von Gallwitz led the German forces during St. Mihiel and Meuse-Argonne.

Secretary of War Newton Baker, wearing a doughboy helmet, poses with a group of American and French officers in Verdun while on a tour of the front in September 1918.

General Pershing arrives at First Army headquarters in Souilly. His driver, Sergeant Caesar Santini, can be seen in the front seat of the Cadillac.

Lieutenant Colonel George S. Patton standing in front of a Renault tank. Patton, who had served as an aid to General Pershing during the Mexican Punitive Expedition, sailed to France aboard the *Baltic* as a staff officer with him before transferring to the Tank Corps. Patton was wounded on the first day of Meuse-Argonne near Cheppy and remained out of action for the entire battle.

Exhausted doughboys from the New York 77th "Liberty" Division rest in a captured German trench.

An American artillery battery fires a French-manufactured 155mm at German positions from the village of Varennes on the Aire River, which was taken by First Army on September 26.

Congested and shell-damaged roads leading to the front required some ambulance drivers to resort to hand-carrying wounded doughboys to the rear on litters.

A wave of doughboys advances across No Man's Land after jumping off in the early-morning hours of September 26, the first day of Meuse-Argonne.

ABOVE: Doughboys in the recently captured village of Montfaucon march by the house that the crown prince used to observe the Battle of Verdun in 1916.

LEFT: Colonel Claude Sweezey rallied the 313th Infantry Regiment, 79th Division, during its two-day ordeal to capture Montfaucon.

Doughboys model captured German armament, including breast plates, Mauser rifles, and a forty-one-pound antitank gun.

Telephone operators, called "Hello Girls," at the switchboard in Souilly. Helmets and gas masks hang on their chairs in the event of an attack. Pershing called them "real soldiers."

In the early-morning fog, First Army military police direct traffic at a crossroads in the Argonne region. The few roads leading to the front couldn't handle the large number of American troops, supply trucks, and ambulances, creating constant congestion during Meuse-Argonne.

"Balloon Buster" Lieutenant Frank Luke was credited with eighteen victories before he was shot down on September 29, 1918.

ABOVE: A group of war correspondents stops for lunch on their way to the Argonne front.

RIGHT: Major Charles Whittlesey, a New York lawyer, led the so-called "Lost Battalion" from the 77th Division during five harrowing days in October 1918.

African American troops, probably from the 92nd Division, march to the front under a canopy of camouflage netting.

Sergeant Alvin C. York from Company G, 328th Infantry Regiment, 82nd Division, a conscientious objector turned war hero, stands in the Argonne woods near Chatel-Chéhéry in February 1919 to point out where he captured 132 German prisoners in October 1918.

Brigadier General Douglas MacArthur led the 84th Brigade of the 42nd "Rainbow" Division during the attack on the Côte de Châtillon in October 1918. In this photo the colorful MacArthur makes himself at home in a French château that he used as his headquarters.

ABOVE LEFT: Father Francis Duffy, chaplain of the 165th "Fighting 69th" Infantry, 42nd Division. Father Duffy was often seen at the front with ambulance litters recovering wounded doughboys.

ABOVE RIGHT: Colonel William "Wild Bill" Donovan, a battalion commander in the 165th Infantry Regiment, 42nd "Rainbow" Division. During World War II he headed the Office of Strategic Services (OSS).

LEFT: On the morning of October 12, 1918, near Cunel, Lieutenant Sam Woodfill of the 60th Infantry Regiment, 5th Division, silenced a German machine-gun nest and wounded and killed several enemy soldiers. For this action Woodfill received the Medal of Honor.

The mayor's office at Souilly, which the French used as an army headquarters during the Battle of Verdun, then turned over to Pershing in September 1918, for use as American First Army headquarters during Meuse-Argonne.

Machine gunners from the 78th "Lightning" Division fire at German snipers near the village of Grandpré, which they captured on October 27, 1918.

Grandpré was heavily contested during the Meuse-Argonne until the 78th Division took the village in October 1918.

Wounded doughboys of the 1st Division receive treatment at a destroyed church in the village of Neuvilly at the Argonne front.

Lieutenant General Hunter Liggett at his desk in Souilly, shortly after he took command of First Army from Pershing in October 1918.

Brigadier General Hugh Drum, First Army chief of staff, at his desk in Souilly.

A former artillery commander in 1st Division, Major General Charles P. Summerall led Fifth Corps during the last phase of Meuse-Argonne and drove the Germans across the Meuse River.

Field Marshal Ferdinand Foch, commander of Allied forces, and General Pershing confer at Chaumont. Throughout the war the two often clashed over the use of American troops.

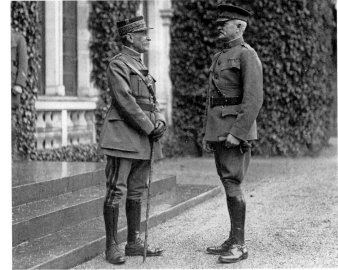

The flamboyant and egotistical Brigadier General William "Billy" Mitchell commanded First Air Service during St. Mihiel and Meuse-Argonne.

Personnel of Pershing's special train. The African Americans on staff were former Pullman porters. Captain Earl L. Thornton, who was in charge of the train, is standing on the far right.

War correspondent Frederick Palmer on board the *Baltic* as it heads to Europe in June 1917. After the war Palmer would write an account of Meuse-Argonne, as well as a biography of Pershing.

Lieutenant General Robert Lee Bullard commanded Third Corps for most of Meuse-Argonne until Pershing appointed him to lead Second Army in October 1918.

Commanders of the German army, Generals Erich Ludendorff and Paul von Hindenburg, pose with staff officers.

A group of doughboys enjoys German cigars and beer inside a captured trench at the Argonne front.

Brigadier General Charles Dawes, a Nebraska lawyer and future vice president, was a longtime friend of Pershing's and was appointed by him as the general purchasing agent for the AEF.

Future Missouri Senator and President of the United States Captain Harry S. Truman commanded a 35th Division artillery battery.

Captain Eddie Rickenbacker stands next to his SPAD plane. Rickenbacker commanded the 94th "Hat in the Ring" Aero Squadron and with twenty-six victories was America's top ace.

A fourteen-inch naval railway gun fires from twenty miles away at a German railway and troop movement center.

Jubilant doughboys on the Argonne front celebrate the armistice on November 11, 1918.

General Pershing stands next to Brigadier General Fox Conner, the AEF Operations officer (G-3), on board the transport *Leviathan* after the war as they enter New York Harbor in September 1919.

Colonel George C. Marshall stands next to General Pershing. Marshall was instrumental in planning the St. Mihiel and Meuse-Argonne battles and became an aid to Pershing after the war.

white cloth attached. He carried a note written in perfect English by Lieutenant Fritz Prinz, who had lived in Spokane, Washington, for four years as a representative of a German company:

Sir,

The bearer of this present, Lowell R. Hollingshead, had been taken prisoner by us. He refused to give the German Intelligence Officer any answer to his questions, and is quite an honorable fellow, doing honor to his Fatherland in the strictest sense of the word.

He has been charged against his will, believing that he is doing wrong to his country to carry forward this present letter to the officer in charge of the battalion of the 77th Division, with the purpose to recommend this commander to surrender with his force, as it would be useless to resist any more in view of the present condition.

The suffering of your wounded men can be heard over here in the German lines, and we are appealing to your humane sentiments to stop. A white flag shown by one of your men will tell us that you agree with these conditions. Please treat Lowell R. Hollingshead as an honorable man. He is quite a soldier. We envy you.

The German Commanding Officer.[13]

When Hollingshead made it back to the Lost Battalion, he was greeted by Whittlesey, McMurtry, and Holderman. Rather than welcoming the soldier, Whittlesey had every reason to have him arrested, since he had left his post without permission; but this was no time to worry about disciplinary measures. Instead, the major read the message aloud to his fellow officers and the three looked at each other with big grins. Whittlesey never responded to the note.[14]

Each day the battalion casualties added up. There was little to do for the wounded, other than provide comfort and stifle their moaning and groaning so as not to attract attention from nearby German machine gunners. Burial proved particularly difficult. Men were too weak to dig graves in the cold soil, so in many cases the dead were covered with brush and a thin layer of dirt, only to be unearthed by artillery shells. At ten thirty a.m. on October 7, Whittlesey sent a message by pigeon: "Germans are still around us, though in small numbers. We have been heavily shelled by mortar this morning. . . . Situation is cutting into our strength rapidly. Men are suffering from hunger and exposure; the wounded are in very bad condition. Cannot support be sent at once?"[15]

That afternoon, Whittlesey's men were subjected to a blistering artillery attack that lasted more than an hour and a half. Adding to the misery was the realization that the shells were sent not by the Germans but by American guns. The cause for the friendly fire was never investigated, but most likely the reason was a miscalculation of the Lost Battalion's coordinates by the 77th artillery spotters. Regardless, the results were devastating. From the top of Hill 198 down to Charlevaux Brook, the ground on which Whittlesey's men lay began to crumble all around them from a combination of high explosives and shrapnel, blasting deep crevices in the soil while spraying jagged steel at the men, who remained bunched together. The Germans observed the fiasco with a great deal of pleasure. Trees that offered some protection from enemy machine-gun and rifle fire were uprooted by the American artillery and left the frightened doughboys exposed. Whittlesey later said thirty men were killed or wounded as a result of the friendly fire. Grabbing his message pad, Whittlesey wrote the following note: "We are along the road parallel 276.4. Our artillery is dropping a barrage directly on us. For heaven's sake, stop it!"[16]

Whittlesey called for Private Omer Richards, who was in charge of the battalion's supply of messenger pigeons. Richards brought a crate containing the last two birds. When the private reached inside, a shell detonated nearby and a startled bird escaped his grasp and went airborne. Richards started to chase after the pigeon, but it was no use, as the bird was quickly out of reach. Returning to the crate, he lifted the last bird, a black-and-gray pigeon named Cher Ami. Holding the bird tightly with one hand, with the other he placed Whittlesey's scribbled message in a little aluminum capsule attached to the bird's leg and then released Cher Ami into the air.[17]

The pigeon flew a short distance and then circled a few times. Likely scared by the shelling, he landed on a damaged tree not far from where he took off. Richards tried to chase Cher Ami away with a stick. When that didn't work, the private jumped up and down, screaming at the bird. Whittlesey and other New Yorkers joined in, but Cher Ami wouldn't budge. As a last resort Richards climbed up the tree and shook the branch, and the pigeon took off, heading toward Allied lines.[18] Thirty minutes after departing from the Lost Battalion, Cher Ami landed at the 77th Division pigeon loft twenty-five miles away at Les Souhesmes-Rampont, worse for the wear. The leg carrying the message capsule was shattered, one wing was badly wounded, and his breastbone was broken. It is unclear if the message stopped the friendly fire, since the 77th's artillery barrages were timed and ended at a set hour.[19]

Meanwhile, Brigadier General Johnson ordered the 308th's new commander, Breckenridge, to launch the attack on October 7. But it was a futile effort. They made it as far as a ravine in front of Hill 198, but could advance no farther; German wire and machine guns were too much, and the vast majority of the regiment was either wounded or killed. Johnson was hit when a machine-gun projectile pierced his leather puttee and penetrated his calf. He received the Distinguished Service Cross for this action.

Around the same time, the 307th Infantry under Colonel Eugene Houghton, a Minnesota lumberman, tried to attack the Germans from the right flank. But Houghton had the same luck as Breckenridge, and the attack failed. The French helped out by striking at La Palette and captured the hill, but they pulled back to Binarville when the Germans counterattacked.[20]

What ultimately freed the Lost Battalion was a plan devised by Hunter Liggett. Recovering from a slight case of diarrhea, a persistent problem during the war, Liggett pored over maps and intelligence reports and concluded that a 1st Division advance on his corps's right was the perfect opportunity to rescue Whittlesey's trapped battalion on its left. A flank attack through the Argonne, between the villages of Apremont and Fléville, Liggett suggested, would drive the stubborn Germans right out of the forest.

Specifically, Liggett proposed that the 82nd Division attack from the northwest across the Aire against Cornay and other ridges while a brigade from the 28th Division would strike at Hill 244 directly in front of them. As Liggett explained it, "the object was not only to force the enemy completely out of the forest, thereby relieving the Lost Battalion, but to protect the new line of the 1st Division, which was enfiladed, or cross-fired, from the eastern flank of the forest above the village of Cornay."[21] Liggett admitted the attack was risky. Doughboys were told to flank-attack upon enemy positions that dominated the Aire River valley "from the height of three hundred feet. These crests were very steep, and in places formed rugged cliffs overlooking the valley road."[22]

Liggett, without the authority to order an attack, had to seek approval from First Army headquarters. He conferred with Drum and McAndrew at Souilly, told them his plan, and received their approval to go forward. Pershing was not at the meeting, nor did he mention the Lost Battalion ordeal in his diary, but no doubt Drum kept him informed of the situation. For the most part the attack worked. Summerall's troops fought their way into Fléville on the Aire. They were followed by the 28th Division, which reached the Aire south of Fléville and held the line, which included the village of Apremont. Neither division let up. Within two days, I Corps's boundaries extended to the eastern fringe of the Argonne Forest to the north of Binarville. The 82nd Division, with only six companies of infantry, stormed the eastern Argonne bluffs overlooking the Aire Valley. They scaled them, took them, and eventually held Châtel Chéhéry and Cornay, "two villages that clung to the heights like Swiss chalets."[23]

On the morning of October 8, Lieutenant John G. Taylor led the 308th's Company K across now-vacated Hill 198 toward the pocket. Taylor's men saw firsthand how the Germans had held out for so long. Some of their trenches were fortified with concrete and surrounded by piles of empty machine-gun cartridges. Taylor observed few shell holes, an indication that American artillery had missed its mark.[24]

When Taylor finally reached Whittlesey, the major appeared "calm, collected, and, he thought, clean-shaven, asking for food and surgeons." Taylor sent his men back across the valley to the rear for rations, and they returned with corn willy, bread, butter, and syrup. The Lost Battalion survivors gulped down the food, their first meal in five days, and promptly vomited it up again. Sick and wounded doughboys were taken to the field hospital either by ambulance or on small narrow-gauge railroad flatcars. Dead soldiers were buried in temporary cemeteries by a detachment of the 53rd Pioneer Regiment.

Among those killed over the harrowing five days was Private Henry

Chinn, a Chinese American from New York City's Chinatown who served in Company H of the 308th.[25] Also killed was the 307th's Captain Eddie Grant from Franklin, Massachusetts, a former Major League baseball player who at various times was on the roster of the New York Giants, the Philadelphia Phillies, and the Cincinnati Reds. Grant was killed by shell fire on October 5 while supposedly waving for stretcher bearers to care for two men struck down by a shell. He was buried in a German cemetery, a few yards from where he fell.[26]

Early on October 8, while Whittlesey and what remained of his Lost Battalion limped out of the Argonne, elsewhere in the forest a corporal from the backwoods of Tennessee, Alvin Cullum York, with the 82nd Division, single-handedly silenced several machine guns, killed around 20 Germans, and took 132 prisoners. While the Lost Battalion's saga made immediate headlines, few outside the 82nd heard about York's bravery until early 1919, when a story published in the *Saturday Evening Post* spun the events of October 8 and York's folksy manner into a larger-than-life tale. Much to his amazement, the Tennessean was catapulted to the status of America's greatest soldier in World War I.

Thirty-year-old York was the third oldest of eleven children raised dirt poor in a one-room cabin on a small farm in Fentress County, near Pall Mall, Tennessee. To make ends meet, his father, William, farmed, hunted, and from time to time worked as a blacksmith. York learned to hunt at a young age and quickly became a marksman. Where York grew up, education wasn't much of a priority and his days in a classroom totaled about nine months. Religion was paramount in this part of Tennessee, and his family were practicing Methodists. But as he grew older, the tall redhead strayed from his faith. Employed as a day laborer on the railroad near his home, York found more pleasure in drinking and gambling than going to church. He seemed to have little ambition and gave no thought to the future. However, in 1914, he witnessed his best friend die in a bar fight, and believed he might suffer the same fate if he didn't change his rebellious ways. On New Year's Day 1915, after attending a revival at the Church of Christ in Christian Union (CCCU), a strict fundamentalist sect that renounced, among other sins, drinking, carousing, swearing, violence, and war, York joined the congregation. Gracie Williams, a young woman who lived across a stream from his family's farm, influenced York's desire to practice Christianity. York wished to court Gracie, but first had to convince her father, Frank, that his wild days were in the past. Attending the CCCU each Sunday helped sway Mr. Williams. York and Gracie became a couple and would be married after the war.[27] York's simple life was interrupted two years later when the United States entered the Great War, and he struggled with his newfound beliefs and a feeling of responsibility to serve his country.

Like all men between the ages of twenty-one and thirty-one, York was required to register for the draft, and in June 1917 he obliged. Because his church discouraged military service, Pastor Rosier Pile told York to answer yes on his registration card where it asked if he claimed exemption from the draft. To emphasize his response, York added, "Don't Want To Fight." The Draft Board denied his request and York filed an appeal at the state level on the grounds that "I am a member of a well organized Religious Sect . . . whose then expending [sic] creed or principles forbade its members to participate in war, etc."[28] Again, York's appeal was turned down. The War Department wouldn't recognize the CCCU as a legitimate Christian religion, and therefore its members were not allowed to declare conscientious-objector status. Shortly thereafter, York was drafted and ordered to Camp Gordon, Georgia, for training. He was assigned to Company G, 328th Infantry of the 82nd, a division that was later called the All-Americans because its ranks were filled with drafted men from "every blood strain" and "every section of the United States," including "cotton pickers from Dixie, and city boys reared in tenements."[29]

With his Southern drawl and country demeanor, York stood out among the Greek, Irish, Italian, Polish, and Jewish recruits in his regiment. He fought off peer pressure from his platoon to carouse and chase women in the nearby city of Augusta, Georgia. Such activity ran counter to his Christian beliefs, but so did carrying a rifle with the purpose of killing Germans. Still, York worked hard at being a soldier, and he actually enjoyed what the Army provided him. He ate three meals a day, slept in a cot that he didn't have to share, and amazed other recruits with his shooting skills at the camp rifle range. Company G commander, Captain E. C. B. Danforth, and Major G. Edward Buxton, who led the 2nd Battalion, were impressed by York, but saw that he needed guidance, and they stepped in to counsel him over his guilt in disobeying the CCCU. Both Danforth and Buxton were also devout Christians, and York was drawn to their wisdom that America was morally obligated to join the war and that serving one's country was acceptable in the eyes of God. This put York at ease and he actually enjoyed being a soldier.[30]

York and the 82nd shipped off to France in April 1918, and saw combat for the first time at St. Mihiel, where the 328th Infantry captured the village of Norroy. Afterward, the 82nd was held at Pont-à-Mousson until September 25, when they were ordered to the Argonne, sixty-two miles away, for placement as a reserve in Liggett's I Corps. They traveled partway to the front by train, marched a bit, and then rode for fourteen hours on a convoy of buses driven by French Indochinese colonial soldiers.[31] Like many uninformed Americans, York, who hadn't ventured too far out of Fentress County, before mustering into the Army, assumed his drivers were Chinese. "I had done never seen a Chinaman before, and I jes couldn't keep my eyes off them," he recalled. "Them Chinamen were the awfulest drivers you ever seed. They must have sorter had the idea they had to get us there before they even started. The way they done tore and bumped those old French buses over those old French roads was enough to make your hair stand up straight."[32]

Along the way, the 82nd was met by Major General George Duncan, who had replaced division commander William P. Burnham. Duncan was a personal friend of Pershing's and at one time had commanded the 77th Division. Although the 82nd fought well at St. Mihiel, Pershing had made up his mind to relieve Burnham, who he felt was too timid with subordinate officers. At midmorning of October 6, Duncan learned from I Corps headquarters that one brigade from his division was to attack and take over a sector in between the 1st and 28th Divisions. The objective was not only to relieve German pressure on the Lost Battalion by cutting enemy supply lines but to drive the enemy from the eastern half of the Argonne, where the 1st was taking heavy losses. Duncan tasked chief of staff Lieutenant Colonel Jonathan Wainwright with drafting the attack order. The 164th Brigade, under the command of Brigadier General Julian R. Lindsey, with the 327th and the 328th Infantry Regiments, would advance northwest across the Aire and attack the village of Cornay and Hills 263, 180, and 223, while keeping close a connection with the right brigade of the 28th Division. There would be no preliminary artillery attack.

Only part of one battalion of the 327th reached its designated position on the morning of October 7, as steady rain and masses of artillery and machine-gun units going in the same direction prevented the other elements of 82nd Division from entering the line. They were soon followed by the 328th Infantry. As it turned out, only six companies from Lindsey's brigade would see action.[33] At around five a.m.

on October 8, the recently promoted Corporal York and the 2nd Battalion—exhausted, wet and cold—passed through the village of Châtel Chéhéry, captured the day before by the 28th Division infantry. York's battalion proceeded to Hill 223 for an attack on Castle Hill and another section of high ground one kilometer to the north, labeled Hill 180 on the Americans' maps, although to the Germans the hill was known as Schöne Aussicht, or Pleasant View. The 2nd Battalion's objective was to cross an open valley and a stream to cut enemy logistic and communications lines. Specifically, the task was to disrupt the narrow-gauge Decauville railroad line that ran on the heights west of the village, behind Hill 223. The railroad, well protected by machine-gun nests, was feeding supplies to German troops attacking the 77th Division.

The hills surrounding York's men were crowded with Germans, including the 125th Württemberg Landwehr, the Guard Elizabeth Battalion, and the 47th Machine Gun Company, under the command of Captain Heinrich Müller.[34] At 6:10 a.m. York's regiment jumped off and headed down the slope of Hill 233 into a valley to the west of Châtel Chéhéry. Company E was on the right and York's Company G on the left. The 327th Infantry, covering the right flank, was to attack a ridge above the village of Cornay, while a brigade of the 28th Division on the left flank was to assault the Germans on Hill 244. Originally the attackers were told to advance westward, but right before the jump-off, the order was changed to head north. All units in line that morning were told this except York's battalion. The runner entrusted with the message was killed on his way to the battalion post command.[35]

Not realizing they were advancing the wrong way, York's 2nd Battalion marched into a valley defended on three sides by German machine guns and rifles. It was a rude awakening. "[The] Germans met our charge across the valley with a regular sleet storm of bullets," York remembered. "The Germans done got us and they done got us right smart."[36] As the morning progressed, casualties mounted until only York and a handful of other doughboys from his unit had survived.

Inflicting the most bloodshed was a machine gun perched on "Humserberg," described as "the hill in the valley behind Châtel Chéhéry." York took it upon himself to destroy the gun. He climbed partway up Humserberg and crossed a supply road about 160 yards from the weapon and got into position. Crouching down, he aimed his rifle and opened fire. Within moments, the machine-gun crew was dead, along with several other Germans standing beside them. All told, nineteen German soldiers were killed.[37]

Acting Sergeant Bernard Early then led a platoon of seventeen men, including York, to the rear of some other German machine-gun nests, where York and the others rounded up about seventy or so prisoners. Germans on a nearby hill signaled to their captured comrades to lie down, and then opened fire on the platoon. The hail of bullets killed six Americans, including York's best friend, Corporal Murray Savage. Also killed were several prisoners, "which caused the surviving captured men to wave their hands wildly in the air and yell, 'Don't shoot—there are Germans here!'"[38]

Sergeant Early was wounded, and only eight of his men were still alive, including York, who was now the only noncommissioned officer in the small platoon. Exposed to enemy fire, they had to act quickly, York knew, or end up slaughtered like the other Company G doughboys. Taking the initiative, he worked his way up the slope toward the machine gunners, who were under command of Lieutenant Paul Vollmer. The gunners, elevated above the American, were forced to expose their heads above their cover to fire down on him. Whenever York saw a German helmet rise, he squeezed the trigger of his .30-caliber rifle, hitting his target every time. In accordance with his beliefs, he killed no man unless necessary, intermittently yelling up at them, "Give up and come on down." But the testy Germans refused to surrender. When a squad of Germans charged York as he passed near their trench while sprinting back down the hill, he instinctively resorted to a hunting skill he had used when facing a flock of turkeys back home. Experience taught him that "if the first soldier was shot, those behind would take cover." Unholstering his Model 1911 Colt .45-caliber semiautomatic pistol, York targeted the men from the back to the front. York later recorded in his diary that he picked off five German soldiers and an officer with his pistol, shooting them down like wild turkeys. The exact number of Germans he killed in the skirmish is unclear, but likely around twenty to twenty-five.

Lieutenant Vollmer, likely stunned by the loss of so many of his men, emerged and shouted to York, "English?" The corporal replied, "No, not English." Vollmer inquired, "What?" "American," York answered. "Good Lord!" Vollmer exclaimed. "If you won't shoot any more I will make them give up." York told him to go ahead. Vollmer blew a whistle and yelled an order up the hill. German soldiers soon trudged down the slope to join the other prisoners.[39]

York ordered Vollmer to line up his men in a column and have them carry out the six wounded doughboys. "He then placed the German officer at the head of the formation, with Vollmer in the lead. York stood directly behind him, with the .45-caliber Colt pointed at the German's back."[40]

As York led the captured German soldiers east along the ridge, York's battalion adjutant, Lieutenant Joseph A. Woods, spotted the group. Fearing it was a German counterattack, Woods assembled as many American soldiers as he could to repulse them. But as the line of men drew closer, he could see that the Germans were unarmed. At the head of the column, a doughboy saluted and said, "Corporal York reports with prisoners, sir."

"How many prisoners have you, Corporal?" Woods asked.

"Honest, Lieutenant," York answered, "I don't know." Woods, not knowing what had occurred, told York to take the POWs back to Châtel Chéhéry, and "I will count them as they go by." The lieutenant tallied 132 Germans taken by York and his men. Later on, York escorted his prisoners to Varennes and didn't return to G Company until the following day while the unit was still occupying positions on the Decauville railroad.

It never dawned on York that he was a hero. Rather, he was deeply affected by what had occurred on October 8. The next day he received permission to return to the site and look for survivors; guilt had overtaken him. Before heading back to the rear, York said a prayer. "I prayed for the Greeks, Italians and the Poles and Jews and others," he recalled. "I done prayed for the Germans too. They were all brother men of mine. Maybe their religion was different, but I reckon we all believed in the same God and I wanted to pray for them." But God, he reasoned, "would never be cruel enough to create a cyclone as terrible as that Argonne battle."

York's exploits were reported to Brigadier General Lindsey and Major General Duncan, and soon after he was promoted to sergeant. Later, he was recommended for the Distinguished Service Cross. But his heroics were nowhere to be found in the historical narratives of 82nd Division, 164th Brigade, or 328th Regiment that covered the action of October 8. Only a field message reports the capture of 132 Germans, without giving credit to York. Other than his DSC citation, Alvin York's story would have been lost to history if it had not been for

Saturday Evening Post reporter George Pattullo. How Pattullo learned about York isn't entirely clear. Most likely his discovery occurred in early 1919, when Company G Commander Captain Danforth sought to upgrade York's award from a DSC to a Medal of Honor. Pattullo was at Chaumont looking for stories about the AEF when Pershing advised him to head over to the 82nd Division headquarters "and ask General Duncan about the man who didn't approve of war." Pattullo soon learned that an investigation was under way to verify York's actions in support of the medal. On a frigid February morning, the reporter tagged along with Major General Duncan and other staff to see the terrain where York had captured the Germans. To the best of his recollection, York showed the party where the action had taken place, and on March 20, 1919, York's Medal of Honor recommendation was approved. A month later, Pattullo's article, "The Second Elder Gives Battle," was published, singling York out among the other brave soldiers of Company G and turning the Tennessee mountaineer into a mythical figure who "sprang from humble origins to greatness."

By the end of October 8 and well into the next few days, the Germans slowly withdrew from the Argonne after they were outflanked by 77th and 82nd Divisions, and put up little opposition. Not until the doughboys heard the clamor of German trucks moving supplies and equipment from the forest were they convinced that the enemy was no longer a threat.[41] But this didn't satisfy Major General Liggett, who complained bitterly that the 82nd managed to get only six companies across the Aire on October 7 to link up with the other troops in the Argonne. If the entire brigade had been reinforced, the enemy could have been captured as they attempted to vacate the forest. Instead, the Germans headed north, across the Aire, by the village of Grandpré, and consolidated forces on the heights east of the Meuse.

Now well into its second week, the Meuse-Argonne became even more of a slugfest, with American casualties mounting. This further increased the strain between Pershing and the other Allied commanders, who already thought he was in over his head. Pershing was also beginning to lose faith. He wrote in his diary of his "hope for better results tomorrow. There is no particular reason for this hope except that if we keep pounding, the Germans will be obliged to give way."[42]

12

REGROUPING FIRST ARMY

While Hunter Liggett's I Corps cleared the Argonne Forest, two other divisions were fighting tenaciously to drive the Germans from the Meuse Heights, east of the river. Machine-gun and artillery fire from this elevated point had menaced the Americans as they tried to advance on the open ground after seizing Montfaucon on September 27. Until the Germans were either removed from the high ground or had their guns at least partially silenced, Pershing's forces would continue to move at a snail's pace. Just how vital the Meuse Heights were to the Germans was not lost in a field order sent from General von der Marwitz to his divisions. A copy was discovered by the Americans in an abandoned German trench and translated by First Army intelligence. "According to the news that we possess the enemy is going to attack the 5th Army and try and push toward Longuyon-Sedan," Marwitz warned, "the most important artery of the army of the West. . . . It is on the invincible resistance of the Verdun

Front, that the fate of a great part of the Western Front depends, and perhaps the fate of our people."[1]

On October 8, the same day Corporal Alvin York performed his heroic action, Pershing ordered the untested 29th "Blue and Gray" Division to attack the toughest defenses on the entire Meuse-Argonne front. The general complained that "those German gunners are sitting there comfortably on top of the hills east of the Meuse without our being able to return our fire," and he expected the Blue and Gray to do something about it.[2]

Composed of National Guard regiments from Delaware, Maryland, New Jersey, Virginia, and Washington, DC, with lineage on both sides during the Civil War, the 29th was led by the iron-fisted Major General Charles G. Morton. For the upcoming assault, Morton's two infantry brigades, the 57th and 58th, were to serve under General Joseph Louis Andlauer's 18th French Division, attached to French XVII Corps, which was also part of First Army. Morton's men had recently moved from Alsace, where the division had been held since before St. Mihiel, to Verdun, where the commanding general took an office, well appointed with fine furnishings and a rug, in one of the upper casements in the city's famous citadel. On the night of October 6, Andlauer arrived in Verdun and addressed Morton and his staff on the upcoming attack. The battle-hardened French general, clad in a long, faded blue greatcoat, his head wrapped in a bandage in an attempt to hide an infection stretching across his face, spoke calmly and deliberately, "without heat or enthusiasm," as he explained the difficulties the Americans should expect to encounter as they attacked. The objective was to seize the heights of Haumont Woods, the Ormont Woods, and the Consenvoye Woods. Three German defensive lines had to be taken, all of which were fortified by veteran divisions, he warned, and the ground over which the 29th would cross was "rough, shell-torn and hilly." Once the Americans made it to the enemy's first line of trenches, they were to pass through a series of woods into open ground identified on the maps as Molleville Farms. The 58th Brigade would jump off first and, after reaching the initial objective, the 57th would take over with fresh troops. Attacking alongside the 29th was Major General George Bell's 33rd Division. After the operation started his men would cross the Meuse and link up with the Blue and Gray on the other side of the river.

At five a.m. on October 8, waves of American battalions went forward toward the German first line of defense. As this was their first time in battle, many of the Blue and Gray nervously lit cigarettes as they advanced under a protective artillery barrage. At first there was minimal response from the Germans, and the first lines of enemy trenches were reached on schedule, ninety minutes later. But these were the outpost lines that the Germans typically held lightly. As the Americans proceeded through the woods and went up Malbrouck Hill, they faced serious resistance and the attack stalled. Meanwhile, the 33rd Division crossed the Meuse at the villages of Brabant and Consenvoye, as planned, after engineers brought up material to construct pontoon bridges in the daylight in plain sight of the Germans, who peppered them with artillery. The bridge at Consenvoye was 156 feet long and had to be built in 16 feet of water while the engineers were forced to don gas masks part of the time.[3] One of the 58th Brigade regiments crossed over the bridge, which almost immediately afterward was destroyed by German artillery and prevented the supply trains from reaching the men. With no water trucks, thirsty soldiers dipped their canteens into the Meuse, which by now was a floating graveyard.[4] Regardless, most of the Americans had made it across the river, and it seemed that the Germans were being pushed back.

When the attack resumed the next day the Germans stiffened their resistance and counterattacked. Any progress gained by the American assault had been stopped. The fighting continued for a week longer, with both the 29th and 33rd Divisions taking enormous losses. Bell's men had more than two thousand gas casualties, more than any other division. Since the Illinois troops had been in line almost continuously since the battle began, "many of them had worn their clothes to shreds," one historian wrote, "the skin on some men's feet peeled off with their filthy socks."[5] Pershing called off the attack, with the Germans barely holding on to the Meuse Heights.

When Pershing wrote about the Meuse-Argonne in his postwar memoirs he emphasized that "the period of the battle from October 1st to the 11th involved the heaviest strain on the army and me."[6] What remained etched in his mind thirteen years later was how easily most of his divisions fell apart after only two days of combat. They became disorganized and fractured, while Gallwitz, who was initially caught off guard by the First Army attack, quickly reinforced his already solid defenses with additional divisions. Even though the Germans had been pushed out of the Argonne, they still had a tight grip on the heights beyond the Meuse. From there, it was easy for machine guns and artillery to target First Army as it tried to attack on the open ground.

Pershing began to wonder if and when his army would finally break through the German lines. He didn't want Meuse-Argonne to turn into a lengthy battle as had the Somme, Verdun, or Ypres. Logistical issues had to be overcome, primarily the clogged roads that kept ammunition, food, and other supplies from reaching the doughboys at the front. More troubling to Pershing was the performance of the division commanders. In his opinion, they lacked the energy and initiative to keep the attacks going. This was true of some generals, and Pershing had replaced and would continue to replace them. But for the most part they were good commanders who lacked experience leading large bodies of men. Much like Pershing, practically all of them had prior combat experience in Cuba and the Philippines, where they had led companies of a few hundred soldiers at most.[7]

While the battle of the Meuse Heights raged, on the evening of October 9, Pershing met with his top advisers: AEF chief of staff James McAndrew, operations commander Fox Conner, and First Army chief of staff Hugh Drum. They sat behind a long table in the Souilly conference room on the second floor, across the hall from Pershing's office. As they spoke, through the windows the "boom-boom of the guns rumbling on the heights of the Meuse" could be heard.[8] It was decided that the way to bring Gallwitz to his knees was to bring more troops to the Meuse-Argonne, and this might mean taking the 27th and 30th Divisions from the British, as well as five divisions—the 2nd, 6th, 36th, 81st, and 88th—who were fighting either in reserve or with the French. McAndrew and Conner went to Bombon the next day to make their case.[9]

At first Foch was impatient with the two American staff officers and dominated the conversation. He complained that First Army was not getting ahead as fast as the British and French were on other fronts and asked why this was so. McAndrew and Conner had no clear response, but instead pointed out that the pressure placed on the Germans in Meuse-Argonne by First Army directly contributed to the success of the Allied armies on other fronts. Foch agreed, but was reluctant to provide more troops. Instead he suggested that they "rely upon the spirit of initiative of the American High Command itself."[10] Foch believed that the "American armies would be fighting with the Stars and Stripes floating over them, under leadership which had always given evidence of magnificent authority, with staffs devoting their talents to the profit of soldiers animated by an uncontestable ardor."[11] "*Tout le monde à la bataille* [Everybody, everyone must fight. Don't let up]," he stressed. "*Combattez! Combattez! Combattez!* [Fight! Fight! Fight!]"[12]

First Army was fighting, and fighting hard, but so were the Germans, and there was no sign they planned to give up. Hindenburg sent divisions to Gallwitz from other fronts, such as Flanders, a clear indication that the Germans were going to hold the Meuse-Argonne defenses for as long as possible. Yet fresh Americans troops also appeared. About 300,000 per month arrived in the French ports and were sent untrained to the battlefield as replacements. By mid-October First Army had over a million men, plus 135,000 French soldiers.[13] The strength in numbers should have been enough for First Army to overwhelm Gallwitz's forces, but the Germans' deadly machine guns and well-aimed artillery took their toll on the American soldiers, and were clearly putting a severe strain on their commander.

During one of his frequent trips to the front, Colonel John G. Quekemeyer, Pershing's Mississippi-born aide-de-camp, riding alongside the general in his Cadillac, watched as the AEF commander covered his face with his hands and mumbled, "Frankie . . . Frankie . . . my God, sometimes I don't know if I can go on."[14] Pershing was not one to openly express his feelings, but these were dark times. Perhaps his sadness triggered thoughts of that horrible day in August 1915 when he lost Frankie and the girls.[15]

Pershing wrote to Bea Patton, "Someone asked me a day or two ago when the war was going to end, and I said: 'I can easily answer that question. I do not know.'"[16] Since the battle commenced, Pershing had been unable to visit Micheline Resco, and this may have contributed to his feelings of frustration and worry. Instead, they communicated frequently by letter and telegram. "I am very sad that I am not able to see you," Pershing assured her in mid-October. "Kiss you, lovingly embrace you. But *la bataille progresse* [the battle progresses]. All to you. J."[17]

Pershing's dour mood was hardly concealed, and it worried the officers who saw him on a frequent basis. Frederick Palmer recalled that the general's skin had turned pale; the deep desert tan from the Punitive Expedition was now gone. His skin now had a ruddy gray complexion and his eyes were tired from an obvious lack of sleep. Colonel George C. Marshall also saw the toll the Meuse-Argonne was taking on Pershing, and in his memoirs rattled off some of the key reasons: "Distressingly heavy casualties, disorganized and only partially trained troops, supply problems of every character due to the devastated zone so rapidly crossed, inclement and cold weather, as well as stubborn resistance by the enemy on one of the strongest positions on the Western Front."[18]

Marshall sided with Pershing that the "officers of high rank" were to blame for First Army's problems. He did not mention any names but implied that those "not in perfect physical condition usually lost the will to conquer and took an exceedingly gloomy view of the situation except when Pershing came around, then they 'bucked up' for the period of his visit, only to relapse into further depths of despondency after his departure."[19] Marshall thought that Pershing "carried himself with an air of relentless determination to push the operation to decisive victory. His presence inspired confidence and his bearing convinced those with whom he came in contact that the weak-hearted would be eliminated and half measures would not be tolerated."[20]

One day in October, Major General Lejeune caught a glimpse of Pershing as his Cadillac sped by 2nd Division. Although his view of Pershing was fleeting, Lejeune could sense something was wrong with the commander in chief. "The thought of the heavy burden which he carried by night and by day saddened me," Lejeune wrote. "It was a burden he could never lay aside. The successful prosecution of the task allotted to his armies and the honor, as well as the security of our country, were always in his thoughts and on his decisions there depended the life or death of thousands of men as well as victory or defeat for our armies."[21]

Pershing had indeed taken on too much by running both the AEF and First Army. The weight of such a burden would have impacted any commander. But Pershing was also resilient and smart. On October 10 he announced a change that was in the best interest of his army and was destined to become the turning point of the Meuse-Argonne. Effective October 16, he was stepping down as First Army commander and would hand over the reins to Major General Hunter Liggett. He would also add a Second Army to be led by III Corps's Major General Robert Bullard. Both were promoted to the rank of lieutenant general. Pershing would oversee both armies as an Army Group commander on a par with France's Pétain and Britain's Haig.

Other command changes were not as significant but impacted the battlefield. Brigadier General Billy Mitchell would oversee both First and Second Armies' Air Service, while George C. Marshall would directly report to Liggett as assistant chief of operations for First Army. His job, which was still "to work out all the details of the operations," as one staff officer put it, hadn't changed, so they were in a clear, workable order that could be "read in poor light, in the mud and rain."[22]

In theory, Pershing now had more time not only to run the entire AEF but to devote himself to his roles as a diplomat and politician, essential duties when dealing with the other Allied commanders.[23] Leaving First Army was a bold but necessary adjustment. Pershing apparently came to this decision on his own accord, and consulted no one. "You never know what is in the C-in-C's mind," one of Black Jack's aides wrote, "and how it is coming out. When it comes, it comes quick and definite—just like the outburst of a bombardment for an offensive which had been weeks in preparation." Frederick Palmer added that Pershing "listened to many counselors; but the decisive counsels he held behind the locked doors of his own mind." Palmer supposed that "those who thought they knew what he was going to do knew least."[24]

First Army needed a boost, and Hunter Liggett was the right commander to provide it. He had all the necessary traits to lead an army that was now more than a million men in strength. A brilliant tactician and corps commander, Liggett impressed Pershing and, for that matter, everyone else in the AEF and French Army. In recent days Liggett had moved his headquarters closer to the front, and now as First Army commander he took over some old French dugouts at Florimont, a tiny village that sat on a hillside along the main road leading down the Aire valley. Years later Liggett said these French dugouts "put on no such airs as the German counterpart. These were merely holes in the hillsides," and were "populated, as Malin Craig [I Corps chief of staff] described it, by rats as big as pack mules and as savage as tigers."[25] On the evening of October 10, Liggett met with Pershing to discuss his new assignment. He recounted very little about the meeting, other than that the commanding general sounded optimistic, telling him "that if we and our Allies could keep up the gait the war would be ended by the close of the year."[26]

Two days later Liggett journeyed to Souilly by rail with Colonel Stackpole, and the men dined with Pershing and Hugh Drum on the train.[27] Pershing made it clear he was still in charge and as army group commander would oversee operations. Current attacks would cease until the reorganization was finalized, then commence on October 16. Sounding much like Foch, Pershing said from that point there would be no letup in the fighting. The next phase of Meuse-Argonne would strike directly at the Kriemhilde Stellung, destroy enemy communications, and take Mézières; it was essentially the same battle plan as the one given on September 26.[28] Afterward, the party retired to Pershing's office for further talk about the next attack. Frederick Palmer was close by in a "stuffy little ante room" at Souilly when Liggett emerged from the meeting, "his face glowing; his eyes sparkling as though he had seen a vision come true." A few minutes later one of Pershing's aides scurried up the stairs to give his boss a message that had just come by telephone from Paris: the new German chancellor, Prince Maximilian of Baden, had provisionally accepted President Wilson's Fourteen Points for peace. Perhaps the war would soon be over.[29]

Pershing also invited Lieutenant General Bullard to Souilly to discuss Second Army.[30] Bullard was told to get his army ready for an attack on both banks of the Moselle in the direction of Metz. Although peace negotiations were in the works with Germany, Pershing insisted that the Allies must keep up the pressure. Bullard informed Pershing that he expected it would take a great deal of time and effort to get support units and full divisions transferred to his front. It would probably be a month before they were ready to launch an assault.[31] With the changes at the top, there was a need for corps commander replacements. John L. Hines was taking over IV Corps for Bullard. Cameron was demoted from V Corps and took over for Hines at the 4th Division, and was replaced by Major General Charles P. Summerall, and Dickman switched from IV Corps to replace Liggett at I Corps.

Now at the helm of First Army, Hunter Liggett quickly encountered the problems associated with command, the very ones that had kept Pershing awake at night. Leading I Corps had been comparatively easy since he had been concerned with only the divisions assigned to him. Yet now, after thirteen days of almost continuous fighting, First Army had taken a severe beating, and casualties tallied somewhere around 75,000 killed and wounded. First Army hospitals were completely overwhelmed treating soldiers who were shot up or gassed. Near the front, field hospitals were no more than "knockdown" shacks always full "with boys suffering from everything from a finger shot off to the more serious injuries."[32] They were staffed by surgical teams or emergency groups, consisting of a surgeon, an assistant surgeon, an anesthetist, and a couple of nurses and orderlies, sent from base hospitals in the rear.

Each division was assigned four field hospitals that followed the units to the front by truck. Mobile hospitals were deployed as close to the front line as possible to care for nontransportable wounded. The seriously wounded who could be moved were sent to base hospitals or specialized psychiatric and gas hospitals run by the Services of Supply.[33] First Army's evacuation hospitals were the official intake for casualties, and were often so busy that the wounded would have to lie on the wet ground while waiting for attention. Nurse Elizabeth Campbell Bickford recalled that one of the hospitals near Verdun had "a long dirty looking room with seven surgical tables, each occupied by a seriously wounded man." To patch them up were "large packing cases of neatly folded gauze squares, large sponges and pads" that had been "put together with loving care by the women back home."[34]

Within walking distance of Pershing's Souilly office, alongside a curved roadway made of cracked stone, was Evacuation Hospital 8. A plain "rough wooden shack" with a blanket over the doorway to shut out cold and keep in light, there was a bare reception area save for an old coal stove and two tables for use by the clerical staff. The hospital was capable of holding eighty stretchers, and to handle an inevitable overflow of patients, four tents were erected to accommodate forty stretchers each. On September 30, the hospital's busiest day on record, the doctors, nurses, and staff treated two hundred cases during a single twelve-hour shift.

Medical staff at the front worked long days, under danger from German artillery that threatened them nearly as much as the doughboys in the trenches and foxholes. One morning a field hospital at Cheppy was shelled for several hours. Despite the bombardment, the Red Cross nurses refused to leave. Two of them, Bertha Cornwall and Ida Ferguson, who comforted the wounded while under fire, were later cited for bravery.[35] Frederick Palmer described nurses such as Cornwall and Ferguson as "the greatest soldiers of all." He added that "their part was to welcome with a smile and professional efficiency the wounded, whether burned by gas or their flesh torn by shells, in their mud and filth and blood-soaked clothes and make them clean and well again or make death easier for them."[36] Nurse Eva Babcock wrote that "during the long hours, we couldn't stop to eat. Just grab a bite off the mess cart, or a cup of coffee. It was awful to see those poor kids strapped on a board with their backs broken, or an arm or both legs off. It was terribly trying on your nerves."

For two sisters from New York—Gladys and Dorothea Cromwell—the strain of treating wounded soldiers during Meuse-Argonne was too painful. They had left their comfortable Manhattan life to volunteer as relief workers for the Red Cross in early 1918, and were assigned to a medical hut at Souilly. There the Cromwells cared for doughboys badly mangled, gassed, and suffering from shell shock. The experience must have haunted Gladys and Dorothea, because on their way back to America in early 1919, they committed double suicide by jumping over the side of the transport ship. Their bodies were recovered and interred in an American cemetery in France.[37]

German POWs received the same medical care as American troops. A linen tag tied in a soldier's buttonhole provided his treatment and diagnosis. If a patient required surgery, he was sent to a general hospital far from the front, out of harm's way. Many of the doctors who treated wounded soldiers came from private and university hospitals, and included some of the best physicians America had to offer. Among them were Colonel George W. Crile, a famous surgeon from Cleveland; Brigadier Generals Charles and William Mayo, cofounders of the famous Rochester, Minnesota, clinic that bears their name; and Colonel Harvey Cushing, a pioneering brain surgeon from Boston.[38]

One hospital in the town of Vittel, one hundred miles south of the front, was continuously packed during the battle. Colonel Henry C. Berry, who was in charge of the facility, recalled, "Our beds were filled to overflowing and as the casualties continued to pour in, we were obliged to line our corridors and halls with cots. In spite of the terrible suffering which these men were enduring, they maintained a brave front, and only by suppressed moans and facial expressions of pain could one appreciate their agony." After visiting Vittel, Major Ray Dillon of the 801st Pioneer Regiment wrote his family back in Detroit, which many of the general hospital's doctors called home, that he had witnessed a doughboy admitted with his face badly cut up. After one of the skilled surgeons was done operating, "all you could see was a small scar."[39] Two weeks into the battle nurse Elizabeth Weaver cared for many soldiers who passed through. "No one realizes the living hell these men go through at the front," she recorded, "unless you are over here and see the results."[40]

To deal with the living hell of combat, often doughboys turned to "the White Slaver," a name given to cigarettes by carmaker and moral reformer Henry Ford. Tobacco was part of a soldier's daily ration, and the American government shipped millions of cigarettes to France during the war. During Meuse-Argonne, when a soldier's ration ran dry, relief agencies such as the Red Cross, the Salvation Army, and the

YMCA, came to the rescue. Pershing encouraged his men to smoke and supposedly stated that cigarettes were as vital to his army as ammunition and food. One of his aides, Major Grayson M. P. Murphy, said, "In an hour of stress a smoke will uplift a man to prodigies of valor: the lack of it will sap his spirit." Another AEF officer remarked, "A cigarette may make the difference between a hero and shirker."[41] A commanding officer in a field hospital recalled that the "very first thing the wounded man wants to quiet his nerves is a smoke. The American Red Cross came to our rescue in passing those God sent smokes to the boys on the operating table or in the evacuation wards."[42] Lieutenant Harry Spring of the 37th Engineers thought the same thing. "Can understand why cigarettes are a necessary asset for a soldier," he told his diary. "It is most soothing to smoke one after getting out of a tight spot."[43] Pershing even enjoyed tobacco on occasion, indulging in the vice when alone at his desk or riding horseback. Instead of cigarettes, he preferred cutting off a small plug of tobacco from a cigar, then sticking it in the back of his mouth.

Adding to the misery of war was a widespread influenza outbreak. In the Argonne that autumn, cold, tired, and wet troops were especially vulnerable to the wrath of the "Spanish Lady."[44] It is believed that the flu originated earlier in the year at Camp Funston, Kansas, though the strain quickly reached Fort Oglethorpe, Georgia. Soldiers from both camps likely transported the flu to Europe, and in spring 1918 the first wave hit the AEF, although few soldiers died from it. In August the flu expanded and took off worldwide.[45] Because the outbreak hit Spain particularly hard in the spring of 1918, one careless newspaper claimed the disease originated there, and tagged it the Spanish flu.[46] At one First Army hospital, sheets were used as screens "to prevent delirious men from expectorating at his neighbor's bed," one Red Cross nurse recalled, "which was fortunate as many of the flu patients had pneumonia."[47]

Although it was possible to die directly from the flu—and plenty of soldiers did—more often the disease developed into pneumonia, driving the death rate higher. How many First Army soldiers were infected is unknown since the Army only counted those who were hospitalized; a good number of doughboys were never admitted for medical care and died untreated in dugouts or shell holes.[48] Alexander Stark, the First Army chief surgeon, stressed the impact of the disease when he wrote: "Influenza so clogged the medical services and the evacuation system, [and] rendered 'ineffective' so many men in the armies that it threatened to disrupt the war."[49]

First Army doctors reported almost 150,000 cases of the flu in mid-October, overwhelming the field and general hospitals. With the flu having an even greater impact on the training camps in the United States, very few replacements were arriving to help fill the depleted divisions. Pershing reacted by reducing the size of companies from 250 to 175 men each. Even the Germans were victims of the outbreak, losing perhaps 186,000 men during the war.[50] By the end of hostilities, it is estimated that between 750,000 and one million doughboys had caught the flu. When it finally ran its course in 1919, twenty-one million people had died from the flu worldwide. Pershing had a mild bout of the flu the week before the Argonne jump-off but was able to weather the illness. A month later, he came down with a more severe case.

Lieutenant General Liggett immediately began to "tighten up" First Army, which was getting sloppy in regards to "inattention and carelessness in saluting and straggling," among other problems that one AEF inspector point out.[51] Straggling especially had gotten out of hand. Liggett claimed that roughly 100,000 troops had left their units during the first month of the battle. He was exaggerating, but the point was well made: too many soldiers were heading to the rear.[52] Exactly why they separated from their units is not entirely clear. Certainly the chief reason was that doughboys simply became lost in the abysmal conditions of constant shell fire, poor roads, and fog. To remedy the situation, Liggett ordered division commanders to post military police at key crossroads and assign file closers behind each platoon.[53] While the vast majority of stragglers accidentally lost touch with their units during combat in the dense Argonne Forest, some left deliberately, and were considered deserters. Many hid in foxholes, ravines, thick underbrush, and abandoned French and German dugouts. Military police units were kept busy rounding up the stragglers, and some eventually faced court-martial.

On Wednesday, October 16, Pershing met with Foch at his Bombon headquarters to go over the changes in American command. General Weygand was there, too, and as usual their conversation was uncomfortable and heated. It seemed that Foch had forgotten what he had told McAndrew and Conner the week before, and lectured Pershing about the Americans' lack of progress in the Argonne, telling him that "results are the only way to judge by: that if an attack is well planned and well executed it succeeds with small losses; that if it is not well planned and well executed the losses are heavy and there is no advance." Change in command was not important, Foch pointed out, "so long as you keep things going at the front."[54]

Then Foch asked Pershing how First Army was progressing. "The Germans are putting up a very determined resistance," Pershing replied. Yes, Foch responded, but "on all other parts of the front [where] the advances are marked, the Americans are not progressing rapidly."

True, Pershing countered, but "no army in our place would have advanced farther than the Americans."

"Every general is disposed to say the fighting on his front is the hardest," Foch shot back. "I myself only consider results."

"Results? In seventeen days we have engaged twenty-six German divisions," Pershing noted. "I shall continue my attacks until the Germans give way." Pausing for a moment, Pershing asked, "Provided, of course, that this is Marshal Foch's desire?"

"By all means," said Foch. Then he advised Pershing on how to fight. "In order for an attack to succeed, a commander must go considerably into details."

Pershing mentioned the difficult terrain in the Meuse-Argonne, and Foch replied, "You chose the Argonne and I allowed you to attack there." At this point Weygand, acting as an intermediary, interrupted and introduced Pershing's plan to create Second Army. Foch approved and the meeting ended on a high note.[55]

Afterward, Pershing seemed more relaxed, his confidence restored. His emotional breakdown before Colonel John G. Quekemeyer appeared to be behind him. Certainly this had much to do with the fact that he still remained in charge of the AEF and the Meuse-Argonne, despite French efforts to undermine him. Other than a mild case of the flu, Pershing remained healthy for the remainder of the war. After one physical, his doctor told him that his "heart and arteries were of a man thirty-five and an eye lens crystal of a boy of eighteen." Earl Thornton, who managed Pershing's train, said "physically and mentally he seemed almost tireless." Exercise was part of the general's daily regimen. If he wasn't horseback riding, Pershing walked every day, no matter the weather, and could be seen running outside even after it had snowed. While at Chaumont he walked the six kilometers from his château to the office, and at Souilly he walked the length of his train for at least an hour. Then he would eat a simple breakfast, usually fruit, wheat cakes, boiled eggs, toast, and tea.[56]

One night, on the way back to Ligny-en-Barrois, where his train was parked, Pershing's Cadillac ran low on gasoline. Santini stopped at a small village to fill up. Watching the AEF commander and his driver was a wrinkled, gray-haired, elderly Frenchwoman, a black shawl draped over her hunched shoulders. Seeing the American flag on the general's car, she shuffled up to the window, peered in at Pershing, and said, *"Monsieur, merci à vous* [Mister, thank you]," then turned and left. It was unlikely she recognized the passenger as General John J. Pershing, but from the flag she knew he was American, and that mattered most of all.[57] Moments like this one gave Pershing the boost he needed. With Liggett doing the heavy lifting as First Army commander, the Meuse-Argonne entered a new phase, and Pershing had reason to feel optimistic.

13

RESUMING THE ATTACK

As the AEF endured a period of organizational changes, First Army had not let up in the fighting. The next phase of Meuse-Argonne started on October 14. In line to the right was III Corps (3rd, 4th, and 5th Divisions), V Corps (32nd and 42nd Divisions) was in the center, and I Corps to the left (77th and 82nd Divisions). They targeted the Kriemhilde Stellung, now held by twenty-seven under-strength, but still lethal, German divisions. Over the past couple of weeks First Army had gotten close to the stellung but never had the strength to push through. The reasons were obvious: besides the horrible landscape of thick woods, deep crevices, and twisted underbrush, the Germans had added three rows of breast-high wire in front of four-foot-deep trenches with machine-gun shelters.[1]

Protected by an intense rolling barrage directed at the German defenses, the three corps of First Army jumped off later than usual, at eight thirty a.m., believing this would catch the enemy off guard. Yet

Gallwitz's artillery and machine guns responded with intensity, shattering the American lines as they advanced. The 5th Division had the most difficult time. Its three attacking regiments—the 60th, 11th and 6th, with the 61st in support—were slow to reach the jump-off line to follow the barrage, and when they finally reached the Cunel-Romagne Road, the Germans were ready for them and inflicted heavy casualties. Eventually Cunel was taken, but that was as far as the division could go that morning. In the afternoon the 32nd took Romagne and the 5th tried to break out, making it as far as the lower third of the Bois de Pultière. By this time almost half of the divisions' four regiments were either killed or wounded.

One bright spot in the 5th Division's attack occurred during the lead-up on October 12, when the "Red Diamond" Division was in the process of relieving the 80th Division smack in the middle of the Romagne and Cunel Heights.[2] First Lieutenant Samuel Woodfill's courage on October 12 ranks next to Alvin York's feat as the most heroic episode of the Meuse-Argonne battle. Born in 1883 in Jefferson County, Indiana, on a corn and tobacco farm owned by his father, Woodfill had sandy hair just like his father, who had served honorably during the Mexican and Civil Wars. When Sam was ten years old his father laid a rifle across a windowsill, painted a small target on a fence twenty-five yards away, and taught his boy how to hold the rifle and shoot. Six years later Woodfill had earned enough money to buy his own long arm.[3]

Near Cunel on First Army's right flank, Lieutenant Woodfill, a regular Army sergeant who was a combat veteran of the Philippines and the Mexican Punitive Expedition, single-handedly attacked a series of machine-gun nests. Pinned down with his company in an open field, he leaped forward into a shell hole to assess the situation. Woodfill could see that the most serious threat came from machine-gun fire from a church tower two hundred yards away. Aiming his rifle, he fired

off five shots. The enemy fire stopped. Woodfill had either killed or wounded the German soldier or scared him off; it didn't matter, because enemy bullets were coming from other directions. He silenced another machine gun shooting from a stable, but fire was still coming from a bush in front of him. Woodfill jumped from his shell hole and scrambled to another nearby. He then crawled toward the flank of another machine gun. Within ten yards of the gunner, he unloaded his rifle, killing him and another five Germans nearby. A seventh German was shot down by Woodfill's pistol.

Advancing deeper into the woods, he shot a German officer who foolishly tried to take his gun. Two other enemy officers saw what happened to their comrade and gladly headed to the rear, their hands raised in the air. Woodfill continued on, wiping out another machine-gun nest and killing five more Germans. He attempted to signal for his company to come forward, but he was too far away. Staggering upon a position manned by two Germans, he killed them with their own pickax. Finally, remnants of his company arrived and they tried to get reinforcements, to no avail. Woodfill was forced to withdraw, but he had cracked the Hindenburg Line. For his achievement that day, Woodfill received the Medal of Honor.[4]

Shouldering the heaviest load on October 14 was the 42nd "Rainbow" Division, specifically the 84th Brigade, commanded by Douglas MacArthur. His men had the unenviable task of attacking the Côte de Châtillon, also known as Châtillon Hill, another high ground the Germans were anxious to retain. There was no one quite like Brigadier General Douglas MacArthur in the U.S. Army—or any army, for that matter. By the Armistice, MacArthur had been awarded the Distinguished Service Cross twice and the Silver Star six times. No other soldier during the Great War had received so many decorations. Not willing to remain in the rear like most staff officers, he led his men into

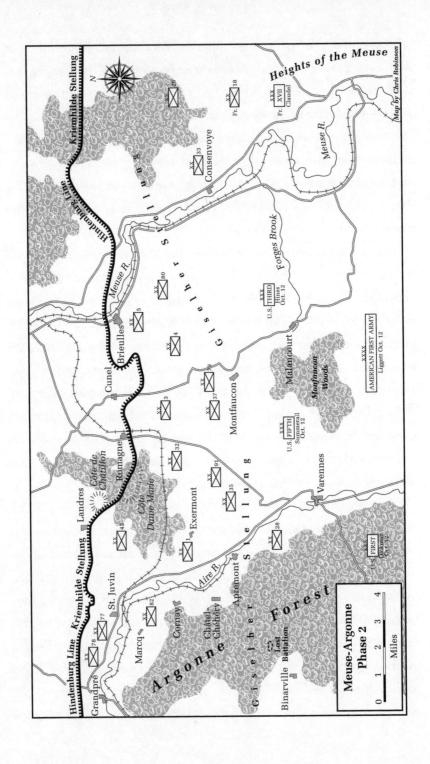

Heights of the Meuse

Fr. XVII Claudel

Fr. XX 18

XX 26

XX 33 Consenvoye

Meuse R.

Forges Brook

U.S. XXX THIRD Hines Oct. 12

XXXX AMERICAN FIRST ARMY Liggett Oct. 12

XX 80

XX 5

Brieulles

Cunel

XX 4

XX 7

XX 37

Montfaucon

XX 3

Malancourt

Montfaucon Woods

U.S. XXX FIFTH Summerall Oct. 12

Meuse R.

Hindenburg Line

Kriemhilde Stellung

Côte de Châtillon

Romagne

Côte Dame Marie

Landres

XX 32

XX 91

XX 35

Varennes

XX 1

Exermont

XX 42

XX 28

U.S. XXX FIRST Dickman Oct. 12

Grandpré

St. Juvin

XX 82

Marcq

Cornay

Châtel, Chéhéry

Apremont

Lost Battalion

Binarville

XX 77

XX 78

Argonne Forest

Giselher Stellung

Aire R.

Meuse-Argonne
Phase 2

0 1 2 3 4
Miles

Map by Chris Robinson

battle from the front. MacArthur was a soldier's soldier, just like his father, General Arthur MacArthur. Douglas not only followed in his footsteps but far too often emulated his father when it came to dealing with superiors. In 1863, during the Civil War, Arthur had won the Medal of Honor for gallantry at the Battle of Missionary Ridge. Thirty-five years later he commanded a division and department in the Philippines. Arthur was promoted to military governor and his star was on the rise. There was talk that he would be appointed Army chief of staff. But he repeatedly clashed with the civilian governor, future president William Howard Taft, on how to run the Philippines, and was sent back to the United States. Although promoted to lieutenant general, which made him the highest-ranking officer in the army, he spent the remainder of his career at uninspiring posts in the West. Arthur retired a bitter man in 1909 and died three years later. For Douglas, his father's downfall was painful to watch, and he took steps to ensure his own career turned out differently. By the time his long Army service came to a halt in 1951, he had become America's best-known general—a well-earned entitlement that began with the attack on the Côte de Châtillon.

That MacArthur and the 84th were tasked with taking such a menacing German position says much about Black Jack's confidence in his young brigade commander. Pershing was well aware of MacArthur, who later recalled vividly the first time they met. Just days after graduating first in the West Point class of 1903, MacArthur was in his father's office in downtown San Francisco when Captain Pershing, then a cavalry officer, came by for a visit. "I shall never forget the impression he made on me by his appearance and bearing," MacArthur reminisced. "He was the very epitome of what is now affectionately called the 'Old Army.'" As Pershing turned to leave, he told Arthur MacArthur, "I am sure Douglas and I will meet again." Pershing could not have been more correct. Their paths crossed often, and MacArthur in many ways modeled his own career after Pershing's. Both men were headstrong and dedicated.

When America entered the Great War in April 1917, MacArthur wanted to be in the thick of the fighting on the battlefield, leading men as his father had done in two wars. Even though he was a Regular Army officer, he saw an opportunity with the National Guard as a way to get overseas early. Assigned to the General Staff in Washington, MacArthur was privy to Army troop deployment plans and knew there were too few regulars to field an immediate expeditionary force; the National Guard would have to pick up the slack. Yet deciding which state units to send overseas was a political nightmare. MacArthur came up with the idea of singling out state regiments with experience on the Mexican border and placing them together to form a composite division. He envisioned units "that will stretch over the whole country like a rainbow." With help from Major General William Mann, the Army's Militia Bureau commander, MacArthur cherry-picked regiments from twenty-six states and the District of Columbia. They were federalized and given the numerical designation of the 42nd Division by the War Department. While Mann took over as its commander, Major Douglas MacArthur secured a slot as division chief of staff.

In November 1917, the Rainbow Division arrived in France as one of the first American units to go overseas. Right away, the division was sent to a so-called quiet sector. Yet it wasn't so quiet. The Germans were well aware that green American doughboys loomed nearby and sent artillery fire and the occasional raid to welcome them to the front. Although a staff officer, MacArthur refused to remain behind when infantry squads retaliated with dangerous nighttime raids on German trenches across no-man's-land. His courage in leading men from the front did not go unnoticed. MacArthur made a name for himself not only as a brave soldier but as a stylish dresser as well. He removed the metal band from the inside of his cap, giving it a jaunty appearance, and the damp autumn climate of France provided the perfect opportunity to don the heavy muffler and bright turtleneck sweater his mother, Pinky, had sent him.

Now a brigadier general in command of the 84th Brigade, MacArthur and the Rainbow Division's moment of truth came on the night of October 11–12, when the 42nd entered the line running from the town of Sommerance eastward through the northern edge of the Romagne Woods. In the ensuing days the division's line extended until it was looming in front of the fortified Kriemhilde Stellung, specifically Hill 288 and Châtillon Hill. MacArthur's headquarters was at a farm east of Exermont, about two miles from the front, yet still within easy range of German artillery. MacArthur had a bad habit of visiting the front without a gas mask. During a reconnaissance mission he was caught in an yperite gas barrage and became violently ill. It was thought that he might need to be hospitalized, but MacArthur insisted on remaining close at hand to lead the troops when the battle commenced. He said that as a result of the gas attack he "was wounded, but not incapacitated, and was able to continue functioning."

MacArthur's forays to the front gave him firsthand exposure to the danger his men would face when they attacked the Côte de Châtillon. First, the attack, set to commence on October 14, required traversing open ground toward heavy German machine-gun fire. MacArthur confessed to the division commander, Major General Charles Menoher, that "he was not certain" his men could take the position. The evening before the assault, Summerall paid a visit to MacArthur's headquarters, telling him, "Give me Châtillon, or a list of five thousand casualties." MacArthur, never at a loss for words, responded, "If this brigade does not capture Châtillon, you can publish a casualty list of the entire brigade with the brigade commander's name at the top."[5]

It was an emotional moment for two veteran soldiers. Both had helped form the Rainbow Division, and now it was about to undertake its most difficult operation of the war. After MacArthur made his declaration, "tears sprang into General Summerall's eyes. He was evidently so moved he could say nothing. He looked at me for a few seconds and then left without a word." MacArthur and the men in his brigade probably slept poorly that night. Not only did German artillery pound the American positions well into the morning but a constant rain would have made rest nearly impossible.

At eight a.m. on October 14, the Rainbow Division jumped off with support of a rolling barrage. The 83rd Brigade was commanded by Brigadier General Michael Lenihan, who was popular with his men but indecisive in combat. Lenihan's brigade was in the lead and at first encountered light resistance, but heavy machine-gun fire from the front and on both flanks halted the troops about a mile from their first objective. MacArthur's 84th Brigade also met heavy fire from the entrenched enemy, but his regiments kept fighting on and captured the crest of Hill 288. Most of the Germans there were killed, although about one hundred lucky ones survived as POWs. It was a costly battle for MacArthur's brigade. Casualties were heavy and it was difficult to transport wounded doughboys to the rear because a lack of roads rendered ambulances impractical, so mules and hand litters were used instead. Intense casualties notwithstanding, the objective of Châtillon Hill was not met, and the 42nd had to try again the next day, which they did with the same results.

On MacArthur's left, the 83rd Brigade was attempting to clear the villages of St. Georges and Landres-et-St.-Georges. If both brigade commanders succeeded, the Kriemhilde Stellung would be in American hands. Fighting with the 83rd on that chilly, rainy October day was Lieutenant Colonel "Wild Bill" Donovan. Before jumping off, he buckled his Sam Browne belt and straightened the ribbons hanging from his left breast pocket. One would have thought he was heading to a formal dinner instead of leading a battalion into a battle that was sure to be costly. Normally officers dress down for such occasions, but in this case many of the doughboys about to follow him across no-man's-land had not yet seen action, and he wanted his men to know who was in charge.[6] Donovan's Fighting 69th, now federalized as the 165th Infantry, had a long lineage. As a regiment of the Union Army during the Civil War, it failed to capture Marye's Heights at Fredericksburg in 1864. "Landres-et-St.-George is our Fredericksburg," Chaplain Francis Duffy said, "and the Kriemhilde Stellung is our Marye's Heights."[7]

The evening before the battle, Lieutenant Colonel Donovan sat in a shell hole while a barber shaved his face with a straight razor, his hand shaking each time a German shell landed nearby. Donovan never flinched, even when a hundred yards away a mule-driven machine cart took a direct hit, blowing up the animal and the gun. Beyond, down the ridge, a valley was littered with American and German dead. "They were an awful sight," a doughboy with the Fighting 69th recalled, "in all the grotesque positions of men killed by violence."[8] The next morning the 165th and a regiment from Ohio jumped off on a front three miles wide. Attacking at the same time were the Alabama and Iowa regiment on the right of the line. At first resistance was strong, but the Americans refused to let up, and the Germans were driven back. Yet as the Rainbow Division advanced, German machine guns concealed in the woods let loose and inflicted heavy casualties. Without mortar support, which lost contact with the infantry soon after the attack commenced, the men had to take out the machine-gun nests with their rifles and hand grenades.

Donovan was livid when he learned his infantry had no artillery support. "What the hell is this all about? Where are the mortars?" he exploded at one runner. "Back toward the rear, sir," the young soldier responded. "We lost direction." "If you got up here, why couldn't the rest of them?" Donovan inquired. "I don't know, sir." By late morning the 42nd halted after advancing about two miles to get within four hundred yards of the defenses protecting Landres-et-St.-Georges. In front of the Rainbow "were acres and acres of barbed wire." When the attack resumed later that day the infantry made several attempts to find a passage through the wire, but the German machine guns repulsed the attackers every time. Under the cover of riflemen and machine guns, engineers scrambled forward with clippers to cut the wire—all of them were either killed or wounded. Finally the mortar unit made it to the front and fired hundreds of shells at the wire without making a dent. Donovan called off the attack to wait for support from heavy artillery and tanks.

At dawn the next day the exhausted Rainbow doughboys woke to the sound of eight clanking Renault tanks as they approached the line with several officers in front serving as guides. When the armored vehicles crept within one hundred yards of the wire, German antitank guns blew up one Renault, and the other seven turned around and headed to the rear, never to be seen again.[9]

Captain Harold Riegelman, a V Corps gas operations officer, helped plan gas attacks on the village of Landres-et-St.-Georges and the Bois de Hazois, where fifteen thousand shells containing bromoacetone and chloroacetone, having a combined lachrymal and asphyxiating effect, were launched. This lethal mix of gases remained potent for at least six hours, forcing the Germans to keep their masks on, "thus impairing the efficiency of their fire," Riegelman recorded, "until our men were well out of the trenches and up the slope." Two hours later a battery of sixty projectors, all the corps had in its arsenal, fired drums of phosgene into the village of Landres-et-St.-Georges. Stunned German soldiers were then treated to high-explosive shells. Riegelman boasted in his diary that "any who survived the phosgene were blown to bits by the succeeding blast." At the same time, more carnage was inflicted upon the hapless Germans who were hunkered down in shell holes east of the village. They were hit by "volley after volley" of high-explosive bombs delivered by Stokes mortars.[10]

After the gas attack, an artillery assault with conventional shells began at three thirty and the infantry jumped off five hours later. They were met by two German planes that fired machine guns at the advancing doughboys.[11] That morning Donovan's battalion left the sunken road north of the Maldah Forest and followed an artillery barrage three hundred yards to the front. Besides shell craters, Donovan's men had to step around the remains of American and German soldiers, victims of earlier assaults. No sooner had they advanced than enemy machine-gun fire peppered the ground, with some better-aimed bullets making direct hits. Donovan shouted, "Where the hell is that coming from?" Yet it was obvious that MacArthur's brigade had failed to silence the Côte de Châtillon's guns. Despite the heavy casualties, Donovan urged his men forward until noon, when they could go no farther.

During the attack, Wild Bill was shot in the leg by machine-gun fire. "Smash! I felt like someone had hit me on the back of the leg with a spiked club," he wrote to his wife. "I felt like a log . . . but managed to crawl into my little telephone hole."[12]

Then "we bivouacked in the woods in the triangle Gesnes-Épinon-ville-Eclisfontaine that afternoon. That was a miserable bivouac. My post command consisted of a big canvas tarpaulin spread out on the wet ground, then doubled over in the middle; one-half serving as an insecure roof propped up at the ends with poles and the whole affair

[was] held to the ground with guy ropes. Five or six of us slept under it, our heads up near the fold. The driest spot was in the center (as the sides were open) and being the senior as well as the oldest I received that prize."[13]

By the third day of fighting, Summerall had lost his patience and took it out on the 84th Brigade commander. After MacArthur's heroic stand on the Côte de Châtillon, early on October 15, Summerall went to follow up with the Rainbow's Lenihan. His observations were maddening. On his right Lenihan's brigade occupied the foot of the hill and partly surrounded La Tuilerie Farm. "My worst apprehensions were realized," wrote Summerall. "At division headquarters, I found that the division commander had never left his command post, which was far to the rear, and knew almost nothing of the situation at the front. The commander of the left brigade was confused and completely unstrung. He knew nothing of why the brigade had not advanced and had never left his command post. I saw that he was in no condition to remain in command and decided to relieve him." Lenihan was now gone, but Summerall didn't stop there. He saw the 165th Infantry commander, Colonel Harry Mitchell, and asked why his unit had not attacked. The colonel responded that he didn't know and had not left his command post to find out. He had heard from a couple of young staff officers that most of his regiment was either killed or wounded, and bodies were hung up in the German wire. Summerall learned this was false and relieved Mitchell as well.[14]

MacArthur could easily have been fired, too, but Summerall gave him until six p.m. on October 16 to take the Côte de Châtillon. MacArthur assured him it would be done. He met with his battalion and regimental commanders, and they devised a plan to send one battalion around the rear while others attacked the front. In the desperate situation, it was their only hope. The fighting started early and lasted for hours, but this time the outcome was different. Châtillon Hill was captured and held by the 84th despite German counterattacks. Supporting the attack with great courage was the 167th Infantry, an Alabama Guard unit that had been in the line for three days and witnessed firsthand the difficult ground of the *côte*. The "atmosphere was tense," wrote the regiment's historian. "Every trail and path in that heavily wooded area of rolling hills was soupy with mud and nearly impassible."[15] Next to them was the 168th, an Iowa regiment. By the end of the day the 167th had made it as far as the German wire protecting the *côté*, although the Germans still controlled two strongpoints, La Musarde and La Tuilerie Farm.[16] At last, the *côte* was in American hands.[17]

MacArthur later recalled that day with satisfaction: "Officers fell and sergeants leaped into the command. Companies dwindled to platoons and corporals took over." Summerall was so happy to hear the great news that he put MacArthur in for the Medal of Honor and a promotion to major general, though Pershing said no to both. MacArthur was, however, awarded his second Distinguished Service Cross. The citation read that MacArthur "displayed indomitable resolution and great courage in rallying broken lines and reforming attacks, thereby making victory possible. On a field where courage was the rule, his courage was the dominant factor."[18]

Major General William Haan's 32nd "Red Arrow" Division attacked to the right of the 42nd Division on October 14, aiming for the Côte Dame Marie. It wasn't expected that Haan's division, exhausted after having been in line supporting attacks elsewhere for a week, could take this heavily fortified hill. All that Pershing hoped for was that the 32nd could hold it long enough to relieve pressure on the 5th Division at Cunel and the Rainbow at the Côte de Châtillon.[19] First, the Red

Arrow would have to make it through the village of Romagne, where the Germans had added on to an old Roman fortress, set up a dressing station, and built a railway station outside of town to bring in supplies.[20]

After jumping off on October 14 behind a rolling barrage, the relentless troops clawed their way up the slopes of the hill, "weaving in and out through the wire." Approaching Romagne, they were surrounded by machine-gun fire, but the brave doughboys didn't let up. More and more of the Red Arrow division drove through Romagne, forcing the Germans through the village, where some took cover in a civilian cemetery. As the Red Arrow Division approached the Côte Dame Marie and attempted a frontal assault, the Germans threw them back. Resourceful, the attackers went around the German flanks, cut through the wire, and engaged in a hand-to-hand battle on the *côte*. Additional waves of Americans scurried up the hill, taking brief cover in ravines, then rushed to aid the soldiers fighting ahead of them. The battle lasted all day and resumed the next as the Germans tried to regain ground they had lost. But in the end, Haan's men held the Côte Dame Marie.[21]

Major General Summerall ordered the 32nd Division to remain in line and advance to the Bois de Bantheville, which some of the Red Arrow reached five days later. The division was now worn-out from heavy combat, and on October 17, General Haan asked Summerall to relieve the unit. "I have received a number of reports from the front today which convince me that my division is exhausted, and to push it any further might result in disaster."[22] A day later Summerall sent Major General William Wright's 89th Division to the Bois de Bantheville and replaced the 32nd. As they poured into the woods from the Sommerance-Romagne Road on the night of October 18–19, the 89th was greeted by a thousand rounds of high-explosive German shells, as well as another one hundred or so shells of various types of gas, including phosgene and mustard.[23] At around the same time, as the 32nd vacated the woods, the Germans got even with Haan's doughboys for taking the Côte Dame Marie by endlessly shelling them over two days. Regiments of the 32nd grew disorganized as men straggled and became intermingled while running from the woods, leaving their dead alongside fallen German soldiers.[24] Summerall ordered the 89th to hold on to this part of the front, which they did while enduring heavy casualties for the next ten days. It was from here that Wright's men would play a key role in attacking the Meuse Heights during the Meuse-Argonne's next phase.

On the I Corps front, the 82nd and 77th had emerged from the Argonne and attacked the Germans near the village of St. Juvin, which was along the Aire and included in the enemy outpost positions. On October 14, St. Juvin was taken by the New Yorkers and with it a large number of German prisoners, but the 82nd had not secured the hills until the fifteenth, when one of its machine-gun companies stopped a vicious counterattack.[25]

After preparing his divisions for the latest attack, Pershing moved out of his Souilly office to make way for the new commander, but much to Liggett's dismay he did not stray very far. Even though he now had the opportunity to spend more time at Chaumont and Paris and attend to AEF affairs, Pershing much preferred to be nearer to the Argonne front so that he could keep watch over the battle, and he made himself a constant fixture at First Army headquarters. "General Pershing is still around at his office on the train and butting into details," an exasperated Stackpole recorded in his diary, "with numerous changes of mind." When he did leave Souilly, Pershing relied on aide Major Edward Bowditch Jr. "to receive reports and to ask [Stackpole about] everything General Liggett does."[26]

Pershing's meddling also bothered Liggett. The First Army commander, who had responsibility for over a million men, eventually told the AEF commander to provide him with his vision for First Army in a directive and "[I] would do all that was humanly possible to carry [it] out."[27] Liggett would learn that even though he was in command of the main tactical unit fighting in Meuse-Argonne, it was still Pershing's battle and he was the subordinate.

14

NOW WE ARE
MAKING HEADWAY

With the battle progressing at a steady pace and the tide turning in First Army's favor after piercing the Kriemhilde Stellung, Pershing ordered the press to ramp up the news to publicize the recent success. More and more correspondents were given permission to visit the Argonne front. Black Jack assigned two American soldiers to work at the Bar-le-Duc post office and help French operators transmit news stories more quickly. The Signal Corps did its part by laying a special American cable under the English Channel that linked London with the western front. Stories were then transmitted from the British capital to the United States.

In Bar-le-Duc, the bar at the Metz et Commerce Hotel was filled with doughboys on leave who were plied with drinks by news-hungry reporters looking for scoops for their hometown papers. One reporter was seen with a Baedeker travel book to use in "describing destroyed or un-destroyed villages and towns, regardless if he had actually seen such places." Reporters complained that people at home weren't getting the truth about the battle; the stories weren't gruesome enough. So correspondents would visit field hospitals "listening to the groans of wounded or the ramblings of the shell-shocked." According to one newsman, they "craved blood and horrors." By mid-October Meuse-Argonne was a fluid operation with few pitched battles. This meant reporters had to cover a vast area of several hundred square miles to uncover news. Thomas Johnson said, "Covering the world's greatest battle was the hardest job American newspapermen had during the war."[1]

American newspapers were also responsible for reporting casualties. They were fed lists of dead and wounded by the Committee on Public Information (CPI) in Washington. It was a monumental task for an agency that had been in business for only slightly over a year. Each list had to be checked and rechecked to assure that the names of dead soldiers were correct. CPI also had to know how to contact the nearest next of kin, "so that relations of other soldiers bearing the same name will not be unduly worried."[2] The lists were sent to the American Red Cross Casualty Bureau in New York City, and the organization contacted the deceased soldier's family directly.

Due to the high number of casualties and the rapid turnover of wounded at the hospitals, First Army had trouble maintaining accurate statistics. By mid-October the AEF's surgeon general reported to Pershing that the base hospitals were overcrowded and wounded men had to wait for beds. On a single day, 1,453 casualties were announced to the war correspondents. The First Army press officer conceded that so far during the offensive "there was no glamour to this advance. It was merely a mixture of death, desolation and drudgery."[3]

In many cases it took weeks for the updated casualty lists to get published, due to delays in transmitting the names from France. At the War Department in Washington, Army Chief of Staff Major General

Peyton C. March blamed the delays on the longer period it took to fact-check at the AEF Central Records Office in France. To no one's surprise there were often errors in the reporting. Men perfectly healthy were reported to be patients in field hospitals. Such was the case for Major William D. Alexander, the son of the 77th Division commander. Major Alexander had been wounded in August 1918, and was sent home for duty in Washington; yet he remained on the casualty rolls some weeks later.[4] More egregious were two hundred men the Red Cross reported as missing. Their relatives had already been notified before the soldiers were found to be alive.[5] Some of the blame for mistaken identity was due to the nature of warfare in the Meuse-Argonne. When a doughboy was badly mangled or decapitated by artillery shells, his remains were often unidentifiable, and the only information the burial parties had to go on was a soldier's round aluminum ID tag, or dog tag, introduced by the Army General Staff in 1913.[6] Each soldier was given a set so if he was killed on the battlefield, one tag was nailed to a temporary grave maker and the other sent back to the command post. The tag was stamped with the soldier's name, rank, and regiment.

Dog tags may have helped identify fallen soldiers, but burial parties had the most difficult job at the front, and their work was heavily scrutinized. To speed up the burial process, Colonel J. W. Grissinger, First Army chief surgeon, said that one company of Pioneer Infantry troops should be assigned to each division. "They are to be used for no other purpose than burial of the dead—men and animals." He further recommended that "they follow up the advancing combatant troops as closely as possible and bury the dead as they find them."[7] First Army followed his advice and placed the burial details under the division chaplains. One of them was Reverend Eugene McLaurin, who left his Presbyterian congregation in Edna, Texas, about one hundred miles southeast of Austin, to serve as a noncommissioned chaplain with a 90th Division supply train.

During the Meuse-Argonne, Chaplain McLaurin led his division's burial details. Carrying grave markers, he would take his men through the muddy battlefields, under the threat of shrapnel and gas attack, to meet with the Graves Registration Service units to administer the burial of both American and German dead. Often the work was carried out at night, when there was less threat of attack. During one of his trips to the front McLaurin encountered "body after body of German soldiers." He recorded in this diary that "most of them were killed by shell fire—our barrage, but a few of them, I noticed had died from our infantry. They had stuck by their machine guns until the very last. And in many a machine gun pit was the body of its last defender."[8]

McLaurin and other chaplains were obligated to bury the German dead, but there were instances when doughboys took souvenirs from deceased Germans before digging their graves. After combat near Châtel Chéhéry, the 82nd Division burial details proceeded to dig graves for German corpses. An inspector general with the burial party reported that the "pockets of all these dead had been turned out, every pocket was rifled and it was perfectly evident that our soldiers had robbed the German dead. Over 200 bodies were buried."[9]

By the third week of October, Liggett's First Army divisions were invigorated and progressing well. On the night of October 21, the 90th Division under General Allen entered the line to relieve the 5th Division, which had made some headway over the past few days and now held the Bois des Rappes. On October 22, the 90th was the only division to attack against the Freya Stellung to gain a good jump-off position for a general attack Pershing ordered the following week.[10] With support on the left from the 89th, holding the Bois de Bantheville, while a regiment of the 90th held the Bois des Rappes, Allen's 179th

Brigade stormed Bantheville and captured it, suffering only twenty casualties.[11] Three days later the Germans counterattacked, first with artillery fire, then with an infantry assault that was repulsed by the 90th with heavy losses. Undaunted, the next day the Germans attempted a second counterattack, which was again driven back by grenades after close fighting. For the next week the Germans continued without letup with sniper and trench mortar fire, which reached the rear areas. POWs captured by the 90th revealed they served with the 132nd Division, which had fought against the 90th at St. Mihiel.

In Hines's IV Corps sector, 5th Division made a strong showing when it seized the Bois des Rappes, along with 150 German prisoners, while the 3rd Division captured Hills 297 and 299. Hines told his diary that "the men are now undoubtedly beginning to feel their own power."[12] During the most recent attack the heaviest combat took place around Grandpré, an area that was heavily contested since the Meuse-Argonne had started because it had been "very difficult to get at."[13] The latest to try and take this "formidable objective" was the 78th, a draft division with men from New Jersey, northern Pennsylvania, and Delaware. They relieved Alexander's 77th Division, exhausted after both the Lost Battalion tribulation and almost a month in combat. At one point Alexander thought his men had Grandpré, but they couldn't hold it. Now it was up to the 78th, under Major General James H. McRae, another of Pershing's West Point classmates, and his untested men, who had been on the western front only since early June. McRae was a tough commander who, according to his chief of staff, Colonel Charles D. Herron, "feared neither God, man, nor the Devil or General Pershing either."[14] The Lightning Division, as the 78th called itself, fought a hand-to-hand battle over four days, but the Germans would not budge.

It was not until October 27 that McRae could report to Pershing that Grandpré was now in American hands, including the shattered town and the cliff on which it stood, known as the Citadel.[15] Seven days later, the 78th's position on the Aire River south of Grandpré and St. Juvin was taken over by the 6th, a division of mostly regulars that had not seen combat lately. Led by Major General Walter H. Gordon, who had yet to prove himself, the 6th was most recently held in a quiet sector in the Vosges Mountain range, a twenty-six-hour train ride to the city of Sainte-Ménehould, south of the Argonne.[16]

On the Second Army front, Pershing had yet to give Bullard the go-ahead for a major offensive. Bullard was growing restless, and so were his men. To keep the Germans guessing about where he would eventually attack, he sent small units on raids and patrols against enemy outposts. For the most part these were minor operations against German regiments protecting the path to the Briey iron fields and Metz, an objective not met during St. Mihiel. During the last two weeks of October, Second Army conducted three hundred of these missions and in the process collected three hundred prisoners.

Bullard's Second Army was given its own Air Service, the 4th Pursuit Group. Only one of the group's squadron's saw action, the 141st Aero Squadron, led by Captain Hobart Amory Hare "Hobey" Baker, a star hockey and football player at Princeton. On October 28, Baker was leading a patrol of three SPAD XIIIs over the lines when they spotted a formation of sixteen Fokkers heading southeast in the direction of Pont-à-Mousson. The gutsy Baker broke formation and headed toward the enemy planes, engaging them in a dogfight at fourteen thousand feet. He squeezed his machine gun's trigger and a solid burst of thirty rounds sent one of the Fokkers on a downward spiral. Baker then went after the other German planes but had to give up when his machine guns jammed. The two other American planes tried to help out, but their aim was poor and the Fokkers went on the offensive.

Outnumbered eight to one, Baker wisely ordered the patrol back to its home field, and luckily the Germans did not give chase. The entire engagement lasted ten minutes.[17]

On October 30, Second Army conducted a ground attack that involved the 56th Infantry Brigade, detached from 28th Division, with support from the 134th Field Artillery Regiment, under the command of forty-six-year-old Colonel Harold M. Bush.* The purpose was to eliminate German machine-gun nests harassing Bullard's troops near the village of Haumont-lès-Lachaussée. Before the infantry jumped off that morning, Bush's regiment exchanged fire with German artillery hidden in the Bois de Bonseil, a cluster of trees near the machine guns. "The sounds of our guns and the steady singing of the shells as they passed overhead raised our spirits a hundred percent," the 134th regimental historian wrote, "for we had all the confidence in the world in the men behind those guns."[18] As the morning wore on, the artillery duel became more intense, with the German guns piercing the American communication lines. Runners were sent forward at great peril to repair the wire. But no sooner were the connections reattached than more enemy fire, directed by observation planes, cut other parts of the line.

The 134th swept the woods with a barrage to quiet the German artillery, but enemy counter-battery continued. The German guns had little impact on the American artillery, however. They "tried in vain" to locate the 134th's guns, "but their shells dropped harmlessly in vacant areas." By late morning the Germans stopped firing, and it was now safe for the regiments of 56th Brigade to attack. The infantry

---

* Also serving in the Meuse-Argonne was President George H. W. Bush's father, and Harold's brother, Captain Prescott S. Bush. He was an information officer with the 158th Field Artillery of the 83rd Division from Ohio.

quickly overran and captured the machine-gun nests. German prisoners were brought to the rear with American bayonets pointed at their backs.[19]

Bullard also had at his disposal the African American 92nd Division. The unit had acquired a bad reputation after falling apart at Binarville in early October, and now Bullard didn't have much faith in their ability to fight. He was of the opinion that African American troops could not be trusted, an attitude shared by many white Regular Army officers. Born in Alabama, Bullard was originally given the name William until he changed it to Robert Lee, after the Confederate icon. Bullard complained in his diary that doughboys of the 92nd Division "have been unable to make a single raid upon the enemy. They are really inferior soldiers: there is no denying it."[20] Bullard later lamented that "the Negro cannot stand bombardment."[21]

While the infantry fought tenaciously, the division commanders continued to protest that their advance was hampered by the fact that the Air Service wasn't providing enough cover. Colonel Conrad S. Babcock, a regimental commander in the 89th Division, complained that "enemy shelling was fairly constant and widely scattered over the area. The trees had lost most of their leaves and enemy planes had little difficulty locating our lines in the too densely populated woods, which increased casualties." The "planes flew over us at all hours and often our own planes were up at the same time," Babcock wrote after the war, "but we never saw them fight each other. It made the foot soldiers furious to see our planes flying about, burning gasoline and doing nothing; that is, nothing that helped the soldier in the trenches or foxholes."[22]

Major General Duncan of the 82nd was with his troops near the village of St. Juvin in mid-October when a group of German Fokkers swarmed over his men. Duncan at first couldn't figure out how the Germans were able to fly in the poor conditions of fog and mist, and then wondered why First Army Air Service wasn't chasing after them. Duncan complained by telegram to Billy Mitchell, who responded with a lengthy reply the next day. Sensitive to criticism, he told Duncan, "It is practically impossible for us to keep all enemy planes away from our sector. To expect this would be like expecting our artillery to prevent a single shell from falling on our sector." He assured Duncan that "we are doing our best to help the infantry in any way we can."[23]

Despite the constant criticism levied against him by the ground troops, these were exciting times for Brigadier General Mitchell, and he was as self-confident as ever. More than a few eyebrows were raised when he showed up at meetings wearing pink breeches and a non-regulation blouse with outside pockets. "He didn't walk like other men," aviator Fred Schrauss recalled. He took "pride in every movement. Even if he had only eight or ten feet to walk, he went at it as though he were marching a mile, and was late. He moved at top speed." Mitchell also drove the same way. Behind the wheel of a Renault racer, provided for his use by the French government, his chauffeur in the backseat, Mitchell pushed the car to ninety miles per hour, motoring from one airfield to another.

Pershing wasn't much interested in Mitchell and his antics, but he remained concerned about his other corps commanders and sent them "some observations, made while commanding the 1st Army and at other times." He addressed issues that covered liaison and the lack of communication between brigade and regimental officers, the failure to reduce enemy machine-gun nests through flanking movements and rifle power. Pershing also pointed out problems with not following through with attack plans, discipline, straggling, even concerns about not properly feeding the troops or caring for the horses. Pershing correctly surmised that many of these difficulties stemmed from the inexperience of young officers and their lack of self-confidence. He urged the division commanders to impress upon them a sense of "decision, aggressiveness and leadership."

Pershing told his commanders "that my sole purpose in writing the above is, by friendly suggestion and perhaps some criticism, to help you, if possible, to meet the great responsibility that rests upon you." His intended audience didn't have to read between the lines to understand that these so-called observations were in reality Pershing's subtle way of saying, "Either follow my instructions, or else." Pershing attached a copy of the memo to a sternly worded letter addressed to each corps commander. "As corps commander," he told Hines, Summerall, and Dickman, "the obligation that rests upon you to increase and maintain the effectiveness of divisions and other troops under your command, of course, must appeal to you strongly, and my only purpose in writing is to give you my personal support. In speaking of the duties of your position, may I not assert that only by the most constant and vigilant oversight and well-ordered direction can the best results be obtained." Furthermore, Pershing reminded them, "it is the corps commander himself who must be held responsible for the success or failure of his troops."[24]

15

THE END IS NEAR

I f Pershing's memo didn't make his corps commanders take notice, his latest round of cleaning out deadweight at the command level certainly did. "Commanders of all grades were falling beneath the sickle of dismissal," as one historian phrased it, "almost as fast as their men beneath the scythe of the enemy machine-guns."[1] One of them was the 5th Division's John E. McMahon, a West Point classmate of Pershing's who, though a bit younger than the AEF chief, looked much older. Pershing accused McMahon of withdrawing one of his brigades from a salient that should have been held. Major General Hines of III Corps inspected the division and didn't like what he saw. "Jumpy," is what he told his diary. Furthermore, he recorded, "It appears that the entire 5th Div. has been used by piling in all remaining reserves, elements are crowded and disorganized," and "they cannot advance."[2] McMahon looked tired, and the strain of the battle made him appear even older. Regardless of their history, in Pershing's mind-set McMahon had to go. In addition, Beaumont Buck of the 3rd Division was blamed for bringing up his reserves unnecessarily, as well as for the poor quality of his unit. After meeting with Buck at the front, Pershing decided at that moment that he, too, was a goner. McMahon was replaced by the 2nd Division's Hanson Ely, while Preston Brown, the IV Corps chief of staff, took over for Buck.

By far the most controversial relief was that of 26th Division's Major General Clarence Edwards. The 26th was one of the AEF's most experienced divisions and most recently performed well at St. Mihiel, but Pershing questioned Edwards's efficiency and thought his division could be even better. Liggett especially didn't like him, which meant he had no allies in First Army. What tipped the scales against Edwards was a recent incident when doughboys from his division fraternized with two German prisoners as Stackpole put it, who came over "to make friends with our men, who had shot them." Edwards downplayed the affair in his report to Liggett, not referring to what had happened as fraternization, but "a very friendly talk between the Germans and our men on peace, etc., and prospects of saving blood by armistice."[3] Liggett fired off a letter to Edwards, telling him, "To my mind, this constitutes a flagrant case of the most insidious and dangerous propaganda we have run up against, its intent being to weaken the fighting determination of our men."[4] Furthermore, as Stackpole recalled, Liggett also told Edwards "to have his men shoot at once instead of parley."[5] As soon as Pershing found out what Edwards had done, he ordered Chief of Staff McAndrew to send out a letter of relief.

After having been relieved as V Corps commander and given a second chance as the head of the 4th Division, Major General Cameron was also fired, sent home with a downgrade in rank. He asked Liggett to intervene, and they met at Souilly. During a "rather long conference," Cameron complained that Pershing was unfair. He had tried to talk with the commander in chief about the tired conditions of his troops, but Pershing "did not want to hear" it. Liggett was repulsed by his moaning, and Cameron left the meeting a beaten man. Stackpole overheard the conversation and called him "a treacherous eel."

Pershing's disdain for incompetent commanders was in many ways little different from the view many of the British and French leaders had of him. Field Marshal Sir Douglas Haig complained in his diary about the "inexperience and ignorance" the American staff officers showed when it came to the "needs of a modern attacking force." British chief of the Imperial General Staff, Field Marshal Sir Henry Wilson, had worse things to say: "The state of chaos the fool [Pershing] has got his troops into down in the Argonne is indescribable." Furthermore, Wilson referred to Pershing as "a vain, ignorant, weak ASS."[6] But this was nothing compared to what Prime Minister Clemenceau wrote. The Tiger wanted desperately to rid the western front of Pershing and he made this painfully clear in a long, rambling message to Marshal Foch on October 21. Clemenceau warned there was a "crisis existing in the American Army." While "the French Army and British Army, without a moment's respite, have been daily fighting . . . our worthy American allies, who thirst to get into action and who are unanimously acknowledged to be great soldiers, have been marking time ever since their forward jump on the first day; and in spite of heavy losses, they have failed to conquer the ground assigned them as their objective." Now, Clemenceau believed, it was "certainly high time to tell President Wilson the truth and the whole truth concerning the situation of the American troops. Indeed, neither you nor I have the right to conceal it from him."[7]

Foch had little affection for Clemenceau, so it was convenient for him to defend Pershing. Noting that there was "no denying the magnitude of the effort made by the American Army," Foch pointed out that "after attacking at St. Mihiel on September 12, it attacked in the Argonne on the 26th." Pershing's troops had struck the Germans "over particularly difficult terrain and in the face of serious resistance by the enemy." Reaction by the Americans to Clemenceau's letter, which Foch shared, was not surprising. Major General James Harbord, Pershing's closest friend in the AEF, thought that Clemenceau was "writing about things of which he had been ignorant even in his splendid prime." Secretary of War Baker crowed that "it would be a long time before any American commander would be removed by any European premier." Pershing called it a "political gesture designed to minimize American prestige at the peace conference."[8] Yet when Pershing and Clemenceau met shortly after the letter was leaked, the French prime minister showered praise on the AEF commander for the fine conduct his army had recently displayed.[9]

Even if Clemenceau and Foch had tried to persuade President Wilson that Pershing should be relieved, the plan would have backfired. Wilson had little interest in the Army's affairs, either in Washington or overseas. Military matters were left up to Baker, who had become quite fond of First Army during his recent trip to the western front. He told a reporter that "at Meuse-Argonne, the American Army had shown it is irresistible and this spirit is unconquerable. It was a smiling army that now made France brown with the khaki American uniform. In hospitals, in the trenches," wherever Baker went as he toured the front, "he found the troops smiling and doing their work with enthusiasm."[10]

Pershing also found himself in a bit of hot water when he attended a conference of Allied commanders at Senlis on October 25 to discuss recent German peace feelers. Tempers flared when the topic of an armistice was brought to the table. Sir Douglas Haig, whose armies to the north of Paris, including two American divisions, had breached the Hindenburg Line but still met stiff German counterattacks, pushed the other commanders to consider lenient armistice terms that were more acceptable to the Germans than the Allies. Haig's troops were bloodied and tired and he just wanted the war over. Pershing, Foch and Pétain downplayed Haig's opinion. The Germans were beaten, they said, but were hanging on to secure the best terms for an armistice. Pershing argued for unconditional surrender, the same terms his hero Ulyssess Grant demanded during the Civil War. Black Jack also voiced his concern that the Germans would use the armistice as a respite from the fighting, then regroup for another effort at victory on the battlefield.

The conference adjourned with no clear solution, although Pershing continued his insistence that the Allies strike the hard hand of war against the Germans. Colonel Clark wrote, "Pershing is the biggest man that the war has produced and should play a leading role at the peace table." Foch and Pershing were absolutely correct about the German Army's ability to keep fighting the war. Sensing defeat, in late September Ludendorff went to Hindenburg's quarters and warned that it was only a matter of time before the Americans would break through and that they must seek an armistice. Hindenburg reflected on the dire situation in his memoirs: "It was plain the situation could not last. Our armies were too weak and too tired. Moreover, the pressure which the American masses were putting on the most sensitive point in the region of the Meuse was too strong."[11]

German Army staff officer Lieutenant Colonel Herman von Giehrl wrote that by the end of October German troops "weren't being replaced by reserves and many of them had not been issued a proper meal, allowed to bathe and delouse for weeks. Morale was shattered and remained that way until the armistice." A major reason for the disenchantment in the lines, according to Giehrl, "were the German troops who had recently arrived from the Eastern Front after Russia capitulated." This included Polish troops who had fought with the Russians and were now forced to serve with the Germans. They "had been exposed too long to the destroying influence of the Russian Revolution and Bolshevist propaganda."

The veteran troops and their "opinions poisoned the character of the Army of the West, which previously had been pretty good." It didn't help that German newspapers printed articles about the potential surrender of their homeland in the eastern German provinces. They had no desire to continue fighting for Germany. Some Landwehr regiments refused to enter the line and were punished as a result. First Army only made enemy spirits plummet even more with steadily harassing artillery.[12] If these weren't enough testaments to prove that the German Army was in decline, news that the kaiser forced Ludendorff to resign on October 26 certainly drove this point home. Hindenburg, who was with his companion that day, also offered to quit, but the kaiser refused the gesture, since he was still valuable to the German people.[13] Many felt that the kaiser would also abdicate, but he refused. Further diminishing the German will to fight were the naval mutinies that erupted in Kiel and spread to Berlin.[14] Then there were the constant food shortages that resulted from the British Royal Navy's blockade of ports in the North Sea.

On the evening of October 30, Colonel T. Bentley Mott was dining with Foch at Bombon when the meal was interrupted by a message from Pershing, directing him to see the AEF commander in Paris immediately. Mott recalled that when he arrived "at the Rue de Varenne I was shown up to his bedroom, where I found him in a dressing gown pacing the floor. Without any preliminary he handed me a paper and asked me to sit down and read it." Pershing "continued to walk backwards and forwards from floor to window, most of the time swearing under his breath and occasionally letting out a furious ejaculation.

Seeing me look up enquiringly, he said: 'Don't pay any attention to my language. I have had a horrible tooth-ache all day. The dentist has been here three times and the only thing he can offer by way of relief is to propose an opiate. I have too much need of all my senses to accept that, so the best I can do is swear. It seems to relieve me a little bit.'" The paper handed to Mott was a letter addressed to Foch and dealing with the question of the terms to be demanded of the Germans in case they asked for an armistice.[15]

In the letter, Pershing outlined thirteen points for consideration of surrender, all of which is summarized in point thirteen: "I believe that complete victory can only be obtained by continuing the war until we force unconditional surrender from Germany; but if the allied Governments decide to grant an armistice, the terms should be so rigid that under no circumstances could Germany again take up arms."[16] Pershing remained in Paris with Charles Dawes by his side, still feeling ill with what he described as the grippe. In actuality it was a bout of flu he could not seem to shake.

Pershing was well enough to send off a copy of the peace plan letter to the Supreme War Council, which made President Wilson furious. Pershing had clearly overstepped his authority. What was more, he had incorrectly assumed that the president would agree with his argument for a negotiated peace. In fact, Wilson's peace plan was more in line with Haig's. The president had already dispatched his chief adviser, Colonel Edward M. House—the title of "colonel" was a nickname; House had no military experience—to meet with the council when they next convened in Paris.

House wrote in his diary: "I cannot understand General Pershing's extraordinary communication. . . . Everyone believes it is a political document and a clear announcement of his intention to become a candidate for the Presidency in 1920."[17] Furthermore, House raged, "I wonder whether he actually knows that he is dealing with a political rather than a military question?" As a matter of protocol, Pershing should have sent his recommendations to House. Instead, it appeared that Black Jack was interfering in political affairs. Pershing backed off and informed House he was only offering military advice and not creating policy on behalf of the president. After Secretary of War Baker was told what his commander had done, he drafted a letter of reprimand, and the matter ended there.

As October came to a close, aviator Eddie Rickenbacker was busy keeping the skies clear of Germans by scoring his final two victories of the war, numbers twenty-five and twenty-six. Rickenbacker thought he had brought down two additional German planes, but they were never confirmed. Frank Luke, his only rival ace, had been dead for about a month, and no other airman would top Rickenbacker's record. His next-to-last conquest occurred while flying toward Grandpré when he was spotted by two Fokkers. Rickenbacker was almost over the town of Emecourt when the Germans approached about a half mile from the east, "like lambs to the slaughter." Rickenbacker waited for the right moment to strike. He let them pass and then immediately "dipped over, swung around, fell and opened up his motor piqued with all speed on the tail of the nearest Fokker" and fired twenty rounds, "all of which poured full into the center of the fuselage."

Rickenbacker removed his hand from the gun's trigger "and watched the Fokker drop helplessly to earth." He saw the other Fokker dive toward the ground and didn't pursue him since he was well within German lines. His next and final kill took place on the way home. Flying over St. Georges, he saw under his right wing an observation balloon on the edge of the little village. It was easy pickings. Rickenbacker flew within a hundred feet of the "sleeping Drachen" and let go with both guns, spraying bullets up and down the length of the gasbag.

As he flew away, Rickenbacker could see "the towering flames light up the sky with a vivid glare."[18]

Rickenbacker's scores were a fitting end to what had started out as a difficult October for Pershing's warriors, but the month ended with great optimism. First and Second Armies were poised to strike on an extended front to launch what was hoped would be the final blow by shredding what remained of the Kriemhilde Stellung and seizing the elusive Meuse Heights. More than 18,000 of Gallwitz's men had been taken prisoner and 370 of his artillery guns had been captured by the Americans, along with 1,000 machine guns and countless other weapons and war material.[19] Fearing for their jobs, Pershing's commanders complied with his demands not to let up when attacking. They were pushing their men hard, keeping in close contact with them at the front. The doughboys responded by performing as well as any veteran British or French soldiers.

On the Champagne front, Major General Smith's 36th Division was still engaged in support of Fourth French Army. Since the first week of October the Germans hadn't budged much beyond the Aisne, and they continually skirmished with American and French soliders holding ground near the town of Blanc Mont. During an attack on October 26, eight members of the Choctaw tribe, who were serving with the 142nd Infantry Regiment of the 36th Division, used a form of code talking over the field telephones to help safely relieve two companies from the front. Aware that German intelligence officers had tapped into the American phone lines, the 142nd's commander knew that any messages sent to the front telling the companies when it was safe to withdraw would be intercepted and his men likely captured or killed. To outwit the enemy, he employed the Choctaws to send messages in code to be translated from "the Indian's vocabulary of military terms." The Choctaw term for *big gun* was substituted for *artillery*, while *little gun shoots fast* was used for *machine gun*. Battalions were referred to with the phrase *one, two, and three grains of corn*. The messages transmitted by the Choctaws completely baffled the Germans, and the two companies of the 142nd made it safely back to the rear.[20]

American troops had performed impressively during the Meuse-Argonne in almost every aspect, and even Marshal Foch could not help but applaud their evolution over the past several weeks. Not since St. Mihiel had he offered Pershing any form of praise about First Army, but now he marveled at the "ability shown by commanders and the energy and bravery of the troops."[21] Major Clark passed on to Pershing the glowing acclaim of General Edmond Buat: the French Army chief of staff, ecstatic over the recent First Army operations, told Clark, "It is work of the first order, it is superfine; it shows excellent management and will continue I am sure."

Liggett felt that way, too, and prepared First Army for a general attack, the largest since September 26. "Every effort was now made to profit by past experiences," he wrote, "and to encourage the fighting spirit of the Army."[22] The French Fourth Army would attack at the same time in Champagne, as they did on the opening day of the battle. Liggett motored to General Gouraud's headquarters to see when his troops would be ready to advance. Pershing wanted the attack to commence on October 28, but First Army wasn't ready—and neither was Gouraud. When the French general was told of Pershing's orders, he threw up his only hand and exclaimed, "I can't possibly move before November 2, the army simply can't be made ready an hour earlier."[23] As it turned out, starting the battle a few days late made no difference at all.

16

FIRST ARMY
HAS COME OF AGE

L iggett divided the operational plan into three stages: first, the attack on November 1, then a pursuit as the Germans fell back, and last, the crossing of the Meuse. "Morale of the First Army was very high," Liggett recorded, "and all were eager to advance. . . . [T]his confidence had permeated through the whole Army, and nobody had any doubts about the success of the coming drive."[1] It was going to be a frontal attack, straight at the German lines, just like the opening offensive on September 26. The only difference was that First Army had come of age, and as Liggett pointed out, they were secure in their knowledge that the Germans were on their last legs. One last thrust would take care of the battle and the war. Everything was coming together.

There was no shortage of supplies. Harbord's SOS "was at last getting its stride across France," as journalist Thomas M. Johnson noted. Sixteen ports were busy day and night unloading cargo shipped from the United States for immediate delivery to the Meuse-Argonne.[2] Liggett's only real concern was that he would not have use of two of the strongest First Army divisions. The week before, when Foch requested two American divisions to fight with the French Sixth Army in Flanders, Pershing sent him the 37th Buckeye and the 91st Wild West divisions as a gesture of goodwill.[3] They remained in Belgium for the rest of the war.

Foch showed great confidence in the Americans, telling Pershing that the objectives were not limited. "Troops thrown in the attack," the marshal instructed, "have only to know their direction of attack. On this direction they advance as far as possible, attacking and maneuvering against the enemy who resists, without any attempts at alignment, the most advanced units working to assist the advance of those who are momentarily halted."[4]

One key to the assault was American artillery, which up to now had had limited impact on the battle. The main blow would take place in the center of the German line by Summerall's V Corps, with Lejeune's 2nd Division leading the attack, well rested after fighting with French Fourth Army at Blanc Mont, followed by Wright's 89th Division. Summerall pointedly asked Lejeune how far he expected his division to advance on the first day. Lejeune, who knew that Summerall had previously commanded 1st Division's artillery and had great affection for the big guns, told the corps commander, "I didn't believe any force could withstand the vigor, power, and speed of its initial attack when backed up by well-directed artillery fire." He also boasted that his division "would be able to take and hold the final objective of the day provided one of its flanks was protected by an adjacent division."[5]

In the days leading up to the attack, five fourteen-inch .50-caliber Mark IV naval guns were deployed. Despite their size, the naval guns were so well camouflaged in orchards, woods, and fields that a soldier wouldn't know they were there until he heard their shells discharged.[6] Each gun, weighing eighty thousand pounds, was mounted on a railway truck built by the Baldwin Locomotive Works in Philadelphia. It was later learned that the guns' impact on German morale was significant. Prior to St. Mihiel, the massive cannons had been used sparingly, but three weeks into the Meuse-Argonne, one Mark IV destroyed a rail center in Mortiers.[7] A shell directly hit a German freight train, lifting a boxcar off the tracks and blasting it thirty feet away. Another shell hit a turnip field, uprooting every one of the bulbous vegetables. Even more devastating was the destruction of a movie house in Laon packed with German soldiers. Rescuers found sixty mangled bodies, and only the dog tags of forty others.[8]

Summerall enjoyed popping into command posts unexpectedly. On the evening of November 10 he appeared before the officers of the 6th Marines and emphatically told the battle-hardened veterans of St. Mihiel and Blanc Mont the consequences they would suffer if the assault was anything less than successful. A platoon commander recalled that Summerall "lashed out as though we were raw, erring recruits. If we failed to take a single objective, he said, he would relieve and send to the rear our regimental commander, and even our deeply-admired and respected division commander. It was a strange performance and one resented by all. General Lejeune's call of 'three cheers for General Summerall' was met with stony silence."[9] That night, feeling a bit anxious over the attack, Lejeune wrote his wife, "I pray God that we may win, and end this war by a decisive victory. Many a poor fellow will give his life to his country tomorrow."[10]

November 1 dawned cloudy and foggy, but with no rain, the weather was better than usual on the Argonne front. The Marines expected a hard fight and didn't need Summerall to point that out. They were about to engage six understrength but tenacious regiments of the German

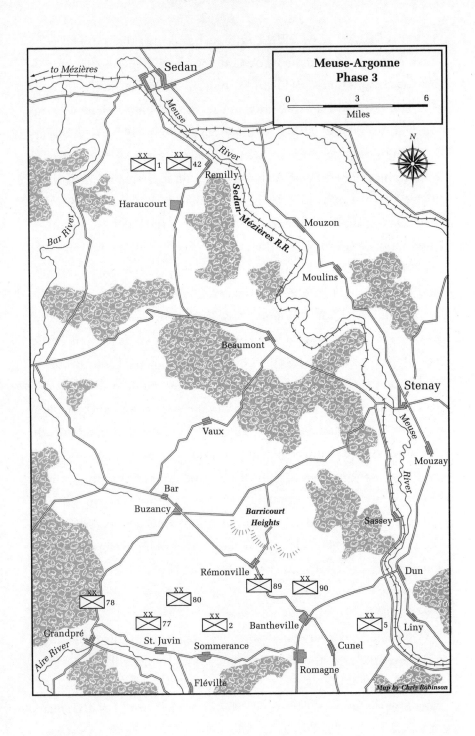

41st and 52nd Divisions, who held a line that ran through the towns Landres and St. Georges. The veteran enemy soldiers were armed with a sizable arsenal of automatic weapons and artillery.[11] The Marines had strength in numbers, but the Germans still maintained the high ground.

Summerall kicked off the attack at three thirty a.m. with a tremendous blast of artillery. More than any other AEF officer, the former artillery brigade commander saw the necessity of having large guns support infantry attacks, and he advised Pershing on the matter, though his recommendation went unheeded.[12] Not only did Summerall's guns pummel enemy positions with high-intensity shells, they inundated German lines with mustard and phosgene gas, catching the enemy by surprise since until now the Americans had been timid in using chemicals.[13] Just before the jump-off, Lejeune moved his men back five hundred yards and had the rolling barrage start from this spot. That way the German machine-gun nests would be destroyed as the Marines attacked. Wright's 89th was to the right of the 2nd, and jumped off in front of some woods, instead of on the edge as the Germans expected. As a result, enemy artillery struck woods that were empty of doughboys.

Rolling along to aid the 2nd Division attack by breaking through the wire were fifteen tanks from the 1st Provisional Tank Company. But the vehicles had little work to do that morning, as the artillery fire effectively blasted away German wire. Other than destroying an occasional machine-gun nest, the tanks were ineffective. By the time Lejeune's Marines reached the Landres-et-St.-Georges Road, only six were still operating. The other nine either broke down or became stuck in trenches and shell holes.[14]

By late evening on November 1, the 2nd had gone five miles and achieved its objective by reaching the Barricourt Heights, while the 89th made it almost as far. As the Americans took over German positions, they discovered that their enemy had poisoned many of the wells. Medical officers purified the water with chemicals, but they left a nauseating taste. As a result, few men drank enough water, and this resulted in dehydration and dysentery.[15] German artillery also gave the leathernecks a tough time, demolishing American guns and killing or severely wounding the crews. Still, morale within the ranks remained high.[16]

At Souilly, First Army staff stood before a large wall map and placed "thumbtacks and red string on places that had seemed once as far away as Berlin." War correspondents gathered next to Colonel Marshall, who "lighted up as he went over with us the colored pencil lines on his own map and talked with happy sureness of where we would be next day."[17] Pershing stayed on board his train, and for the first time in a while kept out of Liggett's way.[18]

In the III Corps sector, the 90th formed a line opposite the Freya Stellung, held in a tight grip by three understrength veteran German divisions: the 28th, 88th, and 107th. They manned positions that included Aincreville, Grand Carré Farm, and Hill 244. Suspecting that an attack against their lines was imminent, the Germans pounded American positions with heavy artillery fire during the early hours of November 1. A Wild West Division regimental post command was destroyed, with twenty-six casualties. Three and a half hours later, American artillery responded and shut down the German guns. Then a brigade of infantry jumped off and immediately drew fire from a "solid nest of machine gunners." Although attempting to go forward in the fog made observation difficult, the thick haze screened the advance of a brigade from the 90th Division so that the Germans couldn't see them coming. By six thirty the brigade had reached the III Corps objective while capturing 719 prisoners, including 14 officers.[19] After five weeks of a steep, costly learning curve, First Army looked polished.

An air of confidence wafted through the ranks, from generals on down to privates. Pershing's warriors seemed invincible.[20]

Showing the tenacity of brave veteran soldiers, the Americans rushed the Germans manning the guns and either captured or killed them with their bayonets. The doughboys then fought their way through the woods and hills that preceded the Freya Stellung. For the next two days the fighting intensified as the Germans withdrew. The enemy fought rearguard actions before escaping across the Meuse, burning the bridges behind them. By November 3, the 90th Division brigades had taken all of the Freya Stellung lines and held the bluffs overlooking the river.[21] Over three days, November 3–5, Ely's 5th Division strode across open ground, and then crossed the Meuse under heavy fire, a movement Pershing considered "brilliant."

Gallwitz observed First Army's impressive assault. Aside from encouraging his tired and depleted troops not to withdraw unless ordered to do so, there was not much else he could do to stem the tide of the American advance. "I clearly saw that the situation could be ameliorated only by counter attacking and throwing the enemy back across the river," Gallwitz wrote after the war. "I lacked artillery enough for such an undertaking, to say nothing of infantry for actual execution of such a plan. All that was left for me, under these circumstances, was to continue to hold out as long as I could."[22]

After keeping abreast of the battle for a few days at Souilly, Pershing had Santini drive him to Paris. Along the way, the chauffeur noted something odd about this trip, as well as other recent excursions to the city. As they drove, the men noticed that the Germans would commence "a long range bombardment or send over a flock of bombing airplanes." No matter what hour of the night or day they reached Paris, the bombardment would begin directly after their arrival and invariably continue for hours. Santini had no idea if the Germans knew when the general was traveling to the city. This was doubtful, since his staff made every effort to keep Pershing's movements a secret.

Due to his illness, Pershing did not see Micheline while in Paris, and she was clearly hurt by his absence. Despite his best efforts to keep his relationship under wraps, rumors of the general's dalliance with a much younger woman were likely widespread within the Army. AEF chief of chaplains Charles Brent, who had been a close friend of Pershing's since their days in the Philippines, was most certainly aware of Miss Resco. In a letter from a 3rd Division chaplain to Brent about morale in the AEF, he asked if a rumor he had heard about Pershing and his mistress was true. Brent, caught off guard by the question, responded that he should keep this matter tight-lipped. "You are quite right in speaking freely to me," Brent advised, "and you will understand that the one reason I do not want your letter to go in the files is because your passage exposes you to criticism of a serious matter."[23]

One of the more remarkable events of the battle of the Meuse-Argonne occurred on November 3. That night, Major General Lejeune permitted the commander of the division's 9th Infantry, Colonel R. O. Van Horn, to lead his regiment into Belval Wood, which lay four miles within the German lines. The regiment moved out at dusk with two thousand men, marching along a narrow road thick with mud. Placed at the head of the column were some doughboys who spoke German. It was pitch-black when the 9th Infantry Regiment finally reached the woods. The bilingual American soldiers quietly snuck up on the enemy. Pretending to be German officers, they lured the startled men from the safety of their dugouts toward the rest of Van Horn's regiment, who took them captive.

Resuming the advance, the 9th crossed a clearing and encountered a large number of Germans digging machine-gun pits by La Forge

Farm. This bunch, however, weren't fooled by the German-speaking Americans, and they grabbed machine guns and fired into the group of doughboys, who charged toward them with only their rifles and bayonets. Vicious hand-to-hand fighting ensued before the Germans retreated to the road in the rear. As the 9th approached the farm, they saw lights flickering from the main building, and heard shouting and singing from within. The Americans rushed through the doorway and the startled, drunk German officers raised their hands to surrender.

As other battalions from the 9th Infantry Regiment arrived at the farm, small groups of Germans appeared from the woods with their arms raised, surrendering. A German sergeant commanding one of the parties spoke to his American captors in perfect English with a New York accent—years before, he had lived in Manhattan and had been on the city's police force.[24] Van Horn sent word to the rear about the capture of 160 Germans.[25]

A great deal of action occurred on November 5. During the night, the 5th Division crossed the Meuse at Dun-sur-Meuse and Brieulles-sur-Meuse and linked up with the 90th Division, which had crossed the river opposite the village of Stenay. The strongly fortified village was to be attacked from the south. Before the war, Stenay had about four thousand inhabitants. Since AEF intelligence thought that many of these people remained, American artillery did not fire upon the town before the infantry charged. According to one war correspondent, "the Americans swept forward against streams of machine-gun bullets and artillery fire from the hills northeast of town. The entire district in the region of Stenay was flooded by the Germans, who dammed the canals and rivers." With the capture of Stenay, the Americans extended their lines northeast of Mouzay, reaching the Bois du Chesnois. The same correspondent reported that the "Germans defended every foot of ground over which the advance was made."[26] All the objectives were reached in the day's fighting, and wherever the enemy attempted to make a stand, he was beaten back by the doughboys.

On the same day, Robert Lee Bullard finally received the orders he had hoped for: Pershing instructed him to prepare Second Army for a major offensive. Second Army was to conduct raids and move toward Briey, in a move that would align forces in the direction of Metz. Pershing made it clear he wanted "the complete destruction of the enemy's armed forces" and set November 14 as the target date for the offensive against Metz. In the meantime, Bullard sent patrols against stubborn German positions, which responded with machine-gun, infantry, and artillery fire. Pershing visited Bullard at his Toul headquarters on November 7 and told him that aerial reconnaissance showed German supply wagons heading toward Metz, which he interpreted to mean an enemy withdrawal from this front.

With more supplies being brought to the front by Harbord's SOS, road congestion remained a serious problem. Pershing told Liggett that during a recent trip to the front he encountered roads that were still jammed with traffic, and warned his First Army commander that he would have difficulty in supplying the divisions. Suggesting that this matter may have slipped by Liggett, Black Jack outlined four points about handling transportation, such as limiting the number of troops in the advance lines to only those actually needed, extending rail facilities, improving the conditions of roads, and, most important, "[instituting] better organization and regulations for handling truck transportation."[27] Pershing failed to take into account that rapid changes to the front were making it difficult for supply trucks to find the divisions. In addition, constant rain kept the roads muddy, while abandoned German material, ammunition, and dead horses created more obstacles.[28]

. . .

Pershing wanted the Americans to capture Sedan and hand it over to the French as a goodwill gesture. The city's importance to the French Army could not be understated. During the 1870 Franco-Prussian War, the Germans had defeated the French in Sedan and in the process arrested their emperor, Louis Napoleon III, a humiliating blow to French pride. To his credit, Black Jack did seek approval from General Paul Maistre, commander of the French Group of Armies, which included Gouraud's Fourth Army, which was on a parallel course with First Army. In the event that American troops reached Sedan first, Pershing thought they should take the city, and Maistre consented.[29]

On November 6, Hugh Drum issued a memorandum on behalf of the AEF commander to the I and V Corps, instructing them that the coveted honor of entering Sedan would fall to First Army. "[General Pershing] has every confidence that the troops of the 1st Corps, assisted on their right by the 5th Corps, will enable him to realize the desire," he wrote. Furthermore, "your attention is called to the favorable opportunity now existing for pressing our advantage throughout the night. Boundaries will not be considered binding."[30] Throughout the Meuse-Argonne offensive, keeping each corps in its designated area (boundaries) during an attack had been problematic. If divisions crossed over one corps boundary to another, it could clog roads, increase straggling, or, even worse, create incidents of friendly fire. But in the advance on Sedan, Drum told the two corps that it was permissible to intersect boundaries if necessary, as long as the objective was met. This decision resulted in confusion and chaos.

Instead of an organized military operation, the pursuit to Sedan turned into a debacle. Summerall decided that 1st Division, which was on the far left flank of his V Corps and attached to I Corps under Joseph Dickman, would capture the city. This meant the Big Red One would have to cross the front and rear of two other divisions, the 42nd and 77th. Summerall wanted this accomplished at night and without Dickman's approval.

Doughboys of the 1st Division, under the command of Frank Parker, headed toward Sedan on the night of November 6. Driving in the pitch-blackness, their headlights turned off, a pool of reporters followed closely behind the doughboys, who marched along slick roads that grew worse from a constant rain. Because the Germans had laid mines at certain intervals, the troops had to take detours. Correspondent Thomas M. Johnson witnessed how little noise the troops made, save the "click of hobnails on the hard gray stone road, the creak of equipment, the word of command."[31] As they approached the historic city, the soldiers saw "glimmers of white flashes from artillery shells." Johnson found a vantage point to watch what happened next.

Along the way, the 1st Division became tangled up with other divisions. One group of soldiers thought another was the enemy and opened fire. Communications and traffic broke down. Nearby, Brigadier General Douglas MacArthur was awoken and told that his 42nd Division was being infiltrated by unknown troops. He immediately dressed and headed to the front. While he stopped to read a map, he was confronted by a 16th Infantry Regiment patrol led by a Lieutenant Black. MacArthur, wearing his trademark floppy hat, muffler, riding breeches, and polished boots, was mistaken as a German officer. Lieutenant Black took him prisoner at gunpoint, but quickly released him with apologies after his true identity was revealed. Decades later, MacArthur downplayed the incident, claiming he was never actually arrested. He recalled that along with his executive officer and an aide-de-camp, he went out to warn the regimental commander of the 167th not to fire on the approaching troops from the 16th Infantry, 1st Division. The party suddenly stumbled on a patrol from the 16th and engaged its commander, who had attended West Point with MacArthur. As they talked, MacArthur noticed that a soldier in the patrol was staring at him. It turned out the doughboy was envious of MacArthur's "dilapidated package" of Camel cigarettes. The general offered the lucky doughboy his carton, telling him, "If you don't get a medal in any event you do get a package of cigarettes." The soldier allegedly responded, "To tell you the truth, General, I would rather have the cigarettes than a medal." MacArthur and his entourage left without incident. The press blew the story out of proportion, he suggested, until it grew into his capture by a patrol.[32]

On their way back, MacArthur and other Rainbow Division officers billeted in an old château at Buzancy where General Georg von der Marwitz had made his headquarters. Despite broken windows and gaping holes in the walls, the Americans made themselves at home. In the evening they sat down to dinner, spreading food out on rough plank tables. Each was lighted by candles placed in narrow German wine bottles. The room was heated by glowing logs in a big fireplace. Johnson recalled that "our brave soldiers were silhouetted by lit cigarettes dangling from their lips."[33]

Much of the blame for the Sedan debacle can be directed at Hugh Drum, who was responsible for drafting the First Army order detailing the advance on Sedan. As one historian has pointed out, Drum's order was "not well written or especially clear as to responsibility for seizing the town." But Summerall deserves some blame as well. He "used this ambiguity to justify ordering the 1st Division to move out of its zone of operations in the 5th Corps area and across the advance of the 42nd Division in the area of the 1st Corps on the left. Considerable chaos and confusion resulted." No doubt "Summerall was not alone in the responsibility for this debacle. But he put his personal feelings, wanting his corps and the 1st Division, in particular, to beat other units to Sedan, above his professional judgment."[34] Liggett pleaded innocence, claiming "he had never heard of the order."[35] One historian summed up the confusion this way: "Pershing wanted to beat the French, Summerall wanted his corps, and the 1st Division in particular, to beat the rest of the American army.[36]

Pershing didn't seem concerned about the Sedan affair and didn't say anything at the time. Stackpole thought he failed to "entirely appreciate the serious consequences which might have resulted."[37] However, a month later, Summerall attended a luncheon at Pershing's Chaumont château with a number of other AEF and French officers. During the meal, Black Jack asked Summerall about the advance of 1st Division at Sedan. Summerall explained the orders he had received and on the tablecloth sketched the route taken by the troops with the towns they marched through. Pershing seemed satisfied.[38]

On November 10, the 92nd Division, in support of the 7th Division, captured the sectors of Bois de la Voivrotte and Bois de Cheminot. At the same time four additional divisions of Second Army attacked on both sides of the Moselle. The attacks gained little and were hampered by a heavy rain and fog that hindered air support and artillery observation. Even though all four divisions made it to German outposts and captured some of the strongpoints, they were cut short by long-range machine-gun and artillery fire. The armistice set for the next day did little to prevent the Germans from defending their positions.[39]

V Corps was ordered to cross the Meuse and advance, but Summerall found that "the army had no boats." So he "ordered the 89th Division to build some catamarans from captured German bridge equipment," and a short time later he "had floating bridges made for the 2nd Division." He chose "9 p.m. November 10, just as the moon went down, for the crossing." He held meetings to make sure "all of the details were understood." On November 9, Summerall received the following order from Foch that came by way of First Army: "The enemy, disorganized by our repeated attacks, retreats along the entire front. It is important to coordinate and expedite our movements. I appeal to the energy and initiative of the commander-in-chief and of their armies to make decisive the results obtained."[40]

Along the Meuse, from the region of Sedan to Stenay, German machine gunners, clinging to the hills overlooking the river, fought as if they had never heard of peace talks, and prevented the Americans from crossing. "Throughout the night the American artillery boomed along the entire front as a signal to the American infantrymen that the war was still on," a newspaper reported, "despite rumors of peace."[41] On November 8, on behalf of the Allied commanders, Marshal Foch and a British naval representative met with a German delegation to discuss a cease-fire. The Germans didn't like Foch's armistice terms, which were in line with what Pershing wanted. Foch demanded that they surrender their weapons and war equipment, and evacuate their forces back to Germany, among other conditions. The Germans refused to give Foch an immediate answer, and in return he refused to grant a provisional armistice. They had three days, until November 11, to consider Foch's terms. Until then the Allies would remain on the offensive.[42]

On the night of November 10, the 2nd Division continued its attack. As soon as darkness fell, Lejeune sent engineers to throw up two bridges just below Villemontry. They were followed by two battalions of the 5th Marines, with two machine-gun companies, a battalion from the 9th Infantry, and a battalion from the 365th Infantry of the

89th Division. It was a dangerous and costly mission, with both engineers and Marines either mowed down by German gunfire or drowned in the river. Yet the majority of Americans made it across the Meuse and occupied an area between Mouzon and Inor. No sooner had they reached the other side of the river than German shells wrecked the bridge.[43]

17

THE BATTLE WILL
BE OVER TODAY

At eight thirty on the morning of November 11, Major General Summerall received orders to cease advancing ninety minutes later, as an armistice had been set for that exact moment. The V Corps commander was "greatly amazed and regarded it as only a delay gained by the Germans." Still, he forwarded the order to his troops, but it didn't reach the leading element of the 89th Division until a half hour after the armistice went into effect. Earlier that day he had instructed his 89th Division engineers to build a bridge across the Meuse so that the corps could keep attacking. When Summerall went forward to see if the work had been completed, he was irritated to find nothing had been done. He sent for the "commanding officer of the engineer regiment and asked why he had not obeyed the order." Summerall was told that it was "against international law," so he "ordered the engineers of 2nd Division to build it."[1] Later on, Summerall learned that the "brigade of Marines in the 2nd Division resented the order to cross the Meuse River, as the Armistice came immediately afterward," and blamed him for their casualties, "which they said were unnecessary."[2]

In the Second Army sector, Robert Lee Bullard was just as aggressive. Each of his divisions attacked, but gained little. George Bell's 33rd Division took the biggest hits, losing fifteen hundred men over the last two days.[3] Bullard was especially disappointed with the African American troops. "The poor 92nd Negroes," he recorded in his diary, "wasted time and dawdled where they did attack, and in some places where they should have attacked, never budged at all. It seems to be as much the fault of the general as of the Negroes."[4]

Above the battlefields, as the armistice dragged closer, American and German airplanes engaged one another one last time. "Very much as the knights used to do in days gone by," Billy Mitchell observed, "they challenged the opposing aviators to individual combat by flying around the hostile airdromes." Major Maxwell Kirby of the 94th Aero Squadron scored the last American victory when he shot down a German aircraft that morning.[5] The German High Command complained to Foch about the fighting that spilled past eleven a.m.: "On the front Stenay-Beaumont and on the Meuse, the Americans continue to attack in spite of the conclusion of the Armistice. Please order the cessation of the hostilities."

At Souilly, Colonel George Marshall narrowly made it through the last day of the war. He awoke at two thirty a.m. to speak by telephone with the division staff officers at the front, then returned to bed for a few hours. At ten o'clock he had breakfast with some British and French officers at 49 Voie Sacrée, a stately house across the street from Liggett's headquarters. As the meal came to a close, the conversation was interrupted by a loud explosion outside a window by the far end of the table. The room shook with such force that Marshall and the others were thrown from their chairs. Marshall's head crashed hard against the thick wall, but miraculously neither he nor anyone else was seriously injured. A few minutes later a young aviator rushed into the room to assess the damage. It seemed that as he was landing in a nearby field, a small bomb stuck to the rack of his plane came loose and fell into the garden.[6] Marshall limped back to his office just before the armistice went into effect.

War artists George Harding and Wallace Morgan attempted to spend what they thought was the last night of the war in their car, positioned reasonably close to the front. However, between the big naval guns on nearby railroad tracks firing continuously and incoming enemy shells, the two were forced to relocate. The next morning, they hitched a ride in an ambulance, going forward two miles before "being forced to walk into a seething, bubbling cauldron straight from hell. Just ahead of them, an enemy plane dropped its bombs, killing three doughboys." As Harding passed by the dead, he noted that one soldier's legs and side were blown open, making him look "like [a] skinned rabbit." Farther forward, they came across a doughboy who had accidentally dropped a live grenade in his own trench, blowing off his testicles and both hands.[7] The gruesome scene demonstrated that even though the German defensive lines had been breached, the enemy continued to resist American attacks.

Leaning against a tree with a cigarette dangling from his lips, dispatch rider Leon George Roth, a Jewish soldier assigned to the 319th Field Signal Battalion, waited near a rail car in Compiègne. He had been sent by Liggett's staff to collect a message. At around five fifteen a.m. an orderly burst through the train's door, carrying a stack of papers that he shoved into a canister and handed to Roth.[8] Told to "drive like mad" and deliver the documents to First Army, Roth took one last drag of his cigarette, mounted his Harley-Davidson motorcycle and sped off toward Souilly. Unbeknownst to the young rider, inside the canister was a copy of the armistice agreement, freshly signed by the Allied and German representatives. Roth's journey was anything but uneventful. At one point he wiped out in a shell hole. With no serious damage to himself or his Harley, he got back up and continued his mission. Shells burst over his head the rest of the way, and after reaching Souilly, Roth discovered a piece of shrapnel lodged in his scalp. He dismounted from his mud-splattered bike and handed the canister to a First Army aide. Then, as Liggett remembered, "probably the most impressive moment of the War was at eleven o'clock on November 11, 1918, when the infernal uproar which had been continuous for a long time suddenly gave way to a silence which was stunning."[9] It was so silent, Private Roth recalled, "I could hear my watch ticking." No staccato bursts of machine guns could be heard, nor the deafening rumbles of artillery shells tearing up the earth. A few planes soared overhead, but they were all Allied, with not a German Fokker in sight. The war, at last, was over.[10]

Many who witnessed the armistice shared their thoughts in writing. Captain Harry Truman was at the front in a farmhouse with his artillery battery. He wrote Bess that he just received "official notice that hostilities would cease at 11 o'clock, but what pleases me most is the fact that I was lucky enough to take a battery through the last drive. The battery has shot something over 10,000 rounds at the Hun and I am sure they had a slight effect."[11] Truman and Battery D had arrived in France with 200 men and came back with 199. One man died of illness.[12]

For Colonel George S. Patton, there were two reasons to rejoice on November 11. Besides the armistice, he celebrated his thirty-third birthday. Having been seriously wounded in the Cheppy Woods on the morning of September 26, his participation in the Meuse-Argonne had amounted to less than a day.[13] Now almost thirty pounds lighter following his convalescence, he had been commanding the Light Tank Training Center at Langres, the same school he had established in February 1918. Despite mild dyslexia, writing poetry was a lifelong passion for Patton, and to celebrate the armistice he drafted an eleven-stanza poem called "Peace-November 11, 1918." It opened with:

> *I stood in the flag-decked cheering crowd*
> *Where all but I were gay*
> *And gazing on their extecy [sic]*
> *My heart shrank in dismay.*[14]

The sadness resonating in Patton's poem reflected his disappointment that the battle was now over and that he had played such a small role. War was everything to Patton and he feared that there might not be another opportunity to see combat. On the other hand, most soldiers embraced the war's end. "It was comical to see the boys throw away their crutches and sing," remembered a nurse at a field hospital.[15] A doughboy in the 80th Division wrote, "Our ears had become accustomed to the bursting of shells. . . . The constant din of firing that turned quiet was bewildering."[16] IV Corps commander Major General John L. Hines wrote in his diary that in Dun "tonight the lights are showing through the smashed walls and windows of this town for the first time in four and a half years."[17]

In Souilly, the reaction to the armistice was more restrained. A band brought in from a nearby regiment played the national anthems of the various Allied nations, as well as other patriotic music, for about an hour. Cheers erupted from trucks motoring back and forth on the Sacred Way, but little else indicated the war was over. One aviator gave a demonstration of stunt flying over the village, a show that ended in tragedy when the wings on one side of the plane collapsed, killing the pilot when the craft crashed.[18] Avery Andrews, by now a brigadier general, celebrated the armistice by drinking champagne served from a German helmet.[19]

Pershing was in Chaumont when Colonel T. Bentley Mott at French headquarters called to say the armistice would go into effect that morning. One of his biographers records that he "stood in front of a large wall map and watched the hands approach 11:00." Part of Pershing still wished that his mighty army had a few more days to crush the Germans even further.[20]

A few hours later, Pershing called on Marshal Foch at Senlis. The two men shook hands and smiled like old friends. There was no longer reason for anger, animosity, or hurt. Each said only nice things about the other. Then they embraced and unabashedly wept.[21] Pershing pinned the Distinguished Service Medal onto Foch's uniform. Afterward, at a glorious lunch, Foch regaled the attendees with stories of how he negotiated an armistice with the Germans.

Pershing soon said his good-byes and left for Paris with Quekemeyer and Dawes. When the party reached the city, they found the streets alive with celebration. "It looked as though the whole population had gone entirely out of their minds," Pershing remembered. Parisians were singing, dancing, and cheering everywhere he looked. As Santini drove through the Place de la Concorde, the Cadillac was mobbed as crowds recognized the automobile as belonging to the American commander. With thick French accents they shouted over and over: "Général Pairshing, Général Pairshing!" Excited Parisians climbed on the Cadillac's running boards, hood and roof. Nearby, a group of doughboys saw that their commander in chief was held up and came to his rescue. Forming a wedge, the troops split apart the throng and Santini squeaked through.[22]

After Pershing finally made it to his Paris residence he wrote General Order 203, a thank-you to all "officers and soldiers of the American Expeditionary Forces who by their heroic efforts have made possible this glorious result." His gratitude extended not just to those who fought at the Meuse-Argonne but to anyone who wore an American uniform during the war. "Your deeds will live forever," he told them, "on the most glorious pages of American history."[23]

A few days after the war ended, Pershing had a chance encounter with Clemenceau. "We fell into each other's arms, choked up and had to wipe away our tears," Pershing recalled. "We had no differences that day." James Harbord later wrote, "The armistice thus ended two wars for us—the one with our friends, the other with our enemies."[24]

With the pleasantries now over, Pershing could relax a bit and reflect on what had happened over the course of battle. Despite so many fits and starts, the Meuse-Argonne was an impressive effort by mostly untested American divisions, ultimately involving 1.2 million American and French troops who used 2,417 guns that fired off 4,214,000 rounds of artillery ammunition. Brigadier General Billy Mitchell's 840 planes had managed to drop one hundred tons of explosives on enemy lines. Yet the battle was fought mostly by soldiers who jumped off from trenches and exposed ground in the face of blistering machine-gun and artillery fire. First Army divisions, inexperienced as they were, penetrated over thirty-four miles, captured 16,059 German POWs, 468 pieces of enemy artillery, and about 3,000 guns and mortars of all types. During the course of forty-seven days, 150 French villages and towns, many of them in ruins, were liberated by Pershing's doughboys at a cost of 120,000 Americans killed and wounded.[25]

From the opening salvos in the early morning of September 26 until the clock struck at eleven a.m. on November 11, Pershing's warriors fought tenaciously and bravely, although at times recklessly, against a far superior opponent. When the smoke cleared, and the battle and the war were declared over, the American soldiers had carried the Allies to victory. For General John J. Pershing, it was his finest hour. The battle of the Meuse-Argonne was not the sole reason the Allies won the war, but it was certainly the deciding factor. Pershing's forces broke the back of the mighty German Army in the most heavily defended section of the western front. Over forty-seven days of brutal combat, the Germans were forced to withdraw and give up the fight.

AFTERMATH

I n early August 1919, Pershing and George Marshall, now serving as the general's aide, boarded Pershing's train in Paris for a trip to Koblenz, Germany, for a visit with American troops on occupation duty. The train stopped over in Verdun, where Cesar Santini picked them up and drove them around the St. Mihiel and Meuse-Argonne battlefields. For two days, with maps in hand, Pershing and Marshall were taken through the villages and towns where First Army had marched, walked the terrain where American soldiers had fought and died, and stood in the trenches and bunkers once held by the Germans. They stopped for a picnic on a hill overlooking Sedan, but the one site that had the greatest impact on Pershing was the temporary cemetery at Romagne where 22,000 doughboys were buried. He was so moved by the rows of wooden markers that he had Santini drive him there a second time before crossing the border into Germany.[1]

Pershing made it a personal mission to protect the legacy of Meuse-

Argonne. After all, it was his persistence that led to the creation of an independent American army, his assertion that his troops be allowed to attack in the St. Mihiel Salient first, and his resolve that saw the Meuse-Argonne through. He documented these operations in 1923 in the War Department–produced *The Report of First Army*, a short monograph of 135 pages and sixteen maps that Pershing and Liggett co-authored. It was intended for publication in 1919, but Pershing was unhappy with the first draft, which was primarily written by Hugh Drum and then turned over to George Marshall for revision. His chief complaint was that it did not give enough credit to the units in the field. Pershing told Marshall in late 1920 that the report "is more-or-less verbose in places, and that there is a tendency to enter too much into the details of what the staff did without setting forth much about what the troops did."[2] Marshall worked on a second draft with help from Drum, who advised on maps, appendices, and rewrites of entire sections. One of Marshall's biographers described the finished product as "dry, factual, pedestrian in style, and without evaluation."[3]

In the immediate years and decades following Meuse-Argonne, Americans commemorated the battle on their own soil. Monuments, memorials, and plaques were erected. Most major cities and quite a few small towns named streets, boulevards, avenues, and buildings after the battle—the Argonne National Laboratory near Chicago and the Argonne Hotel in downtown Lima, Ohio, to name a few.

In 1937, at the age of seventy-seven, Pershing attended the dedication of the Meuse-Argonne cemetery. Set in 130 acres of ground, 14,246 soldiers lie in perpetuity between Romagne and Cunel, where some of the battle's most difficult fighting took place. During his speech that spring day, Pershing summed up the Meuse-Argonne by telling those in attendance, "The morale of the American soldier during this most trying period was superb. Physically strong and virile, naturally courageous and aggressive, inspired by unselfish and idealistic motives, he guaranteed the victory and drove a veteran enemy from his last ditch. Too much credit cannot be given him."[4]

During World War II, George Marshall, by now Army chief of staff, returned to the Meuse-Argonne front in early October 1944 on an inspection trip to see American and Allied commanders. After arriving in Paris, Marshall was flown to Verdun and asked the pilot to dip the plane low over the former Argonne battlefields for a quick glance at the sacred terrain. Later on he drove through St. Mihiel, and then made a point of visiting his old billet in Souilly.[5]

Pershing perhaps summed up the battle best when he wrote, "It presented difficulties, numerous and seemingly insurmountable, which makes the success gained stand as a splendid achievement in the history of American armies."

JOHN J. PERSHING

Pershing returned to America in September 1919 as a celebrated hero. Like Meuse-Argonne, countless cities and towns throughout the United States named a street, park, or building after the American general. Today, Pershing Squares can be found in Los Angeles and New York. A Pershing Road runs through Kansas City, and in Indiana a township in Jackson County is named for him. One could stay at the General Pershing Hotel in Dubois, Pennsylvania, or buy a cast-iron piggy bank or a paperweight with his likeness. The Burlington Railroad renamed its train running between St. Louis and Kansas City the *General Pershing Zephyr*, and a proud horticulturist came up with

General Pershing's Double Red Oleander. To recognize his distinguished service as the commander of the AEF, Pershing was promoted to the special rank of General of the Armies of the United States. No other officer had previously held this title, although George Washington was posthumously promoted to the rank by President Gerald Ford in 1976.

In 1920, Pershing was considered as a possible Republican candidate for president. Although he never actively campaigned, in a newspaper article Pershing was quoted as saying that he "wouldn't decline to serve" if selected by the people. Senator Warren G. Harding won both the party's nomination and the presidential election that year. Clearly Pershing wasn't ready to leave the army, and the following year he was selected its chief of staff, serving for three years before retiring in 1924 at the age of sixty-four. He now spent most of his days as head of the American Battle Monument Commission, ensuring that America's presence in the Great War would not be forgotten. Under his leadership the commission established eight overseas cemeteries and numerous monuments and memorials that dot the western front landscape. In 1937, Pershing published his memoirs, *My Experiences in the World War*, which one of his biographers described as "cold and passionless," as well as "dull, repetitious, finicky and overly wrought."[6]

Slowing down in his later years, Pershing lived at the Carlton Hotel in Washington, DC, two blocks from the White House, before moving to Walter Reed General Hospital in 1941 at the age of eighty-one. There he passed the time as many retired men do, sleeping late, reading newspapers, playing cards, listening to the radio, and visiting with friends. Angered by the Japanese attack on Pearl Harbor, Pershing offered his services to President Franklin D. Roosevelt, but the White House respectfully declined.

Pershing suffered a stroke in September 1944, and although he made a significant recovery, his general health slowly deteriorated. He went into a coma and died in his suite on July 15, 1948, at the age of eighty-eight. Pershing is buried on a hillside at Arlington Cemetery, where a plain marble soldier's headstone sits atop his remains.

MICHELINE RESCO

When Pershing returned to the United States in September 1919, he had promised to bring Micheline to America. But her travel never materialized. His work as chief of staff got in the way. So just like the days when Pershing was stuck in Chaumont or Souilly, running the AEF and First Army, they shared their affection through the mail. "My dear, how I miss you each day and night," Pershing wrote. "I pray for you, your presence, for your kisses, for the many ways you show your tenderness. For the first time we get together again I am sure that we are going to die. I am just going to eat you all up, as I am going to kill you with love."

Micheline finally came to America in 1922, and set up a studio in New York City. While Pershing remained in Washington, they saw each other on the weekends. A few years later she returned to Paris; Pershing would visit on business every four to six months. When World War II broke out in Europe in 1939, Micheline returned to America with her mother and they lived in a Washington hotel. Over the next several years she visited Pershing on a daily basis, and on September 2, 1946, they secretly married in his Walter Reed suite with only two witnesses, her mother and Father Jules A. Baisnée. After Pershing's death, Micheline returned to Paris with her mother. She died in 1968.

HUNTER LIGGETT

After the armistice, Liggett commanded U.S. Third Army in Germany for a year and a half. He returned home and testified before a House committee investigating charges that attacks by American troops on the morning of the armistice had "resulted in needless loss of life." Because two divisions were on both sides of the Meuse and under enemy threat, it "would have been dangerous" to cease the fighting, Liggett argued. Besides, "orders to stop fighting before 11 o'clock," Liggett said, "would have been made only at Marshal Foch's headquarters."[7]

Liggett published two books about his service during World War I: *A.E.F.: Ten Years Ago in France* and *Commanding an American Army*. Both are well-written and accurate accounts of the AEF, and his eventual role of First Army commander with Pershing constantly looking over his shoulder. He was more forthcoming than Pershing in describing the first five weeks of the Argonne offensive: "The defects of the American operation in this battle were such as were humanly inescapable in a not yet fully seasoned army, thrown, on a few weeks' notice, against a first-class enemy at his most vital, and therefore, most furiously defended front, in order to carry out a general strategic plan. We made our mistakes, but given the conditions, acquitted ourselves most honorably, in my judgment."

Liggett died in 1935, only seventeen years after the war. Less than four years later, his widow, Harriett, was destitute. She lived on his government pension of thirty dollars a month in a San Francisco hotel room adorned with photographs of her late husband and places he was posted during his long Army career. A bill to raise the pension to a hundred dollars a month for Mrs. Liggett and eight other widows of ranking officers was passed that year by both houses of Congress, but vetoed by FDR. Harriett died in 1939.

In the general's honor, the U.S. Army designated a post after him during World War II: Fort Hunter Liggett in Monterey County, California.

DOUGLAS MacARTHUR

Following the war, MacArthur served another thirty-three years in the Army. He was superintendent of West Point, headed the American Olympic Committee, and was promoted to general and selected as the Army chief of staff. Later on he retired from the Army, then served as field marshal of the Philippine army. When World War II broke out, MacArthur took command of U.S. forces in the Pacific. Four years later, he accepted the Japanese surrender aboard the USS *Missouri*. President Harry S. Truman appointed him to oversee the occupation and rebuilding of Japan. When the North Korean army invaded South Korea in 1950, MacArthur was placed in command of the newly created United Nations forces. He orchestrated the Inchon landings, considered one of the greatest military operations in history. Yet MacArthur's ego got the best of him, and his public criticism of how the White House was handling the conflict left President Truman with no other choice but to relieve him, in April 1951.

After leaving the Army he considered a run for the presidency on the Republican ticket, but that faded in 1952, when Dwight Eisenhower accepted the party's nomination. During the last years of his life MacArthur and his wife, Jean, resided in New York City, and he was elected chairman of the board for Remington Rand, a business machine manufacturer, and wrote his memoirs, *Reminiscences*. Douglas MacArthur died at Walter Reed on April 5, 1964, at the age of eighty-four.

WILLIAM "BILLY" MITCHELL

Mitchell returned to the United States expecting a promotion as head of the Army Air Service, but instead he never made it beyond deputy chief. Nevertheless, Mitchell took an active role in promoting military aviation and advocated the creation of an independent air force. When this, as well as some of his other suggestions for the Army Air Service, didn't come to fruition, Mitchell publicly attacked his superiors in the military and even went after the White House. He went too far, however, and was court-martialed for insubordination. His punishment was suspension from active duty for five years without pay, but Mitchell instead resigned from the Army in February 1926. As a civilian, Mitchell continued campaigning for an independent air force until his death, on February 19, 1936.

GEORGE C. MARSHALL

Out of all of Pershing's staff officers, Marshall had the most productive and significant postwar career. After serving as aide-de-camp to Black Jack for five years, Marshall held a variety of posts with the Army, both domestically and overseas, culminating with his appointment as chief of staff in 1939. During World War II he was largely responsible for the building, the supplying, and, in part, the deploying of more than eight million soldiers. Under the Truman administration he served as secretary of state, and his most notable achievement in this position was developing the plan for the economic aid of postwar Europe, which was known as the Marshall Plan. He died in 1959.

EDWARD RICKENBACKER

Settling into postwar life, America's greatest fighter ace started an automobile manufacture he called Rickenbacker Motors and later purchased the Indianapolis Motor Speedway, then Eastern Air Lines. In 1941, Rickenbacker almost died in a plane crash, suffering numerous broken bones, a paralyzed hand, and a badly damaged left eye. During the Second World War, Rickenbacker, at the age of fifty-five, inspected Allied air bases in Europe and in the Pacific. When the war ended, he returned to Eastern Air Lines until he was forced out in 1959, but stayed on as chairman of the board until 1963. Rickenbacker died in Zurich, Switzerland, on July 27, 1973, after suffering a stroke. His cousin Adolph helped keep the Rickenbacker name alive by launching a musical instrument business in 1931.

ALVIN YORK

When York returned home from France, the Pall Mall, Tennessee, Rotary Club took pledges to buy a house and farm for him, but not enough cash was raised and York had to take out a mortgage. He married Gracie Williams and they had seven children. Hollywood turned his life story into a movie, *Sergeant York*, which won Gary Cooper an Oscar in 1941. During World War II, the former pacifist volunteered to serve his country once again, but at the age of fifty-four, because he was overweight and in poor health, his enlistment was denied. The Army instead gave him a temporary rank of major in the Signal Corps and sent the war hero on tours of training camps and made him part of the bond drive to support the war effort. He died in September 1962, and is buried in a private Pall Mall cemetery.

CHARLES WHITTLESEY

After his discharge from the Army in 1919, "Galloping Charlie" returned to his law practice in Manhattan, but found it hard to leave the war behind him. He was frequently contacted by former 77th Division servicemen and their families for help, and Whittlesey felt obliged. On November 11, 1921, he was among the honored guests at Arlington Cemetery during an entombment ceremony for the Tomb of the Unknown Soldier. Five days later, unbeknownst to his family and friends, he set sail on a passenger ship journeying to Cuba, the SS *Toloa*. He spent the evening of November 26 drinking at the ship's bar and talking with other passengers. Sometime that night, Whittlesey climbed over the ship's rail and jumped overboard.

SAM WOODFILL

Woodfill returned to the United States in 1919 and was mustered out of the service, even though he "really liked soldiering."[8] The Army allowed him to reenlist as a sergeant so that he could earn enough time to draw a pension later on. In 1921, Woodfill was selected as one of the three World War I veterans to represent the Army at the ceremony to dedicate the Tomb of the Unknown Soldier—Charles Whittlesey and Alvin York were the other two. For most of his life he struggled financially until Congress stepped in to help in 1942, commissioning him to the rank of major to provide him more income. Woodfill died in 1951 of natural causes. Originally buried in a local cemetery, his remains were later removed to Arlington Cemetery.

ROBERT L. BULLARD

After returning home from the war in 1919, Bullard served as commander of the II Army Corps Area and retired from military service in 1925. He was president of the National Security League, an organization dedicated to U.S. war preparedness, and published numerous magazine articles and books. Bullard died in 1947 and is buried at Arlington Cemetery.

FERDINAND FOCH

After the war, Foch played a significant role as military adviser at the Paris Peace Conference. He was also honored as marshal of both Great Britain and Poland. In 1921 he traveled to the United States for the first time and took part in the Liberty Memorial groundbreaking in Kansas City; he then toured much of America, where he received numerous honorary degrees from universities. He died in March 1929 and is buried in Les Invalides, near Napoleon's Tomb.

PHILIPPE PÉTAIN

For the next three decades after the war Pétain held a variety of posts, including minister of war and ambassador to Spain. Hailed as a national hero for his service in the First World War, his good standing with the French people tumbled following the German invasion of France in 1940. At the age of eighty-four, he became premier of France and negotiated an armistice with Germany, then established the Vichy Republic in central France. After the Second World War, Pétain stood trial for treason and was sentenced to death for collaborating with the enemy. The sentence was commuted to solitary confinement, and Pétain was moved to an island off the coast of Brittany, where he died in 1951.

GEORGES CLEMENCEAU

Following the Paris Peace Conference the Tiger was disillusioned over what he perceived as lenient treatment of Germany. He lost a bid for the presidency in 1920 and retired from politics. Clemenceau wrote his autobiography, in which he predicted another war with Germany. He died in 1929 at the age of eighty-eight.

PIERPONT STACKPOLE

In 1919, Stackpole returned to Boston and practiced law as a partner with Warner, Stackpole and Bradlee and served on the board of the New England Conservatory and the Boston Symphony. He died in 1936.

MAX VON GALLWITZ

After the war, von Gallwitz served as Reichstag deputy of the German National People's Party, the primary conservative party in Weimar Germany from 1920 to 1924. Seven years later he aligned himself with other conservative organizations and the Nazi Party. He died on April 18, 1937, while vacationing in Naples, Italy.

HARRY S. TRUMAN

After the war, Truman married his childhood sweetheart, Elizabeth "Bess" Wallace. He opened a hat shop in Kansas City, but the business failed within a few years. In 1922 Truman entered politics, first as a judge, then as a U.S. senator, until President Franklin Roosevelt tapped him as his running mate for his fourth term in 1944. Upon Roosevelt's death, Truman presided over the last few months of World War II and the start of the Cold War after winning reelection in 1948. Truman died in 1973 and is buried in his hometown of Independence, Missouri.

CESAR SANTINI

After the armistice, Santini remained an Army chauffeur for a few months longer, driving President and Mrs. Wilson on several occasions, as well as Foch, Clemenceau, Haig, and King Albert and Queen Elizabeth of Belgium. He went back to the United States, but then returned to France, where he opened an auto repair business. On December 3, 1958, Santini died in Italy.

ACKNOWLEDGMENTS

Researching and writing *Forty-Seven Days* involved the input of many people, and without them the book would have never been completed. It started with my agent, E. J. McCarthy, whose enthusiasm for a story about the Meuse-Argonne was immediately apparent after we first made contact. E. J. helped craft the proposal and assured me that he would find the right editor and publisher. E. J. was true to his word and put me in touch with Brent Howard at New American Library. A contract was signed and the manuscript took off from there. Brent is all I could have hoped for in an editor. He was patient and encouraging and pushed me when I needed pushing and provided tremendous guidance in rewriting chapters and by far improved the manuscript in many ways.

I relied on a number of historians, such as Monique Seefried, Mike Hanlon, Pat Osborn, Richard Slotkin, Taylor Beattie, George B.

Clark, Kevin Hymel, Mark Grotelueschen, and Randy Gaulke to read drafts of the entire manuscript or specific chapters that relate to their fields of expertise. I also benefited from the knowledge of Tim Mulligan, Fred Castier, Guillaume Moizan, David Bedford, Jim Leeke, Wim Degrande, Tony Ten-Barge, Grosvenor Merle-Smith, Barney McCoy, Tom and Margie Nolan, Blaine Pardoe, Betsy Smoot, Ben Byrnes and Steve Harris. I was assisted with scanning documents and photographs and transcribing books by Susan Strange, Lynn Thomas, and Lilith Short. Chris Robinson did another stellar job in creating the maps.

At the National Archives Office of the Inspector General, I counted heavily upon Greg Tremaglio, Dave Berry, Rachel Neil, Tom Bennett, and William Johnson for counsel, support, and, most important, friendship. Other archive colleagues also helped me in many ways, including Rick Peuser, Tim Nenninger, Mark Mollan, Jeff Hartley, Theresa Fitzgerald, Judy Koucke, Holly Reed, Carol Swain, John Hamilton, Jay Bosanko and the staff at the George H. W. Bush Presidential Library. A host of other great people at the archives contributed in one way or another to help me write the book, and I am grateful to them as well.

I am also thankful for the help I received by staff members at the U.S. Army History and Education Center, the Douglas MacArthur Memorial Library and Archives, the Clark County Historical Society, the Women's Memorial Museum and Archives, the Fricke Library, the George C. Marshall Library, the First Division Museum, the John Carroll University Library Special Collections, the Jesuit Archives, the University of Southern Mississippi Library, the University of Chicago Library, the Kansas National Guard Archives, and the Connecticut State Archives.

Throughout the entire process of writing *Forty-Seven Days* I was so lucky to have the patience, support, love, and many other wonderful attributes of Lynn, Lily, and Rosie. As always, my family was there to offer much-needed encouragement.

Despite all of the help and advice I received, I am solely to blame for any errors in the book.

SELECTED BIBLIOGRAPHY

MANUSCRIPTS AND ARCHIVES

The Frick Art Reference Library
Micheline Resco Collection

John Carroll University and the Jesuit Archives
Father Donald Smythe Collection (Correspondence between John J. Pershing and
    Micheline Resco)

George C. Marshall Library and Archives
George C. Marshall Papers
Pierpont Stackpole Diary

Library of Congress Manuscript Division
William Mitchell Papers
Bishop Charles H. Brett Papers
John J. Pershing Papers

Douglas MacArthur Archives and Library
Record Group II, Correspondence

United States Army Heritage and Education Center (AHEC)
Dennis Nolan Papers
Hugh Drum Papers
William Donovan Papers

Clark County Historical Society

Leon Roth Collection

Women's Memorial Archives
Nurses' Manuscripts and Diaries

University of Southern Mississippi Library
Irving Werstein Papers

National Archives and Records Administration (NARA)
Records of the Office of the Quartermaster General (Record Group 92)
U.S. Army Signal Corps Photographic Collection (Record Group III)
Records of the American Expeditionary Forces (Record Group 120)
Records of the War Department and General Staffs (Record Group 165)
General John Pershing Papers (Record Group 200)

Library of Virginia
Virginia War History Commission: World War I History Commission
    Questionnaires

Newspapers
Jewish Floridian
Milwaukee Journal
New York Times
Pittsburgh Gazette Times
Saturday Evening Post
Stars and Stripes
Washington Post
Woodville Republican

BOOKS AND ARTICLES

Adler, Julius Ochs. *History of the Seventy-seventh Division.* New York: W. H. Crawford Company, 1919.

American Battle Monuments Commission, *American Battlefields in Europe.* Washington, DC: United States Government Printing Office, 1938.

———. *1st Division Summary of Operations in the World War.* Washington, DC: United States Government Printing Office, 1944.

———. *2nd Division Summary of Operations in the World War.* Washington, DC: United States Government Printing Office, 1944.

———. *3rd Division Summary of Operations in the World War.* Washington, DC: United States Government Printing Office, 1944.

———. *4th Division Summary of Operations in the World War.* Washington, DC: United States Government Printing Office, 1944.

———. *5th Division Summary of Operations in the World War.* Washington, DC: United States Government Printing Office, 1944.

———. *6th Division Summary of Operations in the World War.* Washington, DC: United States Government Printing Office, 1944.

———. *26th Division Summary of Operations in the World War.* Washington, DC: United States Government Printing Office, 1944.

———. *28th Division Summary of Operations in the World War.* Washington, DC: United States Government Printing Office, 1944.

———. *32nd Division Summary of Operations in the World War.* Washington, DC: United States Government Printing Office, 1944.

———. *33rd Division Summary of Operations in the World War.* Washington, DC: United States Government Printing Office, 1944.

———. *42nd Division Summary of Operations in the World War.* Washington, DC: United States Government Printing Office, 1944.

———. *77th Division Summary of Operations in the World War.* Washington, DC: United States Government Printing Office, 1944.

———. *78th Division Summary of Operations in the World War.* Washington, DC: United States Government Printing Office, 1944.

———. *79th Division Summary of Operations in the World War.* Washington, DC: United States Government Printing Office, 1944.

———. *80th Division Summary of Operations in the World War.* Washington, DC: United States Government Printing Office, 1944.

———. *81st Division Summary of Operations in the World War.* Washington, DC: United States Government Printing Office, 1944.

——. *82nd Division Summary of Operations in the World War*. Washington, DC: United States Government Printing Office, 1944.

——. *89th Division Summary of Operations in the World War*. Washington, DC: United States Government Printing Office, 1944.

——. *90th Division Summary of Operations in the World War*. Washington, DC: United States Government Printing Office, 1944.

——. *91st Division Summary of Operations in the World War*. Washington, DC: United States Government Printing Office, 1944.

——. *92nd Division Summary of Operations in the World War*. Washington, DC: United States Government Printing Office, 1944.

Andrews, Avery DeLano. *My Friend and Classmate John J. Pershing: With Notes From My War Diary*. Harrisburg, PA: Military Service Publishing Company, 1939.

Army Times. *The Yanks Are Coming: The Story of General John J. Pershing*. New York: G. P. Putnam's Sons, 1960.

Beaver, Daniel R. *Newton D. Baker and the American War Effort, 1917–1919*. Lincoln: University of Nebraska Press, 1966.

Berg, A. Scott. *Wilson*. New York: G. P. Putnam's Sons, 2013.

Birdwell, Michael E. "Alvin Cullum York: The Myth, the Man, and the Legacy." *Tennessee Historical Quarterly* 4 (Winter 2012), 318–35.

Blavatasky, H. P. *Theosophical Quarterly Magazine*. Theosophical Society, 1937.

Bonk, David. *St. Mihiel 1918*. Oxford, UK: Osprey Publishing, 2011.

Bourne, John M. *Who's Who in World War I*. London: Routledge, 2001.

Brager, Bruce L. *The Texas 36th Division: A History*. Austin, TX: Eakin Press, 2002.

Braim, Paul F. *The Test of Battle: The American Expeditionary Forces in the Meuse-Argonne Campaign*. Shippensburg, PA: White Mane Press, 1998.

Byerly, Carol. *Fever of War: The Influenza Epidemic in the U.S. Army During World War I*. New York: New York University Press, 2005.

Canfield, Bruce N. *U.S. Infantry Weapons of the First World War*. Lincoln, RI: Andrew Mowbray, 2000.

Casey, Steven. *When Soldiers Fall: How Americans Have Confronted Combat Losses from World War I to Afghanistan*. New York: Oxford University Press, 2014.

Cochrane, Rexmond C. *The 89th Division in the Bois de Bantheville, October 1918*. Army Chemical Center, MD: U.S. Army Chemical Corps Historical Office, 1960.

——. *The 79th Division at Montfaucon, October 1918*. Army Chemical Center, MD: U.S. Army Chemical Corps Historical Office, 1960.

Codevelle, Colonel. *Armistice 1918: The Signing of the Armistice in the Forest Glade of Compiègne* (Friends of the Armistice of Compiègne).

Coffman, Edward M. *The War to End All Wars: The American Military Experience in World War I*. New York: Oxford University Press, 1968.

Conseil Général de la Meuse Histoire et Mémoires. *Les Américains et la Meuse 1914–1918*. Verdun, France: Conseil Général de la Meuse, la Mission Histoire, 2009.

Cooke, James J. *The All-Americans at War: The 82nd Division in the Great War, 1917–1918*. Westport, CT: Praeger, 1999.

———. *Billy Mitchell*. Boulder, CO: L. Rienner, 2002.

———. *Pershing and His Generals: Command and Staff in the AEF*. Westport, CT: Praeger, 1997.

———. *The Rainbow Division in the Great War: 1917–1919*. Westport, CT: Praeger, 1994.

———. *The U.S. Air Service in the Great War: 1917–1919*. Westport, CT: Praeger, 1996.

Cornebise, Alfred Emile. *Art from the Trenches: America's Uniformed Artists in World War I*. College Station: Texas A&M University Press, 1991.

Craig, Lee A. *Jospehus Daniels: His Life and Times*. Chapel Hill: University of North Carolina Press, 2013.

Crocker, H. W., III. *The Yanks Are Coming: A Military History of the United States in World War I*. Washington, DC: Regnery Publishing, 2014.

Davis, William Morris. *A Handbook of Northern France*. Cambridge: Harvard University Press, 1918.

Dawes, Charles C. *Journal of the Great War*. 2 vols. Boston: Houghton Mifflin and Company, 1927.

D'Este, Carlo. *Patton: A Genius for War*. New York: HarperCollins Publishers, 1995.

DeWeerd, Harvey. *President Wilson Fights His War: World War I and the American Intervention*. New York: Macmillan and Company, 1968.

Dos Passos, John. *Mr. Wilson's War: From the Assassination of McKinley to the Defeat of the League of Nations*. New York: Skyhorse Publishing, 2013.

Doughty, Robert A. *Pyrrhic Victory: French Strategy and Operations in the Great War*. Cambridge, MA: Belknap Harvard, 2005.

Duffy, Francis P. *Father Duffy's Story*. New York: George H. Doran, 1919.

Eisenhower, John S. D. *Yanks: The Epic Story of the U.S. Army in World War I*. New York: Free Press, 2001.

Ettinger, Albert M., and A. Churchill. *A Doughboy with the Fighting 69th: A Remembrance of World War I*. Shippensburg, PA: White Mane Publishing Company, 1992.

Evans, Martin Marix. *Retreat, Hell! We Just Got Here: The American Expeditionary Forces in France 1917–1918*. Oxford, UK: Osprey, 1998.

Farwell, Byron. *Over There: The United States in the Great War: 1917–1918*. New York: W. W. Norton & Company, 1999.

Faulkner, Richard K. *The School of Hard Knocks: Combat Leadership in the American Expeditionary Forces*. College Station: Texas A&M University Press, 2012.

Ferrell, Robert H. *America's Deadliest Battle: Meuse-Argonne, 1918*. Lawrence: University Press of Kansas, 2007.

———, ed. *Collapse at the Meuse-Argonne: The Failure of the Missouri-Kansas Division*. Columbia: University of Missouri Press, 2004.

———, ed. *Meuse-Argonne Diary: A Division Commander in World War I, William M. Wright*. Columbia: University of Missouri Press, 2004.

———. *In the Company of Generals: The World War I Diary of Pierpont L. Stackpole*. Columbia: University of Missouri Press, 2009.

———. *The Question of MacArthur's Reputation: Côte de Châtillon, October 14–16, 1918*. Columbia: University of Missouri Press, 2008.

———. *Reminiscences of Conrad S. Babcock: The Old U.S. Army and the New, 1898–1918*. Columbia: University of Missouri Press, 2012.

Finnegan, Terrance J. *"A Delicate Affair" on the Western Front: America Learns How to Fight a Modern War in the Woëvre Trenches*. Stroud, UK: History Press, 2015.

———. *Shooting from the Front: Allied Aerial Reconnaissance and Photographic Interpretation on the Western Front in the World War*. Washington, DC: Center for Strategic Intelligence Research, National Defense College, 2006.

Frazer, Nimrod T. *Send the Alabamians: World War I Fighters in the Rainbow Division*. Tuscaloosa: University of Alabama Press, 2014.

Fuller, J. F. C. *Decisive Battles of the U.S.A.* New York: Thomas Yoseloff, Inc., 1942.

Gavin, Lettie. *American Women in World War I: They Also Served*. Boulder: University Press of Colorado, 1997.

Gawne, Jonathan. *Over There: The American Soldier in World War I*. Mechanicsville, PA: Stackpole Books, 1997.

Giangreco, D. M. *The Soldier from Independence: A Military Biography of Harry Truman*. Minneapolis: Zenith Press, 2009.

Gillett, Mary C. *The Army Medical Department, 1917–1941*. Washington, DC: Center of Military History, United States Army, 2009.

Greenhalgh, Elizabeth. *Foch in Command: The Forging of a First World War General*. New York: Cambridge University Press, 2011.

Gregory, Barry. *Argonne 1918: The AEF in France*. New York: Ballantine Books, 1972.

Grotelueschen, Mark Ethan. *The AEF Way of War: The American Army and Combat in World War I*. New York: Cambridge University Press, 2007.

Hall, Norman S. *The Balloon Buster: Frank Luke of Arizona*. New York: Arno Press, 1972.

Hallas, James. *Squandered Victory: The American First Army at St. Mihiel*. Westport, CT: Praeger, 1995.

Harries, Meirion, and Susie Harries. *The Last Days of Innocence: America at War, 1917–1918*. New York: Random House, 1997.

Harris, Stephen L. *Duffy's War: Fr. Francis Duffy, Wild Bill Donovan, and the Irish Fighting 69th in World War I*. Washington, DC: Potomac Books, 2006.

Hartzell, Arthur E. *Meuse-Argonne Battle (Sept. 26–Nov. 11, 1918)*. General Headquarters, American Expeditionary Forces Second Section, General Staff, 1919.

Hastings, Max. *Catastrophe 1914: Europe Goes to War*. New York: Alfred A. Knopf, 2013.

Haythornwaite, Philip J. *The World War I Source Book*. London: Arms and Armour Press, 1993.

Herris, Jack, and Bob Pearson. *Aircraft of World War I: 1914–1918*. London: Amber Books, 2014.

Hoff, Thomas A. *US Doughboy, 1916–19*. Oxford, UK: Osprey, 2005.

Holt, Major, and Mrs. Holt. *Battlefield Guide: The Western Front—South*. South Yorkshire: Pen & Sword, 2005.

Horne, Alistair. *The Price of Glory: Verdun, 1916*. New York: Penguin Books, 1916.

Howland, Colonel Harry S. *America in Battle: With Guide to the American Battlefields in France and Belgium*. Paris: Herbert Clark, 1920.

Hudson, James J. *Hostile Skies: A Combat History of the American Air Service in World War I*. Syracuse, NY: Syracuse University Press, 1968.

Hurley, Alfred. *Billy Mitchell: Crusader for Air Power*. New York: Franklin Watts, 1964.

Johnson, Douglas Wilson. *Battlefields of the World War, Western and Southern Front: A Study in Military Geography*. New York: Oxford University Press, 1921.

Johnson, Thomas M. *Our Secret War: True American Spy Stories, 1917–1919*. Indianapolis: Bobbs-Merrill Company, 1929.

———. *Without Censor: New Light on Our Greatest War Battles*. Indianapolis: Bobbs-Merrill Company, 1928.

Johnson, Thomas M., and Fletcher Pratt. *The Lost Battalion*. Lincoln: University of Nebraska Press, 2000.

Joint War History Commissions of Michigan and Wisconsin. *The 32nd Division in the World War*. Madison: Wisconsin War History Commission, 1920.

Keegan, John. *The First World War*. New York: Alfred A. Knopf, 1995.

Kennedy, David M. *Over Here: The First World War and American Society*. New York: Oxford University Press, 2004.

Krass, Peter. *Portrait of War: The U.S. Army's First Combat Artists and the Doughboy Experience in WW I*. Hoboken, NJ: John Wiley and Sons, 2006

Lacey, Jim, *Pershing: A Biography*. New York: Palgrave Macmillan, 2008.

Laplander, Robert J. *Finding the Lost Battalion*. Raleigh, NC: Lulu Press, 2007.

Laskin, David. *The Long Way Home: An American Journey from Ellis Island to the Great War*. New York: Harper, 2010.

Lawson, Don. *The United States in World War I*. New York: Scholastic Book Services, 1964.

Lengel, Edward G., ed. *A Companion to the Meuse-Argonne Campaign*. Malden, UK: Wiley Blackwell, 2014.

———. *To Conquer Hell: The Meuse-Argonne, 1918*. New York: Henry Holt and Company, 2008.

Liggett, Major General Hunter. *A.E.F.: Ten Years Ago in France*. New York: Dodd, Mead and Company, 1928.

———. *Commanding an American Army: Recollection of the World War*. Boston: Houghton Mifflin Company, 1925.

Lloyd, Nick. *Hundred Days: The Campaign That Ended World War I*. New York: Basic Books, 2014.

MacArthur, Douglas. *Reminiscences*. New York: McGraw-Hill Book Company, 1964.

Macklin, Elton E. *Suddenly We Didn't Want to Die: Memoirs of a World War I Marine*. Novato: Presidio Press, 1993.

Manchester, William. *American Caesar: Douglas MacArthur, 1890–1964*. Boston: Little, Brown and Company, 1978.

Marshall, George C. *Memoirs of My Service in the World War: 1917–1918*. Boston: Houghton Mifflin Company, 1976.

Mastriano, Douglas V. *Alvin York: A New Biography of the Hero of the Argonne*. Lexington: University of Kentucky Press, 2014.

McCollum, Buck Private. *History and Rhymes of the Lost Battalion*. New York: Buckee Publishing Company, 1937.

Mead, Gary. *The Doughboys: America and the First World War*. New York: Penguin Press, 2000.

Michelin Tire Company. *The Americans in the Great War.* Volume 2, *The Battle of Saint Mihiel.* Clermont-Ferrand: Michelin and Cie, 1920.

———. *The Americans in the Great War.* Volume 3, *Meuse-Argonne Battle.* Clermont-Ferrand: Michelin and Cie, 1919.

Mitchell, William. *Memoirs of World War I: "From Start to Finish of Our Greatest War."* New York: Random House, 1960.

Mortensen, Mark. *George W. Hamilton, USMC: America's Greatest World War I Hero.* Jefferson, NC: McFarland & Company, 2011.

Mroz, Albert. *American Military Vehicles of World War I: An Illustrated History of Armored Cars, Staff Cars, Motorcycles, Ambulances, Trucks, Tractors and Tanks.* Jefferson, NC: McFarland & Company, Inc., 2009.

Muirhead, Findlay, and Marcel Monmarché, eds. *Northeastern France.* London: Macmillan and Company, 1922.

Nenninger, Timothy K. "John J. Pershing and the Relief for Cause in the American Expeditionary Forces, 1917–1918." *Army History* (2005), 21–32.

———. "Tactical Dysfunction in the AEF, 1917–1918." *Military Affairs* (October 1987), 177–81.

———. " 'Unsystematic as a Mode of Command': Commanders and the Process of Command in the American Expeditionary Forces, 1917–1918." *Journal of Military History* 64 (July 2000), 739–68.

Newell, Ben. *Major Sam Woodfill: The Greatest Soldier of WW I.* Baltimore: Publish America, 2008.

Nolan, Thomas J. "Where Sergeant York Won His Medal of Honor: An Example of Allied Geographic Information Science." *Tennessee Historical Quarterly,* No. 4 (Winter 2012), 294–327.

O'Connor, Richard. *Black Jack Pershing.* Garden City, NY: Doubleday & Company, 1961.

Official History of the 82nd Division, American Expeditionary Forces. Indianapolis: Bobbs-Merrill Company, 1919.

Ousby, Ian. *The Road to Verdun: World War I's Most Momentous Battle and the Folly of Nationalism.* New York: Anchor Books, 2002

Owen, Peter F. *To the Limit of Endurance: A Battalion of Marines in the Great War.* College Station: Texas A&M University Press, 2007.

Page, Arthur W. *Our 110 Days Fighting.* New York: Doubleday, Page & Company, 1920.

Palmer, Frederick. *John J. Pershing, General of the Armies: A Biography.* Harrisburg, PA: Military Service Publishing Company, 1948.

———. *Our Greatest Battle (The Meuse-Argonne).* New York: Dodd, Mead and Company, 1919.

Pardoe, Blaine. *Terror of the Autumn Skies: The True Story of Frank Luke, America's Rogue Ace of World War I*. New York: Skyhorse Publishing, 2008.

Paschall, Rod. *The Defeat of Imperial Germany, 1917–1918*. Chapel Hill, NC: Algonquin Books, 1989.

Pershing, John J. *My Experiences*. New York: Frederick A. Stokes Company, 1931.

———. *My Life Before The World War, 1860–1917: General of the Armies John J. Pershing*. John T. Greenwood., ed. Lexington: University Press of Kentucky, 2013.

Pershing, John J., and Lieutenant General Hunter Liggett. *Report of the First Army, American Expeditionary Forces: Organization and Operations*. Fort Leavenworth, KS: General Service Schools Press, 1923.

Persico, Joseph E., *Eleventh Month, Eleventh, Day, Eleventh Hour: Armistice Day 1918, World War I and Its Violent Climax*. New York: Random House, 2004.

Pines, Upton Yale. *America's Greatest Blunder: The Fateful Decision to Enter World War One*. New York: RSD Press, 2013.

Pitt, Barrie. *1918: The Last Act*. New York: W. W. Norton & Company, 1962.

Posey, Brad. "Re-fighting the Meuse-Argonne: Alvin York and the Battle over World War I Site Commemoration." *Tennessee Historical Quarterly*, No. 4 (Winter 2012), 276–93.

Raines, Rebecca R. *Getting the Message Through: A Branch History of the U.S. Army Signal Corps*. Washington, D.C.: United States Army Center of Military History, 1996.

Rickenbacker, Edward V. *Fighting the Flying Circus*. New York: Frederick A. Stokes Company, 1919.

Rohan, Jack. *Rags: The Story of a Dog Who Went to War*. New York: Grosset and Dunlap, 1930.

Sammons, Jeffrey T., and John H. Morrow. *Harlem's Rattlers and the Great War: The Undaunted 369th Regiment and the African American Quest for Equality*. Lawrence: University Press of Kansas, 2014.

Shay, Michael E. *The Yankee Division in the First World War: In the Highest Tradition*. College Station: Texas A&M University Press, 2008.

Simonds, Frank H. *History of the World War*. Volume 5. New York: Doubleday, Page & Company, 1920.

Slotkin, Richard. *Lost Battalions: The Great War and the Crisis of American Nationality*. New York: Henry Holt and Company, 2004.

Smith, Gene. *Until the Last Trumpet Sounds: The Life of General of the Armies John J. Pershing*. New York: John Wiley and Sons, 1998.

Smythe, Donald. *Guerilla Warrior: The Early Life of John J. Pershing*. New York: Charles Scribner's Sons, 1973.

————. *Pershing: General of the Armies.* Bloomington: Indiana University Press, 1986.

Snell, Mark A., ed. *Unknown Soldiers: The American Expeditionary Forces in Memory and Remembrance.* Kent, OH: Kent State University Press, 2008.

Spence, William. *Supplies Used by the American 1st Army in the Meuse-Argonne Offensive.* Fort Leavenworth, KS: Command and General Staff College, 1930.

Stallings, Laurence. *The Doughboys.* New York: Popular Library, 1963.

Summerall, Charles Pelot. *The Way of Duty, Honor, Country: The Memoir of General Charles Pelot Summerall.* Timothy K. Nenninger, ed. Lexington: University Press of Kentucky, 2010.

Tate, Cassandra, *Cigarette Wars: The Triumph of the "Little White Slaver."* Oxford University Press, 2009.

Terraine, John. *To Win a War: 1918, the Year of Victory.* Garden City, NY: Doubleday & Company, 1981.

Thomas, Lowell. *Woodfill of the Regulars: A True Story from the Arctic to the Argonne.* Garden City, NY: Doubleday, Doran & Company, 1929.

Thomas, Shipley. *The History of the A.E.F..* New York: George H. Doran, 1920.

Thomason, Colonel John W., Jr. *And a Few Marines.* New York: Scribner's Sons, 1943.

Thorn, Henry C., Jr. *History of the 313th U.S. Infantry: "Baltimore's Own."* New York: Wynkoop Hallenbeck Crawford Company, 1920.

Toland, John. *No Man's Land: 1918—The Last Year of the Great War.* Garden City, NY: Doubleday & Company, 1980.

Tompkins, Raymond S. *Maryland Fighters in the Great War.* A. S. Abell Company, 1919.

Tucker, Spencer. *The Great War, 1914–1918.* Bloomington: Indiana University Press, 1998.

United States Army Center of Military History. *The United States in World War I.* Washington, DC: United States Army Center of Military History, 1998. CD-ROM.

United States War Department General Staff. *Blanc Mont (Meuse-Argonne-Champagne).* Washington, DC: Government Printing Office, 1921. Monograph.

Vandiver, Frank E. *Black Jack: The Life and Times of John J. Pershing.* 2 vols. College Station: Texas A&M University Press, 1977.

Venzon, Anne Cipriano, ed. *The United States in the First World War: An Encyclopedia.* New York: Garland Publishing, 1995.

Viereck, George Sylvester, ed. *As They Saw Us: Foch, Ludendorff and Other Leaders Write Our War History.* Garden City, NY: Doubleday, Doran & Company, 1929.

Votaw, John F. *The American Expeditionary Forces in World War I*. Oxford, UK: Osprey Books, 2001.

Waller, Douglas. *A Question of Loyalty: Gen. Billy Mitchell and the Court-Martial That Gripped the Nation*. New York: HarperCollins Publishers, 2004.

———. *Wild Bill Donovan: The Spymaster Who Created the OSS and Modern American Espionage*. New York: Free Press, 2011.

War Department Surgeon General's Office. *Medical Department of the United States Army in the World War*. Washington, DC: United States Government Printing Office, 1921–1929.

Werstein, Irving. *The Lost Battalion: A Saga of American Courage in World War I*. New York: W. W. Norton & Company, 1966.

West, William Benjamin. *The Fight for the Argonne: Personal Experiences of a Y Man*. New York: The Abingdon Press, 1919.

Wilson, Dale E. *Treat 'Em Rough!: The Birth of American Armor, 1917–20*. Novato, CA: Presidio Press, 1989.

Woodward, David R. *The American Army and the First World War*. New York: Cambridge University Press, 2014.

Wythe, George, Major. *A History of the 90th Division*. Ninetieth Division Association, 1920.

Yockelson, Mitchell A. *Borrowed Soldiers: Americans Under British Command, 1918*. Norman: University of Oklahoma Press, 2008.

———. *MacArthur: America's General*. Nashville: Thomas Nelson, 2011.

NOTES

Prologue

1. Martin Blumenson, ed., *The Patton Papers,* vol. 2, *1940–1945* (Boston: Houghton Mifflin, 1974), 608.

2. Carlo D'Este, *Patton: A Genius for War* (New York: HarperCollins Publishers, 1995), 163.

3. Frank Vandiver, *Black Jack: The Life and Times of John J. Pershing,* vol. 2 (College Station: Texas A&M University Press, 1977), 958; Cesar Santini, *Warren Tribune,* October 31, 1919; and Frederick Palmer, *Our Greatest Battle* (New York: Dodd, Mead, and Company, 1919), v.

4. Max Hastings, *Catastrophe 1914: Europe Goes to War* (New York: Alfred A. Knopf, 2013), 166.

5. Ibid., 189.

6. Spencer Tucker, *The Great War: 1914–18* (Bloomington: Indiana University Press, 1998), 38–39.

7. Michael Howard, *The First World War* (Oxford: Oxford University Press, 2002), 62.

8. D. Clayton James and Anne Sharp Wells, *America and the Great War: 1914–1920* (Wheeling, IL: Harlan Davidson, Inc., 1998), 28–29.

9. Douglas Wilson Johnson, *Battlefields of the World War, Western and Southern*

Front: A Study in Military Geography (New York: Oxford University Press, 1921), 337.

Chapter 1: Black Jack

1. Johnson, *Battlefields of the World War, Western and Southern Front*, 6.
2. Ibid., 3.
3. Edward M. Coffman, *The War to End All Wars: The American Military Experience in World War I* (New York: Oxford University Press, 1968), 43.
4. Frederick Palmer, *John J. Pershing, General of the Armies: A Biography* (Harrisburg, PA: Stackpole Books, 1948), 24.
5. Joseph Jacque Cesaire Joffre, *The Personal Memoirs of Joffre: Field Marshal of the French Army*, translated by Colonel T. Bentley Mott, D.S.M. (New York: Harper Brothers Publishers, 1932), vol. 2, 578.
6. Donald Smythe, *Guerilla Warrior: The Early Life of John J. Pershing* (New York: Charles Scribner's Sons, 1973), 1–2; John J. Pershing, *My Life Before the World War, 1860–1917*, John T. Greenwood, ed. (Lexington: University Press of Kentucky, 2013), 16–17.
7. Ibid., 23.
8. Palmer, *John J. Pershing, General of the Armies*, 10.
9. Smythe, *Guerrilla Warrior*, 7–8.
10. Ibid., 13.
11. Ibid., 13.
12. Frank Vandiver, "Harmon Memorial Lecture 5" (U.S. Air Force Academy, CO, 1973), 2.
13. Ibid., 12.
14. Gene Smith, *Until the Last Trumpet Sounds: The Life of General of the Armies John J. Pershing* (New York: Wiley, 1998), 21.
15. Ibid., 11.
16. John Perry, *Pershing: Commander of the Army* (Nashville: Thomas Nelson, 2011), 13.
17. Smythe, *Guerilla Warrior*, 29.
18. Smythe, *Guerilla Warrior*, 35; Smith, 42.
19. Vandiver, Harmon Memorial Lecture.
20. Smith, 48.
21. Vandiver, Harmon Memorial Lecture.
22. Jim Lacey, *Pershing: A Biography* (New York: Palgrave Macmillan, 2008), 35.
23. Smythe, *Guerilla Warrior*, 64.
24. Ibid., 47.

25. Lacey, 50–51.

26. Smythe, *Guerilla Warrior*, 121.

27. Vandiver, Harmon Memorial Lecture.

28. Smythe, *Guerilla Warrior*, 126; Smith, 92.

29. Frank E. Vandiver, *Black Jack: The Life and Times of John J. Pershing*, vol. 1 (College Station: Texas A&M University Press, 1977), 593–94.

30. Smythe, *Guerilla Warrior*, 213.

31. John J. Pershing, *My Life Before the World War*. John T. Greenwood., ed. (Lexington: University Press of Kentucky, 2013), 667–68.

32. Edward A. Godeken, "The Dawes-Pershing Relationship During World War I." *Nebraska History* 65 (1984), 113.

33. Smythe, *Guerilla Warrior*, 220.

34. Ibid., 232.

35. Richard O'Connor, *Black Jack Pershing* (Garden City, NY: Doubleday and Company, 1961), 136–37.

36. Vandiver, *Black Jack*, vol. 2, 662.

37. Harvey DeWeerd, *Great Soldiers of the Two World Wars* (New York: W. W. Norton & Company, 1941), 164.

Chapter 2: First Army Is Born

1. Smythe, *Guerilla Warrior*, 21.

2. Ibid., 22.

3. *New York Times*, September 15, 1918.

4. Coffman, 127.

5. Pershing, *My Experiences in the World War*, John T. Greenwood, ed. (Lexington: University Press of Kentucky, 2013), 63.

6. *Pittsburgh Gazette Times*, "Headquarters in France of U.S. Soldiers," December 25, 1918.

7. O'Connor, 198–99.

8. Avery DeLano Andrews, *My Friend and Classmate John J. Pershing: With Notes from My War Diary* (Harrisburg, PA: Military Service Publishing Company, 1939), 165–66.

9. *New York Times*, Sunday, December 16, 1934.

10. American Battle Monuments Commission, *American Armies and Battlefields in Europe* (Washington: U.S. Government Printing Office, 1938), 106.

11. Hastings, 315.

12. James H. Hallas, *Squandered Victory: The American First Army at St. Mihiel* (Westport, CT: Praeger, 1995), 2.

13. Paul Braim, *The Test of Battle: The American Expeditionary Forces in the Meuse-Argonne Campaign* (Shippensburg, PA: White Mane Press, 1998), 62; J. M. Bourne, *Who's Who In World War I* (London: Routledge, 2001), 102.

14. David Bonk, *St. Mihiel 1918: The American Expeditionary Force's Trial by Fire* (Oxford: Osprey Publishing Limited, 2011), 12–13; J. M. Bourne, 102.

15. Pershing, *My Experiences in the World War*, vol. 1 (New York: Frederick A. Stokes Company, 1931), 229.

16. Ibid., 323.

17. John Dos Passos, *Mr. Wilson's War: From the Assassination of McKinley to the Defeat of the League of Nations* (New York: Skyhorse Publishing, 2013), 402.

18. Charles G. Dawes, *A Journal of the Great War*, vol. 1 (Boston: Houghton, Mifflin Company, 1921), 153; James H. Hallas, *Squandered Victory: The American First Army at St. Mihiel* (Westport, CT: Prager, 1995), 42.

19. Pershing, vol. 2, 238.

20. George C. Marshall, *Memoirs of My Services in the World War: 1917–1918* (Boston: Houghton Mifflin Company, 1976), 127.

21. American Battle Monuments Commission, *American Armies and Battlefields in Europe*, 110–11; Braim, 68–69.

22. Most of First Army's divisions were undermanned, at about 25,500 officers and men.

23. Charles Francis King, *General Hunter Liggett* (master's thesis, University of Oklahoma, 1964), 25.

24. Palmer, *Our Greatest Battle*, 358.

25. King, 75.

26. Hallas, 49–50.

27. Pershing, *My Experiences in the World War*, vol. 2, 245–48.

28. Ibid., 247–48.

29. Donald Smythe, *Pershing: General of the Armies* (Bloomington: Indiana University Press, 1986), 176–77.

30. Robert E. Rogge, "304th Tank Brigade: Its Formation and First Two Actions," *eARMOR*, http://www.benning.army.mil/armor/eARMOR/content/issues/2013/JUL_SEP/Rogge.html.

31. William Benjamin West, *The Fight for the Argonne: Personal Experiences of a Y Man* (New York: The Abingdon Press, 1919), 85.

32. John F. Shiner, *Foulois and the U.S. Army Air Corps: 1931–1935* (Washington: Office of Air Force History, 1983), 9–10.

33. Hallas, 19.

34. Burke Davis, *The Billy Mitchell Affair* (New York: Random House, 1967), 45.

35. William Mitchell, *Memoirs of World War I: "From Start to Finish of Our Greatest War"* (New York: Random House, 1960), 237.

36. James J. Cooke, *U.S. Air Service in the Great War, 1917–1919* (Westport, CT: Praeger, 1996), 126.

37. Ibid., 126.

38. Ibid., viii.

39. Ibid., ix.

40. Maurer Maurer, *The U.S. Air Service in the World War*, vol. 3, *The Battle of St. Mihiel* (Washington: Office of Air Force History, 1978–79), 126.

41. Hallas, 32–33.

42. Paul C. Clark to John J. Pershing, September 10, 1918. General John J. Pershing, Record Group 200, National Archives.

43. Hunter Liggett, *A.E.F.: Ten Years Ago in France* (New York: Dodd, Mead and Company, 1928), 145.

44. Ibid., 145–46.

45. Cooke, *U.S. Air Service in the Great War, 1917–1919*, 91.

46. Liggett, *A.E.F.: Ten Years Ago in France*, 146.

47. James Hallas, "Belfort Ruse," in Anne Cipriano Venzon, ed., *The United States in the World War: An Encyclopedia* (New York: Garland Publishing, 1995), 70.

48. Ibid., 71.

49. Laurence M. Stallings and M. S. Wyeth, Jr., *The Story of the Doughboys: The AEF in World War I* (New York: Harper and Row, 1966), 97–98. For a more complete telling of the "Belfort Ruse," see Rod Paschal or Donald Smythe. Col. A. L. Conger to Chief of Staff, AEF, "Operations in the Belfort Sector," September 2, 1918, File 1034, Entry 267, Record Group 120, National Archive.

Chapter 3: St. Mihiel

1. Mitchell, 57.

2. Davis, 41; Hallas, 80.

3. David R. Woodward, *The American Army and the First World War* (Cambridge, UK: Cambridge University Press, 2014), 312.

4. Dale Van Every, *The AEF in Battle* (New York: D. Appleton, 1928), 257.

5. *New York Times*, "Our Attack Launched with a Fleet of Tanks." September 13, 1918.

6. Marshall, 129–30.

7. James Scott Wheeler, *The Big Red One: America's Legendary 1st Infantry Division from World War I to Desert Storm* (Lawrence: University Press of Kansas, 2007), 74.

8. O'Connor, 297.

9. Byron Farwell, *Over There: The United States in the Great War, 1917–1918* (New York: W. W. Norton & Company, 1999), 216.

10. Francis P. Duffy, *Father Duffy's Story* (New York: George H. Doran, 1919), 25.

11. Donovan Diary, September 21, 1918. William J. Donovan Papers, AHEC.

12. Ibid.

13. William Manchester, *American Caesar: Douglas MacArthur: 1880–1964* (New York: Little, Brown and Company, 1978), 101–2; D'Este, 235.

14. Kevin Hymel, http://www.armyhistory.org/ahf2.aspx?pgID=877&id=105&exCompID=56; see also Mitchell Yockelson, *MacArthur: America's General* (Nashville: Thomas Nelson, 2011), 65.

15. Hugh S. Thompson, *Trench Knives and Mustard Gas: With the 42nd Rainbow Division in France*, Robert H. Ferrell, ed. (College Station: Texas A&M Press, 2004), 174–75.

16. A. Lincoln Lavine, *Circuits of Victory* (New York: Doubleday, Page & Company, 1921), 502.

17. Evangeline Cory Booth and Grace Livingston Hill, *The War Romance of the Salvation Army* (Philadelphia: J. P. Lippincott Company, 1919), 238.

18. Lecture by the St. Mihiel town councillor, St. Mihiel, October 5, 2014.

19. Ibid., 242.

20. Goettler Diary, Thursday, September 12, 1918, Harold Goettler Collection, University of Chicago Library.

21. Edward V. Rickenbacker, *Fighting the Flying Circus* (New York: Frederick A. Stokes Company, 1919), 232–33.

22. *New York Times*, "Putnam, American Ace, Killed Near St. Mihiel." September 20, 1918.

23. *New York Times*, "Germans Prepare to Resist Our Men," September 16, 1918.

24. Martin Blumenson, ed., *The Patton Papers*, vol. 1, *1885–1940* (Boston: Houghton Mifflin Company, 1972), 584.

25. *New York Times*, "Tanks a Big Factor in St. Mihiel Victory," September 14, 1918.

26. Ibid.

27. Hallas, 121–22.

28. Pershing Diary, September 12, 1918, Pershing Papers, LOC.

29. Captain Ernest Harmon, "Account of the 2nd Cavalry at St. Mihiel." *Cavalry Journal* (1922). Reproduced in the St. Mihiel *Trip-Wire*: http://www.worldwar1.com/tripwire/smtw.htm.

30. John L. Hines Diary, September 13, 1918, Hugh Drum Papers, AHEC.

31. MacArthur, 63.

32. Marshall, 146.

33. Vandiver, *Black Jack*, 950.

34. John Milton Cooper, *Woodrow Wilson: A Biography* (New York: Alfred A. Knopf, 2009), 438.

35. Smythe, 286.

36. Pershing to Micheline Resco, September 29, 1918. Jesuit Archives, John Carroll University, Cleveland, Ohio.

37. Smith, 192.

38. Mrs. George S. Patton to John J. Pershing, September 13, 1918, Pershing Papers, LOC.

39. Mary Drum to Ernest Brown, managing editor of the *Indianapolis Star*, September 22, 1918, Hugh Drum Papers, AHEC.

40. *New York Times*, "Splendid Victory Is Paris' Verdict," September 16, 1918.

41. http://www.imdb.com/title/tt0190139.

42. Georges Clemenceau, *Grandeur and Misery of Victory* (New York: Harcourt, Brace, 1930), 76.

43. Dale Van Every, *The AEF in Battle* (New York: D. Appleton, 1928), 314.

44. Pershing, *My Experiences in the World War*, vol. 2, 270; General John J. Pershing and Lieutenant General Hunter Liggett, *Report of the First Army: American Expeditionary Forces* (Fort Leavenworth: General Services School Press, 1923), 32.

45. Liggett, *A.E.F.: Ten Years Ago in France*, 159.

Chapter 4: Preparing for America's Greatest Battle

1. Colonel T. Bentley Mott, *Twenty Years as Military Attaché* (New York: Oxford University Press, 1937), 294.

2. *New York Times*, September 16, 1918, "Baker Deeply Stirred by Our Army's Victory."

3. Smythe, 5.

4. C. H. Cramer, *Newton D. Baker: A Biography* (Cleveland: The World Publishing Company, 1960), 14.

5. Smythe, 6.

6. Pershing, *My Experiences in the World War*, vol. 1, 385.

7. Smythe, 166.

8. James G. Harbord to John J. Pershing, September 10, 1918, Pershing Papers, LOC.

9. George C. Marshall, *Memoirs of My Service in the World War*, 147.

10. Michelin & Co., *The Americans in the Great War*, vol. 2, *The Battle of Saint Mihiel* (Milltown: Michelin Tire Company, 1920), 3.
11. Vandiver, 956.
12. *New York Times*, Thornton.
13. Pershing Diary, September 21.
14. Harvey Cushing, *From a Surgeon's Journal, 1915–1918*, September 25, 1918, http://www.ourstory.info/library/2-ww1/Cushing/journal19.html.
15. Palmer, *Our Greatest Battle*, 320–21.
16. Ibid., 543.
17. Stallings, 106.
18. Ibid., 105–6.
19. Smythe, 190.
20. General John J. Pershing and Lieutenant General Hunter Liggett. *Report of the First Army, American Expeditionary Forces: Organization and Operations* (Fort Leavenworth, KS: General Service Schools Press, 1923), 38–39.
21. Harvey Cushing, *From a Surgeon's Journal: 1915–1918*, July 25, 1918, http://www.ourstory.info/library/2-ww1/Cushing/journal19.html.
22. Thomas M. Johnson, *Without Censor: New Light on Our Greatest War Battles* (Indianapolis: Bobbs-Merrill Company, 1928), 169.
23. Lacey, 164.
24. Billy Mitchell, "Air Service in the Meuse-Argonne," *World's Work* (September 1919), 558. Thanks to Christopher M. Rein at the U.S. Air Force Academy for bringing this article to my attention.
25. Marian Baldwin, *Canteening Overseas: 1917–1919* (New York: Macmillan Company, 1920), 131–32.
26. Marshall, 154.
27. Ibid.
28. D'Este, 249.
29. Pershing, *My Experiences in the World War*, vol. 2, 294.

Chapter 5: On with the Battle

1. D'Este, 254.
2. Mark Grotelueschen, *Doctrine Under Fire: American Artillery Employment in World War I* (Westport, CT: Greenwood Press, 2001), 10.
3. Henry C. Thorn, Jr., *History of the 313th U.S. Infantry: "Baltimore's Own"* (New York: Wynkoop Hallenbeck Crawford Company, 1920), 29.
4. Robert H. Ferrell, *Collapse at Meuse-Argonne: The Failure of the Missouri-Kansas Division* (Columbia: University of Missouri Press, 2004), 17.

5. Thomas A. Hoff, *US Doughboy: 1916–19* (Oxford, UK: Osprey Publishing Company, 2005), 18–20.

6. Ibid., 20.

7. Diary of Private Homer E. Simpson, George C. Marshall Foundation Library.

8. http://www.qmfound.com/americas_munitions.htm.

9. Quartermaster Corps School, *Operations of the Quartermaster Corps, U.S. Army During the World War* (Philadelphia: Schuylkill Arsenal, 1929), 34.

10. William Spence, *Supplies Used by the American 1st Army in the Meuse-Argonne Offensive. Solution No. 4* (Fort Leavenworth: Command and General Staff School, 1930).

11. *Operations of the Quartermaster Corps*, 14.

12. Ibid., 24–25.

13. Palmer, *Our Greatest Battle*, 30.

14. Major General Hunter Liggett, *Commanding an American Army: Recollection of the World War* (Boston: Houghton Mifflin Company, 1925), 77.

15. American Battle Monuments Commission, 173.

16. Hines Diary, September 26, 1918, AHEC.

17. 42nd Division Interrogation of Seven Prisoners from the 2nd Company, 14th Assault Battalion. 42nd Division Historical Files, Record Group 120, National Archive.

18. Robert H. Ferrell, *America's Deadliest Battle: Meuse-Argonne, 1918* (Lawrence: University Press of Kansas, 2007), 54–55.

19. Boyd L. Dastrup, *King of Battle: A Branch History of the U.S. Army's Field Artillery* (Fort Monroe, VA: Office of the Command Historian, United States Army Training and Doctrine Command, 1993), 162.

20. Ibid., 1.

21. Robert H. Ferrell, *Collapse at Meuse-Argonne* (Columbia: University of Missouri Press, 2004), 34–35.

22. D. M. Giangreco, *The Soldier from Independence: A Military Biography of Harry Truman* (Minneapolis: Zenith Press, 2009), vii.

23. Alonzo L. Hamby, *Man of the People: A Life of Harry S. Truman* (New York: Oxford University Press, 1995), 66–67.

24. David McCullough, *Truman* (New York: Simon & Schuster, 1992), 118.

25. Exhibit label, National World War I Museum at Liberty Memorial, Kansas City, MO.

26. Harry S. Truman, *The Autobiography of Harry S. Truman*, Robert H. Ferrell, ed. (Columbia: University of Missouri Press, 2002), 48.

27. Giangreco, 175.
28. Charles B. Hoyt. *Heroes of the Argonne: An Authentic History of the Thirty-fifth Division* (Kansas City: Franklin Hudson Publishing Company, 1919), 71.
29. Ferrell, *Collapse at Meuse-Argonne*, 34–35.
30. Hoyt, 76–77.
31. Andrews, 203.
32. Thanks to historian Patrick Osborn for providing copies of the 345th Tank Battalion War Diaries, American Battle Monuments Commission, *28th Division: Summary of Operations in the World War* (Washington: United States Government Printing Office, 1944).
33. *New York Times*, "Brig. Gen. Sigerfoos Is Dead of Wounds," October 25, 1918.
34. *New York Times*, "A Medal of Honor Actor," August 22, 1920. Thanks to historian Patrick Osborn for bringing this article to my attention.
35. Ferrell, *Collapse at Meuse-Argonne*, 35.
36. Dale E. Wilson, *Treat 'Em Rough: The Birth of American Armor, 1917–20* (Novato, CA: Presidio, 1990), 141–43.
37. D'Este, 37–58.
38. Ibid., 120–28.
39. Ibid., 164.
40. John S. D. Eisenhower, *Soldiers and Statesmen: Reflections on Leadership* (Columbia: University of Missouri Press, 2012), 73.
41. John S. D. Eisenhower, *Intervention: The United States and the Mexican Revolution, 1913–1917* (New York: W. W. Norton & Company, 1993), 288–89; D'Este, 173–74; Blumenson, ed., *The Patton Papers*, vol. 1, 355–56.
42. Letter in the possession of Grosvenor Merle-Smith. I am grateful to him for allowing me to copy it and reproduce the contents.
43. Stanley P. Hirshson, *General Patton: A Soldier's Life* (New York: Harper, 2003), 503; Blumenson, ed., *The Patton Papers*, vol. 1, 610–13.
44. " 'Bravest Man in the American Army' Is a Compliment Bestowed on New Jersey Boy by Tank Commander," *Indiana Evening Gazette*, April 4, 1919.
45. Pershing to Bea Patton, October 10, 1918, Pershing Papers, LOC.
46. Peter Krass, *Portrait of War: The U.S. Army's First Combat Artists and the Doughboy Experience in WW I* (Hoboken: John Wiley and Sons, 2006), 239.
47. Robert Lee Bullard, *American Soldiers Also Fought* (New York: Longmans, Green and Co., 1936), 108.
48. Major General Hunter Liggett, *AEF: Ten Years Ago in France* (New York: Dodd, Mead and Company, 1928), 174.
49. Coffman, 306.

50. Raymond S. Tompkins, *Maryland Fighters in the Great War* (Baltimore: Thomas and Evans, 1919), 75.

51. Krass, 227–32.

52. Elbridge Colby, "The Taking of Montfaucon," *Infantry Journal* 47, 134.

53. Thorn, 29.

54. Major General Joseph E. Kuhn, "Two Regiments of Seventy-Ninth Go into Battle," *New York Times*, March 18, 1926.

55. Colonel Conrad H. Lanza, "The Battle of Montfaucon: 26 September 1918— An Artilleryman's View," *Field Artillery Journal* 23, no. 3, May–June 1933, 242.

56. Philip J. Haythornwaite, *The World War I Source Book* (London: Arms and Armour Press, 1993), 200–201.

57. http://apps.westpointaog.or/Memorials/Articles/3474.

58. Tompkins, 82.

59. Coffman, 307.

60. Tompkins, 83.

61. Coffman, 308.

62. James J. Hudson, *Hostile Skies: A Combat History of the American Air Service in World War I* (Syracuse, NY: Syracuse University Press, 1968), 260.

63. Rickenbacker, 269.

64. Ibid., 271.

65. Captain Merian C. Cooper, "Statement," *Gorrell's History of the U.S. Air Service, 1917–1918*, Series E, Record Group 120, National Archives.

66. Interview with First Lieutenant Richardson, in *Gorrell's History of the U.S. Air Service, 1917–1918*.

67. Ezra Bowen, *Knights of the Air* (Alexandria, VA: Time-Life Books, 1980), 172–73.

68. Palmer, *Our Greatest Battle*, 355–56.

69. Emmett Crozier, *American Reporters on the Western Front, 1914–1918* (New York: Oxford University Press, 1959), 252–53.

70. Pershing Diary, September 26, 1918.

71. Liggett, *A.E.F.: Ten Years Ago in France*, 175.

Chapter 6: Advance!

1. Rexmond C. Cochrane, *The 79th Division at Montfaucon, October 1918* (Army Chemical Center, Maryland: U.S. Army Chemical Corps Historical Office, 1960), 21.

2. Historian Wim Degrande graciously provided information on Gallwitz's headquarters. For a description of Longuyon, see Findlay Muirhead and

Marcel Monmarché, eds., *Muirhead's North-Eastern France* (London: Macmillan, 1922), 135.

3. Paul F. Braim, *The Test of Battle: The American Expeditionary Forces in the Meuse-Argonne Campaign* (Shippensburg, PA: White Mane Books, 1998), 85–86; Lieutenant Colonel Wetzell, Fifth Army to Group of Armies Gallwitz, Historical Section German File: 811-33.5, Folder VI: Order. Record Group 165, National Archives.

4. Bleckley War Diary, September 27.

5. Bruce N. Canfield, *U.S. Infantry Weapons of the First World War* (Lincoln, RI: Andrew Mowbray, 2000), 258.

6. John S. D. Eisenhower, *Yanks*, 222–23.

7. Johnson, *Without Censor*, 169.

8. Eisenhower, 223.

9. Tompkins, 89–90.

10. American Expeditionary Forces, *Historical Report of the Chief Engineer: American Expeditionary Forces, 1917–1919* (Washington: U.S. Government Printing Office, 1919), 213.

11. Major General M. W. Ireland, *The Medical Department of the United States Army in the World War:* vol. VII, *Field Operations* (Washington: U.S. Government Printing Office, 1925), 555.

12. Ferrell, *America's Deadliest Battle*, 59.

13. Hines Diary, September 27; Cochrane, *The 79th Division at Montfaucon, October 1918*; U.S. Army Chemical Corps Historical Studies, *Gas Warfare in World War I*, Study Number 19 (Army Chemical Center, Maryland: U.S. Army Chemical Corps Historical Office, 1960), 18–21.

14. Marshall, 162.

15. Marc K. Blackburn, *The United States Army and the Motor Truck* (Westport, CT: Greenwood Press, 1996), 33.

16. Thomas, *Without Censor*, 172.

17. Ireland, 554–55.

18. Harvey Cushing, September 28, 1918. http://www.ourstory.info/library/2-wwi/Cushing/journal19.html.

19. West, William Benjamin, *The Fight for the Argonne: Personal Experiences of a Young Man* (New York: The Abingdon Press, 1919), 45–46.

20. Harvey Cushing, *From a Surgeon's Journal: 1915–1918*, September 27, 1918. http://www.ourstory.info/library/2-wwi/Cushing/journal19.html.

21. Hines Diary, September 28.

22. Arthur W. Hartzell, "Meuse-Argonne Battle." Visitors Bureau, AEF, Second Section, September 23, 1919.

23. Julius Ochs Adler, *History of the Seventy-seventh Division* (New York: W. H. Crawford Company, 1919), 65.

24. Ibid.

25. Ibid.

26. Pierpont Stackpole Diary, September 27.

27. John W. Thomason, *And a Few Marines* (New York: Scribner's Sons, 1943), 131–32.

28. Bourne, 110.

29. Thomas M. Johnson and Fletcher Pratt, *The Lost Battalion* (Lincoln: University of Nebraska Press, 2000), 130.

30. Taylor V. Beattie, "Whittlesey's 'Lost' Battalion." *Army History: The Professional Bulletin of Army History* (Winter 2002), 24.

31. Thomas M. Johnson and Fletcher Pratt, *The Lost Battalion* (Lincoln: University of Nebraska Press, 2000), 17–18.

32. Robert H. Ferrell, *Five Days in October: The Lost Battalion of World War I* (Columbia: University of Missouri Press, 2005), 11.

33. Meirion and Susie Harries, *The Last Days of Innocence: America at War, 1917–1918* (New York: Random House, 1997), 371–72.

34. Ibid., 372.

35. Jennifer D. Keene, "Uneasy Alliances: French Military Intelligence and the American Army during the First World War," http://www.chapman.edu/our-faculty/files/publications/keene-jennifer/Uneasy%20Alliances.pdf, 23.

36. Chad L. Williams, *Torchbearers of Democracy: African-American Soldiers in the World War I Era* (Chapel Hill: University of North Carolina Press, 2010), 350–51.

37. Ibid., 114.

38. Keene, 30.

39. Robert H. Ferrell, *Unjustly Dishonored: An African-American Division in World War I* (Columbia: University of Missouri Press, 2011), 38–39.

40. Military maps designated hills by their proper names if they had them. Otherwise, they were identified by their height in meters. So Hill 198 was 198 meters tall.

41. *Belgium and the Battlefields* (London: Ward, Lock & Co., n.d.), 267.

42. George Sylvester Viereck, ed., "General Erich Ludendorff," in *As They Saw Us: Ludendorff and Other Leaders Write Our History* (New York: Doubleday, Doran & Company, 1929), 39.

43. Max Hastings, *Catastrophe 1914: Europe Goes to War* (New York: Alfred A. Knopf, 2013), 274.

44. Ibid., 273.

45. J. M. Bourne, *Who's Who in World War I* (London: Routledge, 2001), 304–5.

46. Mott, 411–12.

47. Clark to Pershing, September 28, 1918.

Chapter 7: Behind the Lines

1. Timothy K. Nenninger, "John J. Pershing and Relief for Cause in the American Expeditionary Forces, 1917–1918," *Army History* (Spring 2005), 23.

2. Ibid., 20.

3. Ibid., 28.

4. Ibid.

5. Ibid.

6. Allan R. Millett, *The General: Robert L. Bullard and Officership in the United States Army, 1881–1925* (Westport, CT: Greenwood Press, 1975), 401.

7. Stackpole Diary, September 27.

8. Lettie Gavin, *American Women in World War I: They Also Served* (Boulder: University Press of Colorado, 1997), 79.

9. Ibid.

10. Dorothy and Carl J. Schneider, *Into the Breach: American Women Overseas in World War I* (New York: Viking Press, 1991), 269.

11. Ibid., 185.

12. Lavine, 565.

13. Gavin, 88–89.

14. When the Hello Girls returned home after the war, they were refused honorable discharges and veterans' benefits because the War Department considered them civilian employees of the Army. One of the switchboard supervisors, Merle Egan-Anderson of Helena, Montana, lobbied Congress on their behalf. Her effort took sixty years, but in 1978 all seventy surviving telephone operators were given honorable discharges.

15. Schneider, 185.

16. Ibid., 186.

17. "Without Censor," *Theosophical Quarterly Magazine* 34 (1937), 298–99.

18. Lavine, 96–99.

19. Major General A. W. Greely, U.S. Army, "The Signal Corps in the Great War," *New York Times*, May 25, 1919.

20. Ibid.

21. Clark to Pershing, September 30, 1918. Record Group 200, National Archives.

22. Terry M. Bareither, ed., *An Engineer's Diary of the Great War (Lt. Harry Spring, 37th Engineers)* (Purdue, IN: Purdue University Press, 2002), 91.

23. Chester W. Davis, *The Story of the First Pioneer Infantry* (n.p., 1919), 28.

24. Brent Papers, LOC, Box 16.

25. Thomas M. Johnson, *Our Secret War: True American Spy Stories, 1917–1919* (Indianapolis: Bobbs-Merrill Company, 1929), 25.

26. Paul Krech, *Story of a German Prisoner in an American Labor Camp* (Gièvres, 1919). Thanks to Jay Bosanko for providing me a copy of this memoir.

27. George G. Lewis and John Mewha, *History of Prisoner of War Utilization by the United States Army: 1776–1945* (Washington: Center for Military History, 1989), 60–61.

28. Thomas, *Our Secret* War, 33.

29. Ibid., 35.

30. *New York Times*, July 23, 1919.

31. Record Group 120, Entry 177, Box 6009, File #515-16, National Archives.

32. Thomas, *Our Secret War*, 224–25.

33. Ibid., 225.

34. James B. Campbell, "Origins of Aerial Photographic Interpretation, U.S. Army, 1916–1918," *Photogrammetric Engineering and Remote Sensing* (January 2008), 83–86.

35. Terrance J. Finnegan, *Shooting the Front: Allied Aerial Reconnaissance and Photographic Interpretation on the Western Front—World War I* (Washington: NDIC Press, 2007), 127–29.

36. http://www.artic.edu/exhibition/sharp-clear-pictures-edward-steichen-s-world-war-i-and-cond-nast-years.

37. Stackpole Diary, September 28.

38. Ibid.

Chapter 8: No Progress

1. Pershing Diary, September 29, 1918.

2. Herbert R. Lottman, *Pétain: Hero or Traitor?* (New York: William Morrow, 1985), 62.

3. Ibid.

4. Ibid.

5. Pershing, *My Experiences in the World War*, vol. 1, 46.

6. Smythe, 200–201.

7. Pershing, *My Experiences in the World War*, vol. 1, 161–62.

8. Thomas, *Without Censor*, 173.

9. Clark to Pershing, September 29, 1918.

10. Pershing, *My Experiences in the World War*, vol. 1, 100.

11. Smythe, 198–99.

12. *New York Times*, February 18, 1919.

13. Palmer, *Our Greatest Battle*, 145; Ferrell, *America's Deadliest Battle*, 70.

14. Palmer, *Our Greatest Battle*, 145.

15. Booth, 253.

16. Gavin, 226.

17. Ibid., 223.

18. Mary C. Gillett, *The Army Medical Department, 1917–1941* (Washington, DC: Center of Military History, U.S. Army, 2009), 336.

19. Stackpole Diary, September 1918.

20. Johnson, *Our Secret War*, 32.

21. Palmer, *Our Greatest Battle*, 192.

22. Marshall, 164.

23. Coffman, 306.

24. Library of Virginia, Richmond, VA, *Virginia War History Commission* "World War I History Commission Questionnaires, 1919–1928."

25. Smythe, 200.

26. Forrest C. Pogue, *George C. Marshall: Organizer of Victory* (New York: Viking Press, 1973), 177.

27. Marshall, 164–65.

28. Thomas R. Gowenlock, *Soldiers of Darkness* (New York: Doubleday, Doran & Company, 1937), 185.

29. Ibid., 205.

30. Rickenbacker, 229.

31. Ibid., 248–50.

32. Ibid., 280.

33. Bert Frandsen, *Hat in the Ring: The Birth of American Air Power in the Great War* (Washington, DC: Smithsonian Books, 2010), 240–41.

34. Blaine Pardoe, *Terror of the Autumn Skies: The True Story of Frank Luke, America's Rogue Ace of World War I* (New York: Skyhorse Publishing, 2008), 237.

35. Norman Shannon Hall, *The Balloon Buster: Frank Luke of Arizona* (New York: Arno Press, 1972), 174–75.

36. http://acepilots.com/wwi/us_luke.html.

37. Pardoe, 197.

38. Harry S. Truman Presidential Library: http://www.trumanlibrary.org/whistlestop/study_collections/ww.

39. Smythe, 297.

40. Pershing, *My Experiences in the World War*, vol. 2, 306–7

41. Ibid., 168.

42. Donald Smythe, "The Pershing-March Conflict in World War I," *Parameters* 11, no. 4 (1980), 58.

43. George C. Marshall to John J. Pershing, October 24, 1930, *The Papers of George Catlett Marshall*, vol. 1, *The Soldierly Spirit, December 1880–June 1939*, Larry I. Bland, ed. (Baltimore: Johns Hopkins University Press, 1981), 360–61.

44. Richard Slotkin, *Lost Battalions: The Great War and the Crisis of American Nationality* (New York: Henry Holt and Company, 2005), 285.

45. *New York Times*, October 5, 1918.

46. Pershing, *My Experiences in the World War*, vol. 2, 321.

47. Smythe, 200.

48. *New York Times*, April 20, 1919.

49. Pershing, *My Experiences in the World War*, vol. 2, 321–22.

50. Vandiver, 969.

Chapter 9: Fighting in the Argonne

1. Heywood Broun, *Our Army at the Front* (New York: Charles Scribner's Sons, 1922), 279.

2. Buck Private McCollum, *History and Rhymes of the Lost Battalion* (New York: Bucklee Publishing Company, 1937), 48; Irving Werstein, *The Lost Battalion: A Saga of American Courage in World War I* (New York: W. W. Norton & Company, 1966), 46; Irving Werstein Papers, Southern Mississippi Library.

3. Hines Diary, November 4, 1918.

4. Marco Magielse, *Les Secrets de Romagne: '14–'18* (Geldrop, Netherlands: Trench Publishers, 2014), 2, 164.

5. Johnson, *Our Secret War*, 94.

6. Pershing Diary, October 2, 1918.

7. Johnson, 191–92.

8. Caitlin Marie Therese Jeffrey, *Journey Through Unfamiliar Territory: American Reporters and the First World War* (PhD dissertation, University of California, Irvine, 2007), 154–55.

9. "Joseph Timmons of Los Angeles Wounded on American Front," *New York Times*, October 6, 1918.

10. Robert H. Ferrell, *Reminiscences of Conrad S. Babcock: The Old U.S. Army and the New, 1898–1918* (Columbia: University of Missouri Press, 2012), 128–29.

11. Slotkin, 306–7.

12. Ibid., 307.

13. Edward G. Lengel, *To Conquer Hell: Meuse-Argonne, 1918* (New York: Henry Holt and Company, 2008), 224.

14. Werstein, 52.

15. Ibid., 53.

16. Ibid., 55–56.

17. Lavine, 45.

18. Ibid., 45.

19. Liggett, *AEF*, 183.

20. Ferrell, *Five Days in October*, 24.

21. Harries, 375.

22. Johnson and Pratt, 309.

23. Mark E. Grotelueschen, "The Doughboys Make Good: American Victories at St. Mihiel and Blanc Mont Ridge," *Army History* (Spring 2013), 13.

24. Andrews, 207.

25. Stallings, 247–48.

26. Coffman, 276.

27. Ibid., 14.

28. Woodward, 344; Edwin Howard Simmons and Joseph Alexander, *Through the Wheat: The U.S. Marines in World War I* (Annapolis, MD: Naval Institute Press, 2008), 198.

29. Lee A. Craig, *Josephus Daniels: His Life and Times* (Chapel Hill: University of North Carolina Press, 2013), 338.

30. Lieutenant Colonel Ernst Otto, *The Battle of Blanc Mont: October 2–October 10, 1918* (Annapolis, MD: Naval Institute Press, 1930), 1.

31. Thomason, 134.

32. http://www.texasmilitaryforcesmuseum.org/36division/archives/wwi/white/chap5.htm, 2.

33. Ibid., 8.

34. Mark Grotelueschen, *The AEF Way of War: The American Army and Combat in World War I* (New York: Cambridge University Press, 2007), 253.

35. Ibid., 252.

36. Coffman, 157.

37. Van Every, 284.

38. Peter F. Owen, *To the Limit of Endurance: A Battalion of Marines in the Great War* (College Station: Texas A&M University Press, 2007), 161–80; Van Every, 285–86.

39. Van Every, 286.

40. Ibid., 190.

41. Ibid., 157–58.

42. Christopher A. Shaw, "The Battle of Blanc Mont," in Edward G. Lengel, ed., *A Companion to the Meuse-Argonne Campaign* (Malden, UK: Wiley Blackwell, 2014), 66.

43. Grotelueschen, *The AEF Way of War*, 258.

44. Ibid., 258.

45. Thomason, 171.

46. Stallings, 150.

47. Mark Mortensen, *George W. Hamilton, USMC: America's Greatest World War I Hero* (Jefferson, NC: McFarland & Company, 2011), 131.

48. Ibid., 131.

49. Ibid.

50. Ferrell, *Five Days in October*, 25.

51. Don Lawson, *The United States in World War I: The Story of General John J. Pershing and the American Expeditionary Forces* (New York: Scholastic Book Services, 1967), 116.

52. Army Historical Foundation, *Call to Duty: Newsletter of the Capital Campaign for the National Museum of the United States Army* 9, no. 1 (March 2014), 8.

53. Rebecca R. Raines, *Getting the Message Through: A Branch History of the U.S. Army Signal Corps* (Washington, DC: United States Army Center of Military History, 1996), 188.

Chapter 10: There Is Much Fighting Ahead

1. Vandiver, 968; Pershing, *My Experiences in the World War*, vol. 2, 321.

2. Marshall, 161–62.

3. Dawes, vol. 1, 187.

4. Harries, 383.

5. Society of the First Division, *History of the First Division During the World War, 1917–1919* (Philadelphia: John C. Winston Company, 1922)138.

6. Ibid., 217.

7. Ibid., 198.

8. "Hill 240 Our Prize in Desperate Fight," *New York Times*, October 7, 1918.
9. Ibid.
10. Jack Rohan, *Rags: The Story of a Dog Who Went to War* (New York: Grossett & Dunlap, 1930), 72–76.
11. http://amhistory.si.edu/militaryhistory/collection/object.asp?ID=15; Ann Bausum, *Sergeant Stubby: How a Stray Dog and His Best Friend Helped Win World War I and Stole the Heart of a Nation* (New York: National Geographic Books, 2014), 111.
12. Pershing Diary, October 4, 1918.
13. Kevin D. Stubbs, *Race to the Front: The Materiel Foundations of the Coalition Strategy in the Great War* (Westport, CT: Praeger, 2002), 264; Trask, 121, 130.
14. Lengel, *To Conquer Hell*, 233.
15. Nick Lloyd, *Hundred Days: The Campaign That Ended World War I* (New York: Basic Books, 2014), 204–5.

Chapter 11: Progress Was Made

1. "Major George K. Shuler Was Former Post Reporter," *Washington Post*, April 13, 1919.
2. Pershing Diary, October 5, 1918.
3. Elton E. Macklin, *Suddenly We Didn't Want to Die: Memoirs of a World War I Marine* (Novato, CA: Presidio Press, 1993).
4. William Mitchell, "Air Service in the Meuse-Argonne."
5. Johnson and Pratt, 154.
6. Ibid., 155.
7. Ibid.
8. Ibid., 156.
9. Werstein, 164.
10. Lavine, 568–69.
11. Werstein, 154.
12. Johnson and Pratt, 201–2; "History of the 50th Aero Squadron," in *Gorrell's History of the U.S. Air Service, 1917–1918*, Series E, Record Group 120, National Archives, 95–96.
13. Ferrell, *Five Days in October*, 64.
14. Ibid., 64.
15. Ferrell, *Five Days in October*, 32–33.
16. Robert J. Laplander, *Finding the Lost Battalion: Beyond the Rumors, Myths and Legends of America's Famous WWII Epic* (Raleigh, NC: Lulu Press, 2007), 352.

17. Ibid., 353.

18. Ibid.

19. Ibid.

20. Werstein, 164–65.

21. Ibid., 187

22. Liggett, *Commanding an American Army*, 87–88.

23. Johnson, 203; Stackpole, October 7, 1918.

24. Johnson and Pratt, 314.

25. Slotkin, 110.

26. Jim Leeke, *Ballplayers in the Great War: Newspaper Accounts of Major Leaguers in World War I Military Service* (Jefferson, NC: McFarland & Company, 2013), 10–22.

27. Douglas V. Mastriano, *Alvin York: A New Biography of the Hero of the Argonne* (Lexington: University of Kentucky Press, 2014), 23–25.

28. Alvin York, draft registration card, National Personnel Records Center, NARA.

29. *Official History of 82nd Division, American Expeditionary Forces: "All American" Division, 1917–1919* (Indianapolis: Bobbs-Merrill Company, 1919), vi; Stallings, 153.

30. Mastriano, 36–40.

31. Farwell, 222.

32. Mastriano, 73.

33. Coffman, 324.

34. http://www.historynet.com/alvin-york-and-the-meuse-argonne-offensive.htm.

35. Brad Posey, "Re-fighting the Meuse-Argonne: Alvin York and the Battle over World War I Site Commemoration," *Tennessee Historical Quarterly* (Winter 2012), 276–78.

36. Mastriano, 107–8.

37. Ibid.

38. http://www.historynet.com/alvin-york-and-the-meuse-argonne-offensive.htm.

39. Mastriano, 109–13.

40. Ibid.

41. Edward A. Gutièrrez, "Clearing the Argonne," in Lengel, *The Companion to the Meuse-Argonne Campaign*, 100.

42. Pershing Diary, October 14, 1918.

Chapter 12: Regrouping First Army

1. Palmer, *John J. Pershing*, 313.
2. Ibid.
3. Ibid., 156.
4. Ibid., 161.
5. Coffman, 326–27.
6. Ibid., 320–21.
7. Timothy K. Nenninger, "'Unsystematic as a Mode of Command': Commanders and the Process of Command in the American Expeditionary Forces, 1917–1918," *Journal of Military History* 64 (July 2000), 739.
8. Thomas, *Without Censor*, 249.
9. Ibid., 249–50.
10. Ibid., 251–54.
11. Ibid., 433–34.
12. Ibid., 251–52.
13. Coffman, 329.
14. O'Connor, 182.
15. Smythe, 296.
16. John J. Pershing to Bea Patton, October 10, 1918, Pershing Papers, LOC.
17. Pershing to Micheline Resco, October 13, 1918, Jesuit Archives.
18. Marshall, *Memoirs of My Service in the World War*, 208.
19. Ibid., 176.
20. Ibid.
21. Major General John A. Lejeune, *The Reminiscences of a Marine* (Philadelphia: Dorrance Publishing Company, 1930), 373.
22. George C. Marshall Library website, notes to "Education of a Soldier."
23. Nenninger, "'Unsystematic as a Mode of Command,'" 742.
24. Palmer, *Our Greatest Battle*, 356–57.
25. Liggett, *A.E.F.: Ten Years Ago in France*, 198.
26. Ibid., 198–99.
27. Ibid., 198–200.
28. Vandiver, vol. 2, 978.
29. Palmer, *Our Greatest Battle*, 515.
30. Robert Lee Bullard, *Personalities and Reminiscences of the War* (New York: Doubleday, Page & Company, 1925), 281.
31. Allen R. Millett, *The General: Robert L. Bullard and Officership in the United States Army, 1881–1921* (Westport, CT: Greenwood Press, 19), 418–19.
32. Ibid.

33. Sanders Marble, "Medical Support for the Meuse Argonne," in Lengel, *A Companion to the Meuse-Argonne Campaign*, 382.

34. Gavin, 55–58.

35. "Two Nurses Win Citations," *New York Times*, January 29, 1919, 6.

36. Frederick Palmer, *John J. Pershing*, 324.

37. *New York Times*, January 30, 1919; *Washington Post*, January 25, 1919, and February 7, 1919.

38. Robert H. Ferrell, ed., *Meuse-Argonne Diary: A Division Commander in World War I, William M. Wright* (Columbia: University of Missouri Press, 2004), 55.

39. Captain Ray S. Dillon (801st Pioneer Infantry) to his mother, September 30, 1918. Courtesy of John Hamilton.

40. Elizabeth Weaver, ANC, Base Hospital 20, at Châtel-Guyou, Women's Memorial Archives Manuscript Collection.

41. Cassandra Tate, *Cigarette Wars: The Triumph of the "Little White Slaver"* (New York: Oxford University Press, 2009), 71.

42. Ibid., 81.

43. Lt. Harry Spring, *An Engineer's Diary of the Great War*, Terry M. Bareither, ed. (Purdue, IN: Purdue University Press, 2002), 97.

44. Marble, 375; Mary Gillett, *The Army Medical Department: 1917–1941* (Washington, DC: United States Army Center of Military History, 2009), 332.

45. Carol Byerly, *Fever of War: The Influenza Epidemic in the U.S. Army During World War I* (New York: New York University Press, 2005), 6.

46. http://cid.oxfordjournals.org/content/47/5/668.long.

47. Elizabeth Weaver, ANC, Base Hospital 20 at Châtel-Guyou, Women's Memorial Archives.

48. Ibid.

49. Byerly, 108.

50. Farwell, 233–34.

51. Timothy K. Nenninger, "Tactical Dysfunction in the AEF, 1917–1918," *Military Affairs* (October 1987), 180; Coffman, 332.

52. Richard Faulkner, *The School of Hard Knocks: Combat Leadership in the American Expeditionary Forces* (College Station: Texas A&M University Press, 2012), 300.

53. Ibid., 301–3.

54. Elizabeth Greenhalgh, *Foch in Command: The Forging of a First World War General* (New York: Cambridge University Press, 2011), 459; War Department, *United States Army in the World War, 1917–19*, vol. 8 (Washington, DC: U.S. Army Center of Military History, 1988), , 92–94.

55. Farwell, 234–35.
56. Smythe, 242–43.
57. Thomas, *Without Censor*, 300–1; Pershing Diary, October 13, 1918.

Chapter 13: Resuming the Attack

1. Duffy, 265; Smythe, 21–32.
2. Lengel, *To Conquer Hell*, 323.
3. *Washington Post*, November 13, 1921.
4. Farwell, 231.
5. Douglas MacArthur, *Reminiscences* (New York: McGraw-Hill Book Company, 1964), 66.
6. Douglas Waller, *A Question of Loyalty: General Billy Mitchell and the Court-Martial That Gripped the Nation* (New York: HarperCollins Publishers, 2004), 21.
7. Duffy, 276.
8. Albert M. Ettinger and A. Churchill Ettinger, *A Doughboy with the Fighting 69th: A Remembrance of World War I* (Shippensburg, PA: White Mane Publishing Company, 1992), 56.
9. Ettinger, 163–64.
10. "Fifth Corps Gas Attack," *New York Times*, May 27, 1931.
11. Duffy, 268.
12. Farwell, 230.
13. Ferrell, *Reminiscences of Conrad S. Babcock*, 604.
14. Charles Pelot Summerall, *The Way of Duty, Honor, Country: The Memoir of General Charles Pelot Summerall*, Timothy K. Nenninger, ed. (Lexington: University of Kentucky Press, 2012), 144.
15. Nimrod T. Frazer, *Send the Alabamians: World War I Fighters in the Rainbow Division* (Tuscaloosa: University of Alabama Press, 2014), 177.
16. Ibid., 181.
17. Ibid., 187.
18. William Manchester, *American Caesar: Douglas MacArthur: 1880–1964* (Boston: Little, Brown and Company, 1978), 107.
19. Farwell, 232.
20. Magielse, 2, 16, 96, 164.
21. Van Every, 356–57.
22. Rexmond C. Cochrane, *The 89th Division in the Bois de Bantheville, October 1918* (Army Chemical Center, MD: U.S. Army Chemical Corps Historical Office, 1960), 14.
23. Ibid., 19.

24. Ibid., 20.
25. American Battle Monuments Commission, *American Armies and Battlefields in Europe*, 233.
26. Ibid.
27. Stackpole Diary, October 19, 1918.

Chapter 14: Now We Are Making Headway
1. Thomas, *Without Censor*, 297.
2. Steven Casey, *When Soldiers Fall: How Americans Have Confronted Combat Losses from World War I to Afghanistan* (New York: Oxford University Press, 2014), 19.
3. Casey, 29–31.
4. "Reads He Is Wounded," *Washington Post*, November 30, 1918.
5. *New York Times*, January 1, 1919.
6. Casey, 11.
7. http://www.worldwar1.com/dbc/burial.htm.
8. Diary of Chaplain Eugene William McLaurin, November 1, 1918. David F. Beer, ed., *The Journal of the World War One Historical Association* 2, no. 1 (Winter 2013), 20.
9. Nolan Papers, section 6, page 13.
10. Major George Wythe, *A History of the 90th Division* (90th Division Association, 1920), 88.
11. Shipley Thomas, *The History of the A.E.F.* (New York: George H. Doran Company, 1920), 329.
12. Hines Diary, October 21, 1918.
13. Coffman, 333.
14. Ibid., 334.
15. Ibid.
16. David Laskin, *The Long War Home: An American Journey from Ellis Island to the Great War* (New York: HarperCollins Publishers, 2010), 307–8.
17. "Official Records of the 141st Aero Squadron," *Over the Front* 22, no. 4 (Winter 2007), 301.
18. *The Liaison: A History of Regimental Headquarters Company: One Hundred and Thirty Fourth U.S. Field Artillery* (Dayton, OH: Otterbein Press, 1919), 47.
19. Millett, 423.
20. Ibid., 143.
21. Robert Lee Bullard, *Personalities and Reminiscences of the War* (New York: Doubleday, 1925), 320.

22. Ferrell, *Reminiscences of Conrad S. Babcock*, 130, 133.

23. Major General George B. Duncan to Brigadier General William Mitchell, October 17, 1918; Mitchell to Duncan, October 18, 1918. Record Group 120, National Archives.

24. John J. Pershing to Major General John L. Hines, October 28, 1918, Pershing Papers, LOC.

Chapter 15: The End Is Near

1. Timothy K. Nenninger, "John J. Pershing and the Relief for Cause in the American Expeditionary Forces, 1917–1918," *Army History* (2005), 21–33.

2. Lengel, *To Conquer Hell*, 347.

3. Stackpole Diary, October 20, 1918.

4. Coffman, 331.

5. Stackpole Diary, October 20, 1918.

6. Andrew Weist, "The Reluctant Pupil: The American Army on the Western Front, 1917–18," in Matthias Strohn, ed., *World War I Companion* (New York: Osprey Publishing, 2013), 207.

7. Mott, 435–36.

8. Smythe, 216–17; O'Connor, 316.

9. Palmer, *John J. Pershing*, 328.

10. "Secretary Baker Says There Will Be No Relaxation of Any Kind," *New York Times*, October 14, 1918.

11. Joseph E. Persico, *Eleventh Month, Eleventh Day, Eleventh Hour: Armistice Day 1918, World War I and Its Violent Climax* (New York: Random House, 2004), 290.

12. Record Group 165, Entry 320, Box 3, 17–18.

13. Lloyd, 234–35.

14. Barrie Pitt, *1918: The Last Act* (New York: W. W. Norton & Company, Inc., 1962), 265.

15. Mott, 261.

16. Ibid., 265–66.

17. Smythe, 221.

18. Rickenbacker, 348–49.

19. General Fox Conner, "The Meuse-Argonne Operation," G-3 Reports, Entry 296, Record Group 120, NARA.

20. Mitchell Yockelson, "Native Americans in World War I," *National Archives Calendar of Events* (April 1993).

21. Mott, 442.
22. Liggett, *Commanding an American Army*, 102–3.
23. Liggett, *A.E.F.*, 217–18.

Chapter 16: First Army Has Come of Age

1. Liggett, *Commanding an American* Army, 112.
2. Johnson, *Without Censor*, 319–20.
3. Pershing, *My Experiences in the World War*, vol. 2, 385.
4. Pogue, 184.
5. Peter F. Owen, *To the Limit of Endurance: A Battalion of Marines in the Great War* (College Station: Texas A&M University Press, 2007), 185.
6. Ibid., 88.
7. Department of the Navy, *The United States Naval Railway Batteries in France* (Washington, DC: U.S. Government Printing Office, 1922), 12.
8. Lieutenant P. B. Whelpley, U.S.N.R.F., "The Naval Railway Batteries," *Daughters of the American Revolution Magazine* 44, no. 4 (April 1920), 188.
9. Owen, 185–86
10. Lejeune, 382.
11. Ibid., 186–87.
12. Timothy K. Nenninger, review of *To Conquer Hell: The Meuse-Argonne, 1918*, by Edward G. Lengel, ed., *Journal of Military History* (January 2009), 671.
13. Justin G. Prince, "Artillery in the Meuse Argonne," in Lengel, *A Companion to the Meuse Argonne*, 350–51.
14. Wilson, 179.
15. Ibid., 193.
16. 1st Battalion, 6th Marines, Field Messages, November 7, 1918, Record Group 127, National Archives.
17. Johnson, *Without Censor*, 333.
18. Liggett, *Commanding an American Army*, 114.
19. Hines Diary, November 1, 1918.
20. Persico, *Eleventh Month, Eleventh Day, Eleventh Hour*, 311.
21. Ibid., 102–14.
22. Viereck, 281.
23. Charles H. Brent Papers, LOC, Box 16.
24. "The Night March: An Untold War Story," *New York Times*, November 4, 1928.
25. Shipley Thomas, *A.E.F.*, 336–41.

26. "Rainbows in a Dash to Capture Sedan," *New York Times*, November 8, 1918.
27. Pershing to Liggett, November 6, 1918, Pershing Papers, LOC.
28. Hines Diary, November 7, 1918.
29. Smythe, 227–28.
30. Liggett, *A.E.F.: Ten Years Ago in France*, 152.
31. Johnson, 331.
32. Correspondence between Thomas M. Johnson and Douglas MacArthur, February 17 and March 22, 1939. Record Group 1, Correspondence Series, MacArthur Papers. MacArthur Memorial Archives.
33. Shipley Thomas, *A.E.F.*, 331, 387.
34. Charles Pelot Summerall, *The Way of Duty, Honor, Country: The Memoir of General Charles Pelot Summerall*, Timothy K. Nenninger, ed. (Lexington: University of Kentucky Press, 2012), 3.
35. Ibid., 154.
36. Coffman, 353.
37. Stackpole Diary, November 9, 1918.
38. Charles Pelot Summerall, *The Way of Duty, Honor, Country: The Memoir of General Charles Pelot Summerall*, Timothy K. Nenninger, ed. (Lexington: University Press of Kentucky, 2010), 158.
39. Millett, 424.
40. Summerall, 154.
41. "Rainbows in a Dash to Capture Sedan," *New York Times*, November 8, 1918.
42. Smythe, 231.
43. Ibid., 234–36.

Chapter 17: The Battle Will Be Over Today

1. Summerall, 155
2. Ibid., 155.
3. Millett, 425.
4. Bullard, 296.
5. Mitchell, 286.
6. Marshall, *Memoirs of My Service in the World War*, 199.
7. Krass, 259.
8. Roth donated the canister to the Clark County, Ohio, Historical Society, where it is on display.
9. Liggett, *Commanding an American Army*, 125.
10. "The Jewish Courier of the War's End," *Jewish Floridian*, November 18, 1938.

11. http://www.trumanlibrary.org/whistlestop/study_collections/ww1/documents/fulltext.php?documentid=1-26.

12. Ferrell, *Reminiscences of Conrad S. Babcock,* 127.

13. On the evening of December 1, 1918, Patton returned to the field south of Cheppy and took photographs of the shell hole where he was wounded. Blumenson, ed., *Patton Papers,* vol. 1, 657.

14. Ibid., 270–71.

15. Diary of Margaret Connolly Burrows, November 11, 1918. Women's Memorial Archives.

16. Diary of Homer E. Simpson, November 11, 1918.

17. Hines Diary, November 11, 1918.

18. Marshall, 200.

19. Andrews, 209.

20. Smythe, 232; Pershing Diary, November 11, 1918.

21. Smythe, *Pershing: General of the Armies,* 233.

22. Vandiver, vol. 2, 987–88.

23. Ibid., 989.

24. Lacey, 177.

25. Leonard P. Ayres, *The War with Germany: A Statistical Summary* (Washington, DC: U.S. Government Printing Office, 1919), 111.

Aftermath

1. George C. Marshall Papers, "Diary of a Trip over the Battlefields of the Western Front with General Pershing, August 1–18, 1919," George C. Marshall Library.

2. John J. Pershing to Colonel George C. Marshall, October 26, 1920, Record Group 220, Entry 24, "Draft of the First Army," Folder 4, Box 14.

3. Pogue, 223.

4. Ibid., 69.

5. Ibid., 174–75.

6. Smythe, 289.

7. "Liggett Says Truce Put Troops in Danger," *New York Times,* January 21, 1920.

8. Ben Newell, *Major Sam Woodfill: The Greatest Soldier of WW I* (Baltimore: Publish America, 2008), 176.

INDEX

Index

Index